T0368408

THE
ULTIMATE
BLACK
HISTORY
TRIVIA BOOK

CURTIS CLAYTOR

THE ULTIMATE BLACK HISTORY TRIVIA BOOK

iUniverse books may be ordered through booksellers or by contacting:

iUniverse
1663 Liberty Drive
Bloomington, IN 47403
www.iuniverse.com
1-800-Authors (1-800-288-4677)

Because of the dynamic nature of the internet, any web addresses or links contained in this book may have changed since publication and may no longer be valid. The views expressed in this work are solely those of the author and do not necessarily reflect the views of the publisher, and the publisher hereby disclaims any responsibility for them.

Any people depicted in stock imagery provided by Getty Images are models, and such images are being used for illustrative purposes only.
Certain stock imagery © Getty Images.

ISBN: 978-1-5320-4988-0 (sc)
ISBN: 978-1-5320-4990-3 (hc)
ISBN: 978-1-5320-4989-7 (e)

Library of Congress Control Number: 2018906725

Print information available on the last page.

iUniverse rev. date: 03/20/2020

Contents

Introduction...vii

History...1
Music..257
Sports...359
Television, Arts, and Literature....................................461
Famous People and Events..563

Sources...615

Introduction

The Ultimate Black History Trivia Book is filled with educational, entertaining, and fun questions and answers that will test and increase your knowledge of black history. It is a celebration of the achievements of numerous well-known African Americans and of the accomplishments of many who are lesser known.

Most of us learn in school about the accomplishments of Martin Luther King Jr., Harriet Tubman, and George Washington Carver. But do you know the name of the first self-made American woman millionaire? She was, in fact, a black woman named Madam C. J. Walker, and she earned her fortune in the early 1900s selling hair-care products for black women.

Ida B. Wells was one of the greatest and most courageous figures in US history, but many people do not know who she was. She was an educator, a journalist, and a fierce antilynching advocate. In 1883 she refused to sit in the Jim Crow section of a train that was assigned to blacks. *Every* American should know about Ida B. Wells. They should also know that the gas mask and the three-signal stoplight were invented by the same black man.

As you work through *The Ultimate Black History Trivia Book*, not only will you learn about history, but also you will have numerous fun questions. Who scored 101 points in the first half of a high school basketball game? According to the Whodini song, when do the freaks come out? What is Fred Sanford's middle initial? These are just a few of the interesting questions in *The Ultimate Black History Trivia Book*.

The book has two thousand multiple-choice questions in four categories. The categories are history; music; sports; and television, arts, and literature. There are eight hundred history questions and four hundred questions in each of the other three categories. If you want to learn black history, and have fun doing it, this book is for you.

History

1   Who was the first man killed at the Boston Massacre in 1770 protesting British treatment of colonists?

A   Henry Flipper
B   James Armistead
C   Benjamin Banneker
D   Crispus Attucks

Black Saga, page 44

2   The trip from Africa to North America for slaves is known as the _____.

A   Slave Voyage
B   Ride of Horrors
C   Third World
D   Middle Passage

Africana, page 1302

3   Which of the following escaped slavery by being mailed in a box from Richmond, Virginia, to Philadelphia?

A   Quaco Walker
B   Henry Brown
C   Frederick Douglass
D   Phillis Wheatley

The Timetables of African American History, page 122

4   Married couple Ellen and William Craft escaped slavery. Ellen disguised herself as a _____and William as her _____.

A   Prisoner, prison guard
B   Slave, elderly white master
C   Elderly white master, slave
D   Prison guard, prisoner

African American Lives, page 196

5   How old was famous poet Phillis Wheatley when she was kidnapped in Africa and sold as a slave?

A   Seven
B   Ten
C   Sixteen
D   Two

Africana, page 1988

6   The savage beating of which slave led to the abolishment of slavery in Massachusetts?

A   Henry Brown
B   Gustavus Vassa
C   Henry Blair
D   Quaco Walker

Black Saga, page 57

7 Lucy Bagby Johnson was the last fugitive slave to be captured in a free state and returned to his or her master in a slave state. In what state was she captured?

A Pennsylvania
B California
C Ohio
D Illinois

Black Saga, page 185

8 How many of the first twelve presidents of the United States were slave owners?

A Two
B Ten
C Five
D Three

Civil War Chronicle, page 34

9 Sojourner Truth was an abolitionist, preacher, and women's rights advocate. What was her birth name?

A Sojourner Brown
B Linda Brent
C Lucille Truthlinberg
D Isabella Baumfree

African American Lives, page 820

10 Approximately how many slaves died on the trips from Africa to North America?

A   Five hundred thousand
B   One million eight hundred thousand
C   Seven hundred
D   One million

Africana, 1302

11 In what year did the US House of Representatives apologize for slavery?

A   2008
B   1866
C   1865
D   1903

And Still I Rise, page 238

12 Who was the author of the first slave narrative?

A   Lucy Terry
B   Frances Harper
C   Briton Hammon
D   Phillis Wheatley

Black Firsts, page 725

13 Which of the following was the last ship to bring slaves to the United States?

A   *Rainbow*
B   *Clothide*
C   *Mayflower of Liberia*
D   *Planter*

The Timetables of African American History, page 140

14 Which state did Congressman George Henry White, the last former slave in the United States Congress, represent?

A   Virginia
B   North Carolina
C   Florida
D   South Carolina

Black Saga, page 281

15 Which of the following presidents of the United States was not a slave owner?

A   Martin Van Buren
B   George Washington
C   John Adams
D   Thomas Jefferson

Civil War Chronicle, page 34

16 Which of the following presidents of the United States was not a slave owner?

A William Henry Harrison
B Andrew Jackson
C Andrew Johnson
D John Quincy Adams

Civil War Chronicle, page 34

17 Which of the following presidents of the United States was not a slave owner?

A Rutherford B. Hayes
B John Tyler
C Zachary Taylor
D Ulysses S. Grant

Civil War Chronicle, page 34

18 The first attempted revolt in the colonies by white servants and black slaves occurred in Virginia. What was the year?

A 1704
B 1663
C 1710
D 1831

Black Saga, page 16

19   In 1800 Gabriel Prosser attempted a slave revolt. Prosser, his family, and twenty-four others were executed after two house slaves revealed the plot. In what state did this occur?

A   Virginia
B   South Carolina
C   Tennessee
D   Maryland

Black Saga, page 77

20   In 1822, Denmark Vesey, a free black, attempted to lead a slave revolt. Vesey and his followers were captured and executed after another slave revealed the plot. In what state did this occur?

A   Virginia
B   Arkansas
C   Tennessee
D   South Carolina

Black Saga, page 93

21   Which of the following led the slave mutiny and revolt on the ship *Amistad*?

A   Joseph Cinque
B   Toussaint L'Ouverture
C   Cato
D   Morris Brown

African American Almanac, page 16

22 In what year did Haiti gain its independence from France?

A   1804
B   1811
C   1807
D   1808

Black Saga, page 78

23 What former US president defended the slaves during the trial of their mutiny and revolt on the *Amistad*?

A   James Monroe
B   Thomas Jefferson
C   James Madison
D   John Quincy Adams

African American Lives, page 169

24 What is the name of the 2016 movie about the Nat Turner revolt?

A   *12 Years a Slave*
B   *The Nat Turner Revolt*
C   *The Birth of a Nation*
D   *Revolution*

25 Nat Turner led a slave revolt in 1831 that killed sixty whites. Turner and his followers were captured and executed. In what state did the revolt occur?

A North Carolina
B Virginia
C South Carolina
D Maryland

African American Lives, page 828

26 In what city or town was Nat Turner, the leader of an 1831 slave revolt, executed?

A Roanoke, Virginia
B Martinsville, Virginia
C Richmond, Virginia
D Jerusalem, Virginia

Black Saga, page 109

27 After Nat Turner was executed, which of the following items were made from his remains?

A shoe polish
B cat food
C grease
D dog food

African American Lives, page 829

28 Which of the following was Dred Scott's original name?

A Sam Blow
B James Scott
C Dred Jackson
D Scott Brown

Africana, page 630

29 Dred Scott's master took him to slave states and a free state. Scott went to court seeking his freedom because he had lived in a free state. In what year did the Supreme Court rule he was still a slave?

A 1855
B 1853
C 1857
D 1851

Civil Rights Chronicle, page 29

30 To which free state did Dred Scott and his master move, prompting Scott to ask for his freedom?

A Missouri
B Ohio
C Illinois
D Michigan

African American Lives, page 751

31 John Brown, a white abolitionist, led a raid on Harpers Ferry in an attempt to obtain weapons for a massive slave revolt. In what year did the raid occur?

A   1862
B   1859
C   1856
D   1853

Civil Rights Chronicle, page 24

32 How much money did Mary Pleasant give John Brown, a white abolitionist, to help the cause?

A $30,000
B $20,000
C $10,000
D $40,000

African American Lives, page 674

33 Which of the following men was a wealthy black abolitionist and advocate for women's rights and peace?

A   Prince Hall
B   John Brown
C   James Forten
D   Jack Sisson

African American Lives, page 305

34 Harriet Tubman helped numerous slaves to their freedom through the Underground Railroad. What was her birth name?

A Harriet Bradley
B Amanda Roosevelt
C Araminta Ross
D Harriet Johnson

African American Lives, page 822

35 What role did Harriet Tubman play for the Union forces during the Civil War?

A cook and waitress
B pilot
C prison guard
D nurse and spy

Black Saga, page 142

36 In what state was Harriet Tubman born?

A Virginia
B Georgia
C South Carolina
D Maryland

Afromation, September 14

37 In what state did Harriet Tubman lead a mission as a Civil War spy that resulted in the freeing of 756 slaves?

A South Carolina
B Georgia
C Virginia
D Tennessee

African American Lives, page 824

38 In what year did Harriet Tubman die?

A 1876
B 1899
C 1913
D 1915

African American Almanac, page 21

39 How did Frederick Douglass, abolitionist, author, and leader, disguise himself to escape slavery?

A As a sailor
B As a pilgrim
C As a tiger
D As a priest

Black Saga, page 126

40 Frederick Douglasses' speech asserted the hypocrisy of the Fourth of July celebrations (slavery existed eighty-eight years after July 4, 1776). In what year was he born?

A   1830
B   1817
C   1837
D   1777

African American Quotations, page 143 and Afromation January 5

41 Frederick Douglass was an abolitionist, author, and black leader. In what state was he born?

A   Virginia
B   Georgia
C   Nebraska
D   Maryland

Macmillan Encyclopedia: The African American Experience, page 175

42 What was the name of the abolitionist newspaper founded by Frederick Douglass?

A   *Mirror of Liberty*
B   *Appeal*
C   *Freedom's Journal*
D   *North Star*

African American Lives, page 239

43 Seventeen months after Frederick Douglass's wife died, he married his white secretary. What was her name?

A Helen Reddy
B Helen Pitts
C Mary Todd
D Susan B. Anthony

Africana, page 628

44 Where was the main station for William Still's part of the Underground Railroad?

A Boston
B Philadelphia
C Washington, DC
D Richmond, Virginia

African American Lives, page 790

45 How did James Forten, black abolitionist and advocate for women's rights and peace, obtain his wealth?

A As an artist
B As a clockmaker
C By gambling
D By working as a sail maker

African American Desk Reference, page 53

46 Sojourner Truth was an abolitionist, preacher, and women's rights advocate. In what state was she born?

A New York
B Virginia
C Maryland
D New Jersey

Afromation, January 15

47 What colony made a 1663 law that a white woman and her offspring would become slaves if she married a black man?

A Virginia
B Florida
C South Carolina
D Maryland

The Timetables of African American History, page 14

48 Which colony made a 1723 law stipulating that freed slaves could not vote or carry weapons?

A Kentucky
B Pennsylvania
C South Carolina
D Virginia

The Timetables of African American History, page 26

49 Which colony was the first to abolish slavery?

A Vermont
B New Hampshire
C Pennsylvania
D Maine

Black Saga, page 53

50 Which colony made a 1780 law that all offspring of slaves became free at age twenty-eight?

A Rhode Island
B Ohio
C Maine
D Pennsylvania

Black Saga, page 55

51 What year did the US Supreme Court rule grandfather clauses (racist laws to prevent blacks from voting) unconstitutional? (The grandfather clause stipulated that if your grandfather did not vote, you could not vote. Therefore, blacks could not vote.)

A 1883
B 1915
C 1920
D 1954

Black Saga, page 308

52 For what crime did a 1712 South Carolina law make it legal to cut off a slave's ear?

A Being a three-time runaway gone for thirty days
B Being a four-time thief
C Being a five-time runaway
D Being a two-time runaway

Black Saga, page 27

53 Which colony made a 1780 law that gave a slave to each man who enlisted in the army?

A Virginia
B Maryland
C North Carolina
D South Carolina

Black Saga, page 55

54 According to a 1716 South Carolina law, who was allowed to vote?

A Christian white men
B Everybody of voting age
C All Christians of voting age
D All whites of voting age

The Timetables of African American History, page 24

55   How many lashes was a white woman ordered to receive for having a black baby, according to the decision of a 1690 Pennsylvania court case?

A   Fifty
B   Ten
C   Thirty
D   Twenty-one

The Timetables of African American History, page 17

56   How much could you be fined, in addition to being sentenced to a year in jail, for hiding a runaway slave, according to a 1739 South Carolina law?

A $200
B $1000
C $10
D $20

Black Saga, page 28

57   According to a 1691 Virginia law, how long did a mixed child with a white mother continue to be a ward of the state?

A   Ten years
B   Thirty years
C   Five years
D   Twenty years

The Timetables of African American History, page 18

58 Which colony made a 1735 law decreeing that any freed slave who returned to the colony within seven years would become a slave again?

A   Maryland
B   North Carolina
C   South Carolina
D   Virginia

The Timetables of African American History, page 28

59 Which colony made a 1729 law that made the decapitation of a slave legal as punishment for some crimes?

A   North Carolina
B   Maryland
C   South Carolina
D   Virginia

Black Saga, page 33

60 Which colony made a 1739 law stating that no slave could work over fifteen hours per day in the summer or fourteen hours in the winter?

A   Maryland
B   Virginia
C   Kentucky
D   South Carolina

Black Saga, page 28

61 Which colony made a 1691 law that levied a fine of £15 (fifteen pounds of sterling) on any white woman for having a black baby?

A   Maryland
B   Virginia
C   South Carolina
D   Tennessee

Black Saga, page 20

62 Which colony made a 1774 law stating that a slave who served three years as a soldier would be freed?

A   Rhode Island
B   New Jersey
C   New York
D   Vermont

The Timetables of African American History, page 42

63 What colony made a 1680 law stating that slaves could be executed for carrying arms?

A   South Carolina
B   Maryland
C   Virginia
D   Georgia

The Timetables of African American History, page 16

64 Which colony made a 1705 law decreeing that any black would be beaten severely for striking a white?

A   Massachusetts
B   Georgia
C   Vermont
D   Pennsylvania

The Timetables of African American History, page 21

65 What colony made a 1641 law decreeing that white and black runaway servants would be branded?

A   Virginia
B   Mississippi
C   South Carolina
D   North Carolina

The Timetables of African American History, page 11

66 Which colony made a 1770 law decreeing that a white man must be present at any gathering of six or more blacks?

A   Virginia
B   Maryland
C   South Carolina
D   Georgia

Black Saga, page 28

67 How long did a freed slave have to leave the colony of South Carolina according to a 1735 law?

A Three months
B One year
C Two years
D Six months

The Timetables of African American History, page 28

68 What colony enacted a 1770 law that made assaulting a white a capital offense for a black?

A Georgia
B Mississippi
C South Carolina
D Virginia

Black Saga, page 28

69 Which colony made a 1753 law ordering that slaves be publicly whipped for breaking streetlamps?

A Rhode Island
B Connecticut
C New York
D Massachusetts

The Timetables of African American History, page 32

70 For what crime did a 1712 South Carolina law make it legal to execute a slave?

A   Being a two-time thief
B   Being a four-time thief
C   Being a three-time runaway
D   Being a two-time runaway

Black Saga, page 27

71 Which colony made a 1724 law stating that runaway slaves could be punished by being branded or having their ears cut off?

A   Alabama
B   Louisiana
C   Texas
D   Mississippi

Black Saga, page 33

72 Which colony made a 1715 law that prevented blacks from selling oysters?

A   New York
B   Massachusetts
C   New Jersey
D   Rhode Island

The Timetables of African American History, page 24

73 Which colony made a 1792 law that sentenced any white who married a black to six months in jail?

A   North Carolina
B   Maryland
C   South Carolina
D   Virginia

The Timetables of African American History, page 61

74 Which colony made a 1662 law stating that white Christians who had sex with blacks would pay double the fine of other offenders?

A   Virginia
B   Maryland
C   South Carolina
D   North Carolina

The Timetables of African American History, page 14

75 Which colony made a 1730 law decreeing that white males must carry arms to church?

A   Texas
B   South Carolina
C   Virginia
D   Florida

The Timetables of African American History, page 27

76 Which state allowed all men the right to an education and the right to vote in its 1820 constitution?

A   New York
B   Maine
C   New Hampshire
D   Vermont

The Timetables of African American History, page 82

77 What year was the import of slaves outlawed in the United States (even though the law was not enforced)?

A   1855
B   1831
C   1852
D   1808

Black Saga, page 81

78 What year did South Carolina make a law to punish ($100 fine and six months in jail) anyone who gave alcohol to a slave?

A   1739
B   1720
C   1779
D   1802

Black Saga, page 28

79 Which state made an 1832 law that said any free black unable to pay his or her fine would be sold as a slave?

A Maryland
B Florida
C South Carolina
D Virginia

Black Saga, page 111

80 Which state made an 1806 law stipulating that all freed slaves had to leave the state within a year?

A Florida
B Georgia
C Virginia
D South Carolina

The Timetables of African American History, page 70

81 In 1780 which state was the first to allow interracial marriage by repealing the law against it?

A Maine
B New York
C Pennsylvania
D Vermont

The Timetables of African American History, page 50

82 Which state made an 1840 law stipulating that one could receive ten to twenty years in jail for having an interracial marriage?

A Iowa
B Indiana
C Georgia
D Michigan

The Chronological History of the Negro in America, page 170

83 In what year were laws against interracial marriages ruled unconstitutional by the Supreme Court?

A 1961
B 1964
C 1967
D 1969

Civil Rights Chronicle, page 328

84 The Boswell Amendment said voters must be able to explain any part of the US Constitution to a poll worker in order to vote. This Alabama law was used to prevent blacks from voting. What year did it become law?

A 1946
B 1940
C 1948
D 1950

Black Saga, page 374

85 Which state made an 1842 law stipulating that blacks coming in from any other state would be whipped and deported?

A   South Carolina
B   Tennessee
C   Mississippi
D   Virginia

The Timetables of African American History, page 114

86 What year was segregation in Washington, DC, restaurants banned by the Supreme Court?

A   1953
B   1947
C   1954
D   1960

The Timetables of African American History, page 268

87 Which state made an 1840 law stipulating that a minister could be levied a fine up to ten thousand dollars for performing an interracial wedding?

A   Ohio
B   Georgia
C   Illinois
D   Indiana

The Chronological History of the Negro in America, page 170

88 Which state made an 1832 law stipulating that a slave could be executed for burning more than fifty dollars' worth of wheat?

A Maryland
B Virginia
C South Carolina
D North Carolina

Black Saga, page 111

89 Which court case ruled that excluding blacks from juries violated black defendants' rights?

A United States v. Cruikshank
B Roberts v. Boston
C Richmond v. J. A. Croson
D Neal v. Delaware

African American Desk Reference, page 309

90 Which city had its cemeteries zoned in 1835 (one for whites, one for free blacks, and one for slaves)?

A Dallas
B Memphis
C New Orleans
D Richmond, Virginia

The Timetables of African American History, page 100

91 According to an 1810 law in New York, who was required to read the Bible?

A   Slave children
B   White women
C   Eskimos
D   Native Americans

Black Saga, page 82

92 Which state made an 1807 law decreeing that all blacks must pay a five-hundred-dollar good behavior bond?

A   Vermont
B   Illinois
C   Pennsylvania
D   Ohio

Black Saga, page 79

93 Which state made an 1832 law stipulating that a slave could be executed for assaulting a white?

A   North Carolina
B   South Carolina
C   Tennessee
D   Virginia

Black Saga, page 111

94 Which state made an 1811 law decreeing that any black who entered must leave within ten days or be fined $10 per week?

A   South Carolina
B   Georgia
C   Delaware
D   Virginia

Black Saga, page 82

95 Which state made an 1800 law prohibiting free blacks from entering?

A   Georgia
B   Florida
C   South Carolina
D   Virginia

The Timetables of African American History, page 66

96 Which city had an 1841 law stipulating that blacks and whites must be sworn in on different Bibles in court?

A   New Orleans
B   Memphis
C   Atlanta
D   Richmond, Virginia

The Timetables of African American History, page 112

97 In 1784, Connecticut passed a law stating that no one could be held in slavery after they were what age?

A   Twenty-five
B   Fifty
C   Forty
D   Thirty-five

The Timetables of African American History, page 54

98 Which of the following laws made harboring a runaway a crime?

A   Runaway Slave Bill
B   Fugitive Slave Law
C   Slave Return Acts
D   The Lucy Bagby Law

Black Saga, page 71

99 Which state made an 1841 law decreeing that black and white mill workers could not look out of the same window?

A   Virginia
B   Maryland
C   North Carolina
D   South Carolina

The Timetables of African American History, page 110

100 Which state made an 1805 law stating that all freed slaves must leave the state?

A   Virginia
B   North Carolina
C   Illinois
D   Ohio

Black Saga, page 79

101 Which state made an 1851 law that made a free black a slave if he or she stayed in the state for a year?

A   South Carolina
B   Missouri
C   Virginia
D   North Carolina

The Timetables of African American History, page 126

102 What did an 1832 law in Virginia make it illegal for free blacks to purchase?

A   Guns
B   Ships
C   Alcohol
D   Slaves

Black Saga, page 96

103 A jenny coupler is a device that attaches one train car to another. Which of the following received a patent for the jenny coupler?

A   Rufus Stokes
B   Elijah McCoy
C   Lonnie Johnson
D   Andrew Beard

A Salute to Black Scientists and Inventors, page 11

104 Which of the following received a patent for an automatic traffic symbol (the three-color traffic light)?

A   Garrett Morgan
B   Frederick Jones
C   James Adams
D   Granville Woods

African American Lives, page 603

105 Garrett Morgan invented the national safety hood. What is it commonly known as?

A   Gas mask
B   Oxygen mask
C   Hoodie
D   Motorcycle helmet

African American Lives, page 603

106 Who invented the induction telegraph system, which allowed trains to communicate with each other, thus preventing collisions?

A   Elijah McCoy
B   Garrett Morgan
C   Andrew Beard
D   Granville Woods

African American Lives, page 909

107 Who made the first clock in the American colonies?

A   Benjamin Banneker
B   Henry Flipper
C   James W. Smith
D   Wesley Brown

African American Firsts, page 288

108 Who was the first person to perform a successful open heart surgery?

A   Edwin Adom
B   Louis Sullivan
C   Daniel Hale Williams
D   Roseau Lee

Black Saga, page 278

109 What is the name of the first black-owned hospital in the United States?

A   Chicago Hospital for Negroes
B   Provident
C   Williams Memorial
D   DC Colored Hospital

Afromation, August 30

110 Madam C. J. Walker was a millionaire when she died at the age of fifty-two. What did she sell to obtain her wealth?

A   Hair-care products
B   Records
C   Oil
D   Cleaning products

Black Saga, page 302

111 Benjamin Banneker played a major role in the surveying and design of which city?

A   Philadelphia
B   Boston
C   New York
D   Washington, DC

African American Almanac, page 395

112 Which of the following was a slave who taught whites how to vaccinate against smallpox?

A   Sojourner Truth
B   Onesimus
C   Pedro Nino
D   Pompey Lamb

Black Saga, page 33

113 What year did the Tuskegee Syphilis Experiment (government experiments on black men with syphilis) end?

A   1972
B   1960
C   1967
D   1943

Black Saga, page 458

114 Who resigned as head of a plasma drive because soldiers were permitted to receive blood only from donors of their own race?

A   William Cardozo
B   Louis Sullivan
C   Louis Wright
D   Charles Drew

Africana, page 632

115 How many years did the Tuskegee Syphilis Experiment (government experiments on black men with syphilis) last?

A   Forty
B   Five
C   Thirty
D   Nine

Africana, page 1903

116 Which of the following men became famous for his scientific discoveries using soybeans?

A   George Washington Carver
B   Thomas Jennings
C   Percy Julian
D   William Ruth

African American Desk Reference, page 279

117 Which of the following received a patent for ice cream?

A   Madeline Turner
B   Bertram Fraser-Reid
C   Hyram Thomas
D   Augusta Jackson

Almanac of African American Heritage, page 164

118 In what year did the Red Cross stop segregating blood?

A   1950
B   1918
C   1957
D   1964

African American Lives, page 246

119 Which of the following black men received a patent for his invention of a folding bed?

A   Charles Richey
B   Leonard Bailey
C   Cap Collins
D   Harry Hopkins

Almanac of African American Heritage, page 163   •

120 Which of the following received a patent for a corn sheller?

A   Lockrum Blue
B   Elijah McCoy
C   Marjorie Joyner
D   Ruane Sharon Jeter

Almanac of African American Heritage, page 163

121 Which of the following received a patent for a miner's lamp bracket?

A   Lloyd Hall
B   Joseph Lee
C   J. R. Watts
D   Norbert Rillieux

African American Desk Reference, page 275

122 Who received a patent for a lock in 1889?

A   Leander Coles
B   W. A. Martin
C   Ozzie Williams
D   Barbara Sizemore

Black Firsts, page 595

123 Who was the first female president of a bank in United States history?

A   Madam C. J. Walker
B   Sojourner Truth
C   Ursula Burns
D   Maggie Walker

African American Lives, page 844

124 In what year did Richard Spikes, engineer and inventor, develop the multiple-barrel machine gun?

A   1940
B   1880
C   1976
D   1931

125 Which of the following received a patent for a stair-climbing wheelchair?

A   Rufus Weaver
B   George Grant
C   Patricia Bath
D   Ruane Sharon Jeter

Almanac of African American Heritage, page 167

126 George Washington Carver was an agriculturist and inventor. In what state was he born?

A   Alabama
B   Maryland
C   Missouri
D   South Carolina

Macmillan Encyclopedia: The African American Experience, page 123

127 Which of the following received a patent for a low-fuel helicopter engine?

A   Joseph Logan
B   James Earl
C   Joseph Lee
D   Linneaus Dorman

Almanac of African American Heritage, page 167

128 Which of the following received a patent for a mortician's table?

A   William Barnes
B   Tanya Allen
C   Louis Wright
D   Leander Coles

Almanac of African American Heritage, page 164

129 Who was the first physician to aid President Garfield after he was shot?

A   Edwin Odom
B   Charles Purvis
C   Daniel Hale Williams
D   Irene Duhart Long

The Timetables of African American History, page 181

130 Who was the first African American to receive a PhD in chemistry?

A   Benjamin Banneker
B   Charles Purvis
C   Saint Elmo Brady
D   Ben Carson

African American Desk Reference, page 272

131 Who was the first director of the American Red Cross Blood Bank?

A   Daniel Williams
B   Charles Drew
C   Louis Sullivan
D   Colin Powell

Afromation, August 20

132 Who developed many products from peanuts?

A   Clarence Carter
B   Carter Woodson
C   George Washington Carver
D   Benjamin Banneker

Africana, page 389

133 Which company was cofounded by Frederick Jones?

A   Frigid Freeze
B   Jones and Jones
C   Thermo King
D   Frederick Freeze

Afromation, June 5

134 Who was the first black woman to obtain a medical degree in the United States?

A   Susie King
B   Mae Chinn
C   Mary Jane Patterson
D   Rebecca Crumpler

African American Firsts, page 291

135 Which of the following received a patent for an automatic train lubricator?

A   Elijah McCoy
B   James Earl
C   Joseph Logan
D   Linneaus Dorman

African American Firsts, page 292

136 Percy Julian, renowned chemist, created synthetic physostigmine in a lab. What condition does it treat?

A   Diabetes
B   Pink eye
C   Glaucoma
D   Hemorrhoids

Afromation, June 6

137 In what year was Provident Hospital, the first black-owned hospital, founded?

A   1907
B   1804
C   1891
D   1876

Africana, page 1996

138 Which of the following received a patent for a hearing aid?

A   Julia Hammonds
B   Harry Hopkins
C   Mary Moore
D   Valerie Thomas

Almanac of African American Heritage, page 164

139 Which of the following men's invention of a toggle harpoon greatly improved the whaling industry?

A   Elijah McCoy
B   George Crum
C   Lewis Temple
D   Lewis Latimer

African American Desk Reference, page 280

140 Which of the following invented the Super Soaker water gun?

A   Richard Spikes
B   Elijah McCoy
C   Michel Molaire
D   Lonnie Johnson

"Miracles" poster no. 61

141 Which of the following men received a patent for the vacuum pan evaporator, a device that revolutionized the sugar industry?

A   Lewis Temple
B   Frederick Jones
C   George Washington Carver
D   Norbert Rillieux

Africana, page 1620

142 Who received a US patent for the first elevator in 1887?

A   Rufus Stokes
B   Clarence Eldor
C   Hyram Thomas
D   Alexander Miles

Almanac of African American Heritage, page 165

143 Which of the following received a patent for an airplane propeller?

A   James Adams
B   Alfred Bishop
C   Benjamin Montgomery
D   Garrett Morgan

Almanac of African American Heritage, page 163

144 Who was the first African American female neurosurgeon?

A   Alexa Canady
B   Shirley Ann Jackson
C   Fannie Elliott
D   Joycelyn Elders

African American Firsts, page 309

145 What year was sickle cell anemia, an inherited blood disease most common in blacks, discovered?

A   1910
B   1914
C   1924
D   1934

Encyclopedia of Black America, page 714

146 Which of the following received a patent for a toaster?

A   Marjorie Joyner
B   Ruane Sharon Jeter
C   James Adams
D   Rufus Weaver

Almanac of African American Heritage, page 167

147 Which of the following received a patent for potato chips?

A   Leander Coles
B   Bertram Fraser-Reid
C   Hyram Thomas
D   Madeline Turner

Almanac of African American Heritage, page 166

148 Who received a US patent for a lawn sprinkler in 1897?

A   Joseph Smith
B   Joseph Logan
C   Robert Spikes
D   J. R. Burr

Almanac of African American Heritage, page 165

149 Which health problem did Solomon Fuller fight as a doctor?

A   Sickle cell anemia
B   Heart disease
C   Alzheimer's disease
D   Syphilis

African American Desk Reference, page 233

150 Which of the following men received a US patent for inventing a lawn mower in 1899?

A   Raymond Burr
B   J. R. Watts
C   J. C. Watts
D   J. A. Burr

Almanac of African American Heritage, page 163

151 In which state was the great inventor Garrett Morgan born?

A   Ohio
B   Kentucky
C   Tennessee
D   Virginia

African American Almanac, page 408

152 Who was the first black president of the American Medical Association?

A   Gloria Randle Scott
B   Arnette Hubbard
C   Roselyn Payne Epps
D   Barbara Lorraine Nichols

The Timetables of African American History, page 355

153 Who was the first black male surgeon general?

A   Ronald Dellums
B   Louis Sullivan
C   John Conyers Jr.
D   David Satcher

Almanac of African American Heritage, page 219

154 Who founded a hospital for blacks in Nashville in 1916?

A   Lucy Craft Lane
B   Millie Hale
C   Matilda Evans
D   Susie King

African American National Biography, vol. 4, page 10

155 Who was the first black nurse to enroll with the Red Cross?

A   Susie King
B   Mary Ann Shadd Cary
C   Sojourner Truth
D   Frances Elliott Davis

Black Firsts, page 617

156 Which of the following received a patent for a portable electric light?

A   Richard Spikes
B   Henry Sampson
C   Michael Molaire
D   Cap Collins

Almanac of African American Heritage, page 164

157 Which of the following received a patent for a radar search beacon?

A   Mary Kenner
B   Edmond Berger
C   Joseph Logan
D   Ozzie Williams

Almanac of African American Heritage, page 166

158 How old was Jan Matzeliger, inventor of a shoe-lacing machine, when he died of tuberculosis?

A   Thirty-seven
B   Twenty-eight
C   Thirty
D   Forty-seven

African American Firsts, page 294

159 Which of the following received a patent for a spark plug?

A   Ozzie Williams
B   Joseph Logan
C   Leander Coles
D   Edmond Berger

Almanac of African American Heritage, page 163

160 Which of the following black inventors created a refrigeration system for trucks?

A   Clarence Eldor
B   Frederick Jones
C   Cap Collins
D   Rufus Stokes

Almanac of African American Heritage, page 164

161 Which of the following received a patent for a guided missile device?

A   William Ruth
B   John Allen
C   Joseph Logan
D   Otis Boykin

Almanac of African American Heritage, page 166

162 Which of the following men was the engineer who received a patent for a carbon filament for the electric lamp (light bulb)?

A   Leander Coles
B   Lewis Temple
C   Lewis Latimer
D   Norbert Rillieux

African American Almanac, page 406

163 Who founded three hospitals with nurse training schools, and a free clinic in Columbia, South Carolina, before 1935?

A   Millie Hale
B   Lucy Craft Lane
C   Susie King
D   Matilda Evans

African American National Biography, vol. 3, page 205

164 Who was known as the "Baby Doctor" because she delivered more than 7000 babies?

A   Rebecca Crumpler
B   Nannie Burroughs
C   Rebecca Cole
D   Justina Ford

Black Firsts, page 605

165 Which health problem did William Cardoza fight (as a doctor)?

A   Sickle cell anemia
B   Heart disease
C   Alzheimer's disease
D   Syphilis

African American Desk Reference, page 232

166 Which of the following received a patent for a machine to knead dough?

A   Ruane Sharon Jeter
B   J. R. Watts
C   Marjorie Joyner
D   Joseph Lee

Almanac of African American Heritage, page 165

167 Which of the following received a patent for a golf tee?

A   Rufus Weaver
B   George Grant
C   Patricia Bath
D   Joseph Logan

African American Desk Reference, page 274

168 Which of the following received a patent for a permanent waving machine?

A   Tanya Allen
B   R. B. Spikes
C   Ruane Sharon Jeter
D   Marjorie Joyner

Almanac of African American Heritage, page 165

169 Which of the following received a patent for a feeding device for the handicapped?

A   Rufus Weaver
B   George Grant
C   Patricia Bath
D   Bessie Blount

"Miracles" poster no. 4

170 Which of the following received a patent for a shoe-lasting machine that dramatically increased the production of shoes?

A   Jan Matzeliger
B   Dewey Sanderson
C   Elijah McCoy
D   Benjamin Banneker

African American Lives, page 570

171 Which of the following received patents for corn and cotton planters in 1836?

A   Henry Blair
B   I. O. Carter
C   James Forten
D   Meredith Gourdine

Almanac of African American Heritage, page 163

172 Which of the following received a patent for tissue tests for cancer prevention drugs?

A   Mary Kenner
B   Julia Hammonds
C   Jane Cooke Wright
D   Valerie Thomas

Almanac of African American Heritage, page 167

173 Who was the founder of Provident Hospital?

A   Edwin Adom
B   Louis Sullivan
C   Roseau Lee
D   Daniel Hale Williams

Africana, page 1996

174 Which of the following received a patent for a beer keg tap?

A   Elijah McCoy
B   Lawrence Roy
C   Richard Spikes
D   Paul Brown

Almanac of African American Heritage, page 165

175 Which of the following received a patent for an overhead conducting system for electric railways?

A   Henry Blair
B   Frederick Jones
C   Garrett Morgan
D   Granville Woods

A Salute to Black Scientists and Inventors, page 43

176 Which of the following is Shirley Ann Jackson's profession?

A   Scientist
B   Explorer
C   Inventor of Hair Care Products
D   Automobile Designer

Africana, page 1022

177 Which state was the first to secede from the Union?

A   Georgia
B   South Carolina
C   North Carolina
D   Virginia

178 In what year was the Constitution of the Confederate States of America written?

A   1963
B   1873
C   1861
D   1857

Encyclopedia of the American Civil War, page 489

179 According to the Confederate Constitution, in what year could slavery be abolished?

A   1875
B   2000
C   Never
D   2500

Encyclopedia of the American Civil War, page 489

180 In what state did Confederate soldiers massacre women, children, and 238 black soldiers at Fort Pillow?

A   Virginia
B   South Carolina
C   Kentucky
D   Tennessee

Black Saga, page 200

181 Which Confederate general ordered the massacre of hundreds of black soldiers, women, and children at Fort Pillow?

A   Robert E. Lee
B   Stonewall Jackson
C   J. E. B. Stuart
D   Nathaniel Bedford Forrest

Black Saga, page 201

182 In what state did Confederate soldiers massacre the black troops that were captured at Poison Springs?

A   South Carolina
B   Arkansas
C   Tennessee
D   Virginia

Black Saga, pages 201 and 202

183 During the Civil War, what was the location of the first battle involving a black regiment?

A   Island Mound
B   Gettysburg
C   Fort Pillow
D   Fort Wagner

The Timetables of African American History, page 146

184 Which of the following was a female recruiter in the Civil War?

A   Sojourner Truth
B   Phillis Wheatley
C   Mary Ann Shadd Cary
D   Mary Bethune

Africana, page 390

185 Which of the following wars had the largest total number of American deaths.

A   World War I
B   World War II
C   Vietnam
D   Civil War

186 For what Civil War battle did the first black receive the Congressional Medal of Honor for his heroism?

A Gettysburg
B Vicksburg
C Fort Wagner
D Island Mound

The Timetables of African American History, page 148

187 Who was the first black casualty of the Civil War?

A Nicholas Biddle
B Sergeant Crocket
C William Carney
D William Reed

Black Saga, page 185

188 Which of the following blacks was a Civil War surgeon?

A Dennis Bell
B James Armistead
C Milton Olive
D Alexander Augusta

African American Desk Reference, page 231

189 Which state was called the Bleeding State because of fights between proslavery and antislavery groups?

A   Kansas
B   Missouri
C   Virginia
D   West Virginia

Black Saga, page 162

190 In what year did a slave named Robert Smalls become a Civil War hero by sailing a Confederate ship into Union territory and surrendering?

A   1861
B   1862
C   1864
D   1865

Africana, page 1735

191 Robert Smalls became a Civil War hero by sailing a Confederate ship into Union territory and surrendering. What is the name of the ship?

A   *Clothide*
B   *Mayflower of Liberty*
C   *Planter*
D   *Rainbow*

Afromation, September 13

192 In what state was Robert Smalls, Civil War hero and a member of the United States Congress, born?

A   Tennessee
B   Maryland
C   South Carolina
D   North Carolina

Afromation, September 13

193 Robert Smalls was a Civil War hero. How many terms did he serve in the US Congress after the war?

A   Seven
B   One
C   Four
D   Five

Black Saga, page 192

194 Which amendment to the US Constitution abolished slavery?

A   Second
B   Fourteenth
C   Twenty-Fourth
D   Thirteenth

Civil Rights Chronicle, page 26

195 In what year did the United States ratify the amendment to the US Constitution that abolished slavery?

A   1837
B   1865
C   1965
D   1872

Civil Rights Chronicle, page 26

196 The Fourteenth Amendment to the Constitution made blacks citizens of the United States. What year was it ratified?

A   1854
B   1865
C   1868
D   1877

Civil Rights Chronicle, page 28

197 Which amendment outlawed the use of poll taxes, which were frequently used in the South to prevent blacks from voting?

A   Twenty-Fifth
B   Seventh
C   Twenty-Fourth
D   Thirty-First

The Timetables of African American History, page 290

198 What year was the amendment which outlawed the use of poll taxes, ratified?

A   1964
B   1960
C   1967
D   1968

Civil Rights Chronicle, page 258

199 Which of the following adult groups was guaranteed the right to vote in 1870 by the Fifteenth Amendment to the Constitution?

A   Everyone living in the United States
B   All male citizens of the United States
C   All citizens of the United States
D   All white citizens of the United States

Civil Rights Chronicle, page 28

200 What was the first year in the twentieth century with no known lynchings?

A   1952
B   1941
C   1947
D   1975

Black Saga, page 385

201 What year was Michael Donald lynched in Alabama?

A   1970
B   1961
C   1981
D   1951

Black Saga, page 487

202 More than one hundred blacks were lynched or killed in the year of the Red Summer. What year was Red Summer?

A   1944
B   1900
C   1968
D   1919

The Timetables of African American History, page 222

203 Which of the following was a former slave and sponsored the first antilynching bill in the US Congress?

A   Josiah Walls
B   Robert Smalls
C   George Henry White
D   Ebenezer Bennett

Black Saga, page 282

204 Which of the following is Ida B Wells best known for?

A   helping slaves escape
B   nursing soldiers during the war
C   antilynching campaign
D   pole dancing

Africana, page 1983

205 Ida B. Wells refused to leave the first-class section of a _____ and was arrested.

A   wagon train
B   railroad car
C   restaurant
D   steam ship

African American Lives, page 864

206 Ida B. Wells protested the hanging of thirteen black soldiers after the 1917 riots in what city?

A   New York
B   Chicago
C   Dallas
D   Houston

African American Lives, page 865

207 In which of the following cities did racist burn down the newspaper offices of Ida B. Wells?

A   Chicago
B   New York
C   Memphis
D   Detroit

African American Lives, page 864

208 In what year was Ida B. Wells fired from her teaching job for writing an article about black female teachers being sexually harassed by white board members?

A   1883
B   1891
C   1903
D   1864

African American Lives, page 864

209 In 1893 the Ida B. Wells Club (with Wells as president) founded one of the first black _____ in Chicago.

A   railroads
B   banks
C   kindergartens
D   nursing schools

African American Lives, page 865

210 Ida B. Wells compiled statistics and analyses that disputed racist justifications for the _____ of blacks?

A   high unemployment
B   lynching
C   incarceration
D   rapes

African American Lives, page 864

211 Booker T. Washington was the first black to be honored by having his likeness appear on a _____?

A   U. S. Coin
B   candy bar
C   U.S. Flag
D   dollar bill

Black Firsts, page 471

212 Booker T. Washington was a prominent leader of blacks in the late 1800s and early 1900s. He was the founder of which of the following colleges?

A   Virginia State
B   Howard
C   Hampton University
D   Tuskegee

Encyclopedia of Black America, page 821

213 What is the title of Booker T. Washington's autobiography?

A   *Up from Slavery*
B   *You Can't Keep a Good Man Down*
C   *The Autobiography of Booker T. Washington*
D   *The Best You Can Be*

African American Lives, page 847

214 In which state is Tuskegee University located?

A   Mississippi
B   Virginia
C   Alabama
D   Texas

215 What does the middle initial "T" stand for in Booker T. Washington's name?

A   Taliaferro
B   Theodore
C   Tuskegee
D   Timothy

Afromation, April 14

216 In what year did Booker T. Washington die?

A   1915
B   1913
C   1865
D   1920

African American Almanac, page 51

217 What is the name of a book authored by W.E. B. DuBois?

A   The Souls To The Polls
B   The Souls of Black Folks
C   The Suffering of Black Folks
D   The Souls of Colored People

Afromation, October 21

218 W. E. B. DuBois was an educator, an author, and a cofounder of the Niagara Movement. In what state was he born?

A   New Jersey
B   Maryland
C   Delaware
D   Massachusetts

Afromation, October 21

219 Who joined W. E. B. DuBois as cofounder of the Niagara movement to promote racial equality?

A   Marcus Garvey
B   Booker T. Washington
C   Walter White
D   William Trotter

African American Lives, page 819

220 Which of the following nations did W.E.B. DuBois become a citizen of after he moved there in 1961?

A   Kenya
B   Congo
C   Ghana
D   Ethiopia

Afromation, October 21

221 W.E.B. DuBois was the first black to earn a PhD from which of the following colleges?

A   Harvard
B   Notre Dame
C   Brown
D   Yale

Afromation, October 21

222 What year was the National Association for the Advancement of Colored People (NAACP) founded?

A   1917
B   1866
C   1909
D   1953

Civil Rights Chronicle, page 50

223 Charles Houston was an attorney for the NAACP. He played a major role in setting the strategy for legal battles to overturn racist laws. In what city was he born?

A   Chicago
B   Detroit
C   New York City
D   Washington, DC

Afromation, July 20

224 In what state was Julian Bond, civil rights leader, politician, and chairperson of the NAACP, born?

A   Tennessee
B   Maryland
C   Kentucky
D   Virginia

African American Lives, page 89

225 Who was executive director of the NAACP from 1977 to 1992?

A   Julian Bond
B   Benjamin Hooks
C   Roy Wilkins
D   Vernon Jordan

Africana, page 964

226 Who was the youngest president of the NAACP in the history of the organization?

A   Ben Jealous
B   Roy Wilkins
C   Benjamin Hooks
D   Benjamin Chavis

African American Almanac, page 106

227 Who was the national field secretary of the NAACP, 1935–1947?

A   Daisy Lampkin
B   Eunice Rivers
C   Jane Bolin
D   Johnetta Cole

Great African-American Women, page 150

228 Who was the executive director of the NAACP from 1955 to 1977?

A   Vernon Jordan
B   Ralph Abernathy
C   Whitney Young
D   Roy Wilkins

African American Lives, page 885

229 Edgar Nixon was the president of the NAACP in which state?

A   Alabama
B   Mississippi
C   Florida
D   Georgia

African American Lives, page 629

230 What year were Harry Moore, president of the Florida NAACP, and his wife murdered when racists bombed their home on Christmas?

A   1968
B   1955
C   1963
D   1951

Civil Rights Chronicle, page 116

231 How old was Emmett Till when he was brutally murdered ?

A   20
B   11
C   14
D   17

African American Lives, page 815

232 Emmett Till was visiting relatives in Mississippi when he was brutally murdered for whistling at a white woman. Where did he live before visiting his southern relatives?

A   Chicago
B   New York
C   Detroit
D   Philadelphia

Civil Rights Chronicle, page 128

233 What is the name of the town or city in Mississippi where Emmett Till was lynched?

A   Tupelo
B   Jackson
C   Philadelphia
D   Money

Civil Rights Chronicle, page 128

234 The murderers of Emmett Till admitted to his murder in which magazine?

A   *Newsweek*
B   *Life*
C   *Look*
D   *Time*

We Shall Overcome, page 16

235 Which magazine put a picture of the mutilated Emmett Till in his coffin on its cover to show the world how horrific the murder was?

A *Life*
B *Jet*
C *Look*
D *Ebony*

We Shall Overcome, page 11

236 What is the name of the black high school in Prince Edward County, Virginia where students protested in 1951 because the school had inferior facilities to the white schools?

A Geoge Washington Carver High School
B Paul Robeson High School
C Robert R. Moton High School
D Booker T. Washington High School

African American National Biography, vol. 4, page 543

237 What is the name of the sixteen year old student who led the protest at a Prince Edward County, Virginia high school in 1951?

A Delores Johns
B Debra Johns
C Barbara Johns
D Linda Johns

African American National Biography, vol. 4, page 543

238 Homer Plessy bought a first-class train ticket and refused to sit in coach. In what state was he arrested?

A   Louisiana
B   Texas
C   Indiana
D   Mississippi

Black Saga, page 282

239 In what year did the Plessy v. Ferguson court case rule that "separate but equal" was legal?

A   1907
B   1901
C   1896
D   1954

Civil Rights Chronicle, page 39

240 In what year was the Brown v. Board of Education court case that ruled "separate but equal" was not legal?

A   1954
B   1951
C   1896
D   1956

Civil Rights Chronicle, page 121

241 Which president sent federal troops to Little Rock, Arkansas, to protect black students integrating the schools?

A   Harry Truman
B   Dwight Eisenhower
C   Lyndon Johnson
D   John Kennedy

Black Saga, page 395

242 What year did Little Rock, Arkansas, close its public schools in opposition to integration?

A   1954
B   1956
C   1958
D   1960

Civil Rights Chronicle, page 160

243 In what year did Prince Edward County, Virginia, close its public schools in opposition to integration?

A   1964
B   1956
C   1959
D   1961

Civil Rights Chronicle, page 166

244 Rosa Parks became known as the "mother" of what movement for refusing to give up her bus seat to a white man?

A   Bus riders
B   Civil rights
C   Birmingham
D   The NAACP

Africana, page 1499

245 What was Rosa Parks' occupation at the time she refused to give up her bus seat to a white man in 1955?

A   Housekeeper
B   Secretary
C   Cook
D   Seamstress

Africana, page 1499

246 Rosa Parks refused to give up her seat on the bus to a white passenger. What year did this occur?

A   1954
B   1955
C   1962
D   1963

Civil Rights Chronicle, page 130

247 How much was Rosa Parks's fine, including court costs, for her refusal to give up her seat on a bus to a white man?

A $25
B $7
C $14
D $100

We Shall Overcome, page 50

248 Who paid Rosa Parks's bail after she was arrested for refusing to give up her seat to a white man on a bus in Montgomery, Alabama?

A   Martin Luther King Jr.
B   Martin Luther King Sr.
C   Fannie Hamer
D   Edgar Nixon

African American Lives, page 656

249 After moving to Detroit in 1957, Rosa Parks served on the staff of a US congressman. Who was he?

A   John Conyers
B   Coleman Young
C   Charles Rangel
D   Ron Dellums

African American Almanac, page 49

250 Rosa Parks's refusal to give up her bus seat to a white man in 1955 is a topic of ridicule in what movie?

A   *Get on the Bus*
B   *Fridays*
C   *Barbershop*
D   *No Country for Tired Women*

251 Martin Luther King Jr is the first black to be honored by having a memorial at which of the following Washington, DC, locations?

A   Smithsonian Institute
B   National Mall
C   White House
D   Capitol Building

And Still I Rise, page 257

252 What is the date of Martin Luther King Jr.'s birth?

A   .January 15,1929
B   .August 3, 1950
C   .April 10, 1930
D   .March 9, 1940

Afromation, March 8

253 In what state was Martin Luther King Jr. born?

A   Virginia
B   Maryland
C   Nebraska
D   Georgia

Afromation, March 8

254 "I Have a Dream" is Martin Luther King Jr.'s most famous speech. What year did King deliver the speech in Washington, DC?

A   1964
B   1962
C   1963
D   1967

Macmillan Encyclopedia: The African American Experience, page 403

255 Martin Luther King Jr.'s nonviolent pursuit of civil rights earned him what prestigious award in 1964?

A   Nobel Peace Prize
B   The Academy Award
C   *Newsweek* Magazine Man of the Year
D   Peace Lovers Peace Award

African American Almanac, page 45

256 What was the date of Martin Luther King Jr.'s assassination?

A .July 5, 1968
B .April 4, 1968
C .January 5, 1970
D .December 24,1967

Afromation, March 8

257 Who became president of the Southern Christian Leadership Conference after Martin Luther King Jr. was assassinated?

A Ralph Abernathy
B Fred Shuttlesworth
C Andrew Young
D Whitney Young

African American Almanac, page 37

258 Martin Luther King Jr. was murdered on the balcony of a motel in Memphis, Tennessee. What is the name of the motel?

A Memphis
B Colored People's
C Blue Boys
D Lorraine

Civil Rights Chronicle, page 143

259 What now occupies the site of the old motel where Martin Luther King Jr. was assassinated?

A   The Grand Canyon
B   The King Center
C   Nothing
D   The National Civil Rights Museum

Black Saga page 540

260 Who was shot and killed at Ebenezer Baptist Church in Atlanta, Georgia, on June 30, 1974?

A   Malcolm X
B   Ralph Abernathy
C   Martin Luther King Jr.'s mom, Alberta
D   Martin Luther King Jr.'s dad, Martin

Black Saga, page 466

261 Who sang "Take My Hand, Precious Lord" at Martin Luther King Jr.'s funeral?

A   James Cleveland
B   Mahalia Jackson
C   Etta James
D   Marian Anderson

African American Lives, page 437

262 When Martin Luther King Jr. was assassinated in 1968, what were the ages of his children?

A   Six, seven, thirteen, and twenty
B   Ten, fourteen, fifteen, and sixteen
C   Five, seven, ten, and twelve
D   Nine, ten, twelve, and eighteen

263 Which of the following men delivered a eulogy at Martin Luther King Jr.'s and Whitney Young Jr.'s funerals?

A   Jesse Jackson
B   Benjamin Mays
C   John Lewis
D   Ralph Abernathy

African American Lives, page 572

264 Which state was the first to observe the Martin Luther King holiday?

A   Massachusetts
B   New Jersey
C   Illinois
D   New York

King Center (chronology)

265 Who was the firstborn child of Coretta Scott King and Martin Luther King Jr.?

A Yolande
B Dexter
C Bernice
D Martin III

African American Lives, page 500

266 What city lost the rights to host the 1993 Super Bowl because the state did not honor Martin Luther King's holiday?

A New Orleans
B Houston
C Phoenix
D Birmingham

Black Saga, page 534

267 Whose song "Happy Birthday to You" is a tribute to Martin Luther King Jr.?

A Marvin Gaye's
B Curtis Mayfield's
C Michael Jackson's
D Stevie Wonder's

268 Who married Martin Luther King Jr.?

A   Coretta Scott
B   Coretta Johnson
C   Coretta Jackson
D   Coretta Smith

Civil Rights Chronicle, page 139

269 What was Malcolm X's last name at birth?

A   Biggs
B   Little
C   Jackson
D   Small

Afromation, March 15

270 In what state was Malcolm X born?

A   New York
B   Georgia
C   New Jersey
D   Nebraska

Afromation, March 15

271 Who is the author of *The Autobiography of Malcolm X*?

A   Alex Haley
B   Maya Angelou
C   Ralph Ellison
D   William Wells Brown

Civil Rights Chronicle, page 308

272 Where did Malcolm X convert to Islam?

A In college
B In prison
C On a vacation in Saudi Arabia
D In high school

African American Almanac, page 27

273 In what year was Malcolm X assassinated?

A 1971
B 1963
C 1968
D 1965

Civil Rights Chronicle, page 284

274 Which state was Malcolm X murdered in?

A Mississippi
B New York
C New Jersey
D Tennessee

Afromation, March 15

275 Who delivered eulogies at Martin Luther King Jr.'s and Malcolm X's funerals?

A   T. Thomas Fortune
B   Muhammad Ali
C   Elijah Muhammad
D   Ossie Davis

Africana, page 568

276 Which of the following organizations was Fannie Hamer a founding member?

A   NAACP
B   Urban League
C   Mississippi Freedom Democratic Party
D   Southern Christain Leadership Conference

Africana, page 915

277 Where was civil rights activist Fanny Hamer severely beaten by policemen?

A   On the Edmund Pettus Bridge
B   At church
C   In jail
D   At the University of Mississippi

African American Lives, page 369

278 How many brothers and sisters did civil rights leader Fanny Hamer have?

A   Eleven
B   Nineteen
C   Fifteen
D   Twenty-two

Africana, page 915

279 In what year was Medgar Evers, civil rights activist and field secretary for the NAACP, murdered?

A   1963
B   1961
C   1965
D   1968

Afromation, March 3

280 In what state was Medgar Evers, civil rights activist and field secretary for the NAACP, murdered?

A   Georgia
B   Mississippi
C   Alabama
D   Tennessee

Civil Rights Chronicle, page 238

281 When Medgar Evers was assassinated in 1963, what were the ages of his children?

A   Eight, ten, and twelve
B   Fourteen, sixteen, and seventeen
C   Nine, eleven, and sixteen
D   Three, eight, and nine

282 In what year was Byron Dela Beckwith convicted for the murder of Medgar Evers and sentenced to life in prison?

A   1969
B   1987
C   1963
D   1994

And Still I Rise, page 170

283 The movie _____ *of Mississippi* is about the murder of Medgar Evers?

A   Martyrs
B   Ghosts
C   Blacks
D   Racists

And Still I Rise, page 171

284 Who was the first female chairperson of the NAACP?

A   Shirley Chisholm
B   Ida Burnett
C   Daisy Lampkin
D   Myrlie Evers-Williams

Great African-American Women, page 69

285 What are the 1965 beatings of civil rights marchers on the bridge in Selma, Alabama, known as?

A   The Selma Massacre
B   Terrible Tuesday
C   Bloody Sunday
D   The Bridge Beatings

Civil Rights Chronicle, page 287

286 What is the name of the bridge where the beatings of the civil rights marchers took place?

A   Jefferson Davis
B   Stonewall Jackson
C   Jeb Stuart
D   Edmund Pettus

Civil Rights Chronicle, page 287

287 Which of the following men was beaten badly with the civil rights marchers on the bridge?

A   Julian Bond
B   Malcolm X
C   Jesse Jackson
D   John Lewis

Civil Rights Chronicle, page 287

288 The famous bridge in Selma, Alabama, was named for Edmund Pettus. Who was he?

A   Klansman and confederate general
B   Football coach and teacher
C   Abolitionist and NAACP member
D   Confederate spy and farmer

Smithsonian.com

289 What year was James Reeb, a white minister, murdered by white racists in Selma, Alabama?

A   1965
B   1967
C   1963
D   1961

Free at Last, page 78

290 Which of the following men was killed in Alabama by state troopers during the civil rights movement?

A   Trayvon Martin
B   James Earl Chaney
C   Jimmy Lee Jackson
D   Yusef Hawkins

Free at Last, page 76

291 What was the name of the church where four young girls died in a 1963 bombing?

A   Sharpville
B   Central
C   M Street
D   Sixteenth Street

Civil Rights Chronicle, page 253

292 Which of the four girls murdered in the 1963 Birmingham, Alabama, bombing was eleven years old? (The other three were fourteen.)

A   Denise McNair
B   Carole Robertson
C   Addie Mae Collins
D   Cynthia Wesley

Civil Rights Chronicle, page 253

293 Which artist has a song title "Birmingham Sunday" about the church bombing that killed four young girls?

A   Aretha Franklin
B   Rhiannon Giddens
C   Common
D   Mahalia Jackson

294 What is the name of the thirteen-year-old who was murdered by a racist in Birmingham shortly after the church bombing (on the same day)?

A   John Earl Reese
B   Roman Ducksworth
C   Virgil Ware
D   Mack Parker

Free at Last, page 64

295 In what city or town were three civil rights (James Chaney, Andrew Goodman, and Michael Schwerner) workers murdered in 1964?

A   Atlanta, Georgia
B   Jackson, Mississippi
C   Birmingham, Alabama
D   Philadelphia, Mississippi

Black Saga, page 424

296 What were the three civil rights workers doing in Mississippi in 1964 when they were murdered?

A   Robbing people
B   Integrating a sports team
C   Integrating a school
D   Registering blacks to vote

Black Saga, page 424

297 Why was Lamar Smith murdered by racists in 1955?

A   For beating a white
B   For registering voters
C   For robbing banks
D   For marrying a white

Free at Last, page 42

298 Why was Reverend George Lee murdered by racists in 1955?

A   For marrying a white
B   For beating a white
C   For robbing banks
D   For registering voters

Free at Last, page 40

299 Why was Herbert Lee murdered by racists in 1961?

A   For registering voters
B   For marrying a white
C   For robbing banks
D   For beating a white

Free at Last, page 52

300 Why was Vernon Dahmer murdered by racists in 1966?

A   For stealing money
B   For marrying a white
C   For registering voters
D   For raping a white

Free at Last, page 90

301 Why was Viola Liuzzo, a white civil rights activist, murdered by white racists?

A   For robbing banks
B   For transporting marchers
C   For marrying a black man
D   For teaching blacks

Free at Last, page 80

302 In what year was civil rights supporter Viola Liuzzo, who was white, murdered by the KKK?

A   1965
B   1962
C   1958
D   1960

Free at Last, page 80

303 Why was Samuel Younge Jr. murdered in 1966?

A   For murdering someone
B   For interracial dating
C   For robbing someone
D   In a dispute over a whites-only restroom

Free at Last, page 88

304 Where did the 1966 murder of Samuel Younge Jr. occur?

A   Birmingham, Alabama
B   Tuskegee, Alabama
C   Philadelphia, Mississippi
D   Jackson, Mississippi

Free at Last, page 88

305 How many Vietnam War protestors were killed at Jackson State by law enforcement officials?

A   Two
B   Zero
C   Four
D   Thirty-eight

Civil Rights Chronicle, page 369

306 In 1968, three black students were killed and twenty-seven wounded by local policemen at what university?

A   South Carolina State
B   Virginia State
C   Kent State
D   Albany State

Civil Rights Chronicle, page 339

307 What is the 1968 killing of three students (with twenty-seven wounded) by white policemen known as?

A   South Carolina State Massacre
B   Columbia Murders
C   Orangeburg Massacre
D   Charleston Killings

America I Am Black Facts, page 165

308 Which of the following men was murdered by a white mob in Bensonhurst, New York?

A   Yusef Hawkins
B   James Earl Chaney
C   Jimmy Lee Jackson
D   Rodney King

Black Saga, page 515

309 Who was the first black to have a national monument in his honor?

A   Martin Luther King Jr.
B   Frederick Douglass
C   Booker T. Washington
D   George Washington Carver

African American Firsts, page 297

310 Despite a video showing a store owner killing fifteen-year-old Latasha Harlins with a gunshot to the back of her head, a judge did not give the shooter any jail time. Where and what year did this occur?

A   Birmingham, Alabama, 1989
B   Jackson, Mississippi, 1947
C   Los Angeles, California, 1991
D   Selma, Alabama, 1963

Los Angeles Times, October 1, 1991

311 In what city did a white racist murder nine blacks at a church in 2015?

A   Savannah, Georgia
B   Charlotte, North Carolina
C   Birmingham, Alabama
D   Charleston, South Carolina

312 How was James Byrd Jr. murdered by racists in 1998?

A   Burned alive
B   Dragged with a truck
C   Hung
D   Shot

And Still I Rise, page 194

313 In the history of Florida, what was the first year a white person was executed for killing a black?

A   1865
B   1788
C   2017
D   1993

314 A group of blacks were falsely accused of raping two white women in Alabama in 1931. They would become known as the Scottsboro Boys. How many Scottsboro Boys were there?

A   Nine
B   Two
C   Eleven
D   Five

315 Before 1951, the state of Virginia had executed forty-five men for rape. How many were black?

A Seven
B Forty-three
C Forty-four
D Forty-five

Richmond Times Dispatch, February 6, 2011

316 What happened to the three white lacrosse players from Duke University who were falsely accused of rape?

A They were lynched by a mob
B They were castrated
C They were executed
D They were briefly jailed

317 What is the name of the black woman who was abducted at gunpoint and raped by six white men in Alabama in 1944?

A Hannah Cofield
B Recy Taylor
C Claudette Colvin
D Viola White

The Root, September 26, 2017

318 How many whites have been executed between 1619 and today (in the colonies and the United States) for the rape of blacks?

A   1
B   21
C   5,280
D   0

319 How many blacks were executed after the 1951 rape of a white woman in Martinsville, Virginia?

A   Seven
B   Six
C   Two
D   Nine

Richmond Times Dispatch, February 6, 2011

320 Which civil rights icon helped with the investigation of the 1944 rape of Recy Taylor by six whites in Alabama?

A   Julian Bond
B   Marin Luther King Jr.
C   John Lewis
D   Rosa Parks

The Root, September 26, 2017

321 In what year was black motorist Rodney King badly beaten by Los Angeles policemen during a routine traffic stop?

A   1991
B   1992
C   1994
D   1995

Civil Rights Chronicle, page 410

322 What is the name of the white motorist who was badly beaten at the beginning of the 1992 Los Angeles riots?

A   Mark Fuhrman
B   Gil Garcetti
C   Kato Kaelin
D   Reginald Denny

And Still I Rise, page 162

323 Where did white mobs burn 1,115 black homes and businesses and murder over 200 people in 1921 riots (according to Red Cross statistics)?

A   Tulsa, Oklahoma
B   Los Angeles
C   East Saint Louis, Missouri
D   Jackson, Mississippi

Africana, page 1893

324 In what state did a white mob destroy a black orphanage in 1863?

A   New Jersey
B   New York
C   South Carolina
D   Virginia

The Timetables of African American History, page 148

325 In which of the following years was there a major race riot in Detroit?

A   1967
B   1942
C   2016
D   1897

Black Saga, page 437

326 A black boy who ventured into the "white section" of Lake Michigan drowned after whites threw rocks at him. What year did this cause a major riot in Chicago?

A   1954
B   1919
C   1968
D   1944

Civil War Chronicle, page 406

327 Approximately two hundred blacks were murdered by white mobs in 1868 in which following town or city?

A   New Orleans
B   Opelousas, Louisiana
C   New York City
D   Floyd, Virginia

African American History for Dummies, page 116

328 In which of the following years was there a major race riot in East Saint Louis?

A   1873
B   1905
C   1917
D   1936

Chronology of African American History, 2nd ed., page 126

329 In which of the following years was there a major race riot in New York City?

A   1863
B   1914
C   1927
D   1956

Black Saga, page 198

330 Who were Franklin McCain, Joseph McNeil, David Richmond and Ezell Blair, Jr.?

A Black senators
B The men who started the Woolworth sit-in
C Church-bombing victims
D The Four Tops

Civil Rights Chronicle, page 170

331 The March on Washington was a massive protest during the civil rights movement. More than two hundred thousand protestors demonstrated for freedom and equality. What year did this occur?

A 1963
B 1960
C 1966
D 1969

Civil Rights Chronicle, page 246

332 Four freshmen from what college began the Woolworth sit-ins in 1960?

A North Carolina A&T
B Johnson C. Smith
C North Carolina State
D North Carolina Central

Black Saga, page 405

333 Which duo protested United States racism at the 1968 Olympics by giving the black power salute during the medals ceremony?

A   Vincent Matthews and Wayne Collett
B   Fred and Lamont Sanford
C   John Carlos and Tommie Smith
D   Bill Russell and Oscar Robertson

Black Firsts, page 703

334 Which of the following refused to be inducted into the military?

A   Colin Powell
B   Muhammad Ali
C   Ossie Davis
D   T. Thomas Fortune

African American Almanac, page 421

335 Who among the following was the conscientious objector who spent two and a half years in jail?

A   Jack Trice
B   Carl Hansberry
C   Bayard Rustin
D   Muhammad Ali

Black Saga, page 415

336 Whitney Elaine Johnson died when she was 19 hours old and was buried in a white cemetary. The deacon's board wanted her body because her father was black. In what year and state did this occur?

A   1962 Mississippi
B   1996 Georgia
C   1943 Alabama
D   1954 South Carolina

New York Times (Rick Bragg)

337 In which of the following years was there a major riot in Watts?

A   1970
B   1965
C   1975
D   1955

The Timetables of African American History, page 294

338 What is the name of the movement, led by Reverend William Barber, that protests for justice and equality?

A   Wonderful Wednesdays
B   Terrific Tuesdays
C   Moral Mondays
D   Super Sundays

339 In what year were the Freedom Rides (blacks and whites traveled on buses to the south together to protest segregation of interstate transpotation)?

A   1967
B   1955
C   1961
D   1965

Civil Rights Chronicle, page 196

340 The Freedom Riders were often beaten in cities. In what city or town was their bus firebombed?

A   Anniston, Alabama
B   Montgomery, Alabama
C   Jackson, Mississippi
D   Albany, Georgia

Civil Rights Chronicle, page 196

341 H. Rap Brown was a leader in the black power movement and elected chairman of SNCC in 1967. What is his first name?

A   Hubert
B   Henry
C   Harry
D   Hampton

African American National Biography, vol. 1, page 607

342 In what city was the Black Panthers founded?

A   New York
B   Chicago
C   Oakland
D   Los Angeles

Black Saga, page 429

343 Who founded the Black Panthers?

A   Huey Newton and Bobby Seale
B   Muhammad Ali
C   Ossie Davis
D   T. Thomas Fortune

Black Saga, page 429

344 At which of the following colleges did the US Army start a school for black pilots?

A   Morehouse
B   Tuskegee
C   North Carolina A&T
D   Howard

Black Saga, page 363

345 What is the nickname of the those pilots?

A   Red Tails
B   Red Skymen
C   Black Skymen
D   Black Tails

346 No flight school in the United States would give Bessie Coleman flying lessons, so she obtained her pilot's license in what country?

A   England
B   Saudi Arabia
C   Japan
D   France

African American Lives, page 183

347 Who was the first black NASA astronaut to walk in space?

A   Ron McNair
B   Guion Bluford
C   Mae Jemison
D   Bernard Harris

Almanac of African American Heritage, page 171

348 Who was the first African American woman in space?

A   Bessie Coleman
B   Mae Jemison
C   Condoleezza Rice
D   Jill Brown

And Still I Rise, page 164

349 How is astronaut Frederick Gregory related to Dr. Charles Drew?

A   He is his uncle
B   He is his nephew
C   He is his son
D   He is his son-in-law

African American Almanac, page 402

350 Who was the first person to have an international pilot's license?

A   Eugene Bullard
B   Bessie Coleman
C   Percy Sutton
D   Willa Brown

Black Saga, page 325

351 Which black astronaut died when the *Challenger* space shuttle exploded, killing all seven aboard, in 1986?

A   Mae Jemison
B   Guion Bluford
C   Ron McNair
D   Frederick Gregory

Black Firsts, page 621

352 Who was the second black American astronaut in space?

A Frederick Gregory
B Ron McNair
C Guion Bluford
D Bernard Harris

Afromation, June 9

353 Who was the first black commander of a NASA space shuttle?

A Mae Jemison
B Guion Bluford
C Ron McNair
D Frederick Drew Gregory

Black Firsts, page 621

354 What is the name of the NASA space shuttle that Frederick Drew Gregory commanded?

A *Challenger*
B *Columbia*
C *Discovery*
D *Atlantis*

Black Firsts, page 621

355 Mae Jemison is the first African American female astronaut to enter space. In what state was she born?

A   Alabama
B   Maryland
C   South Carolina
D   Virginia

African American Almanac, page 405

356 Mae Jemison has a medical degree from Cornell. Where did she earn her engineering degree?

A   University of California, Berkeley
B   Stanford
C   MIT
D   Harvard

African American Almanac, page 405

357 In what year were the first three blacks accepted to NASA?

A   1982
B   1893
C   1980
D   1978

The Timetables of African American History, page 331

358 Who was the first black female in the United States to have a commercial pilot's license?

A   Bessie Coleman
B   Jill Brown
C   Marcella Hayes
D   Willa Brown

Black Firsts, page 464

359 Where do the women work in the movie *Hidden Figures*?

A   Gentlemen's clubs
B   NAACP
C   NASA
D   NCAA

360 Which of the following was a cofounder of the Student Nonviolent Coordinating Committee?

A   Al Sharpton
B   Jesse Jackson
C   Marion Barry
D   Vernon Jordan

Africana, page 190

361 In what city was the Student Nonviolent Coordinating Committee founded in 1960?

A   Charlotte, North Carolina
B   Greensboro, North Carolina
C   Raleigh, North Carolina
D   Birmingham, Alabama

Black Saga, page 404

362 What presidential award did Whitney Young, executive director for the National Urban League, receive in 1968?

A   Medal of Freedom
B   Purple Heart
C   Pulitzer Prize
D   Nobel Peace Prize

African American Almanac, page 60

363 In what state was Ralph Abernathy, civil rights leader and head of the Southern Christian Leadership Conference, born?

A   South Carolina
B   Maryland
C   Missouri
D   Alabama

Africana, page 4

364 Which of the following was an executive director of the Urban League?

A   Andrew Young
B   Ralph Abernathy
C   Roy Wilkins
D   Whitney Young

Afromation, July 15

365 Who was the founder of the United Negro College Fund?

A   Tony Brown
B   Martin Luther King Jr.
C   Frederick Patterson
D   William Gray

Black Saga, page 372

366 In what year was the United Negro College Fund founded?

A   1953
B   1935
C   1944
D   1961

Black Saga, page 372

367 Who was the founder of PUSH (People United to Save Humanity)?

A   Jesse Jackson
B   Roy Wilkins
C   Vernon Jordan
D   Whitney Young

African American Almanac, page 43

368 Which female was the executive director of PUSH (People United to Save Humanity) from 1986 to 1989?

A   Daisy Lampkin
B   Willie Barrow
C   Myrlie Evers Williams
D   Coretta Scott

Great African-American Women, page 274

369 The Hale House was a home that cared for drug-addicted babies. In what year was it founded by Clara Hale?

A   1970
B   1990
C   1993
D   1996

African American National Biography, vol. 4, page 8

370 In what year was the United Negro Improvement Association founded?

A   1914
B   1908
C   1963
D   1924

Afromation, March 4

371 In which city was Madame Bernard Couvent's school for orphans located?

A   New York
B   Chicago
C   Philadelphia
D   New Orleans

Black Saga, page 154

372 Who founded the United Negro Improvement Association?

A   Marcus Garvey
B   Frederick Douglass
C   W. E. B. DuBois
D   William Trotter

1001 Things Everyone Should Know about Black History, page 49

373 According to the motto of the United Negro College Fund, what is a terrible thing to waste?

A   A glass of milk
B   An education
C   An opportunity
D   A mind

374 Who was the first black member of the Daughters of the American Revolution (DAR)?

A   Susie King
B   Charlayne Hunter-Gault
C   Carol Moseley-Braun
D   Karen Farmer

The Timetables of African American History, page 332

375 Which college had the first black graduate?

A   Howard
B   Middlebury
C   Morehouse
D   Tuskegee

Black Firsts, page 161

376 Who was the first black lawyer approved to practice before the US Supreme Court (but never did)?

A   Thurgood Marshall
B   John Menard
C   John Rock
D   Samuel R. Lowery

Black Firsts, page 306

377 In what state did Jane Bolin, the first black woman judge, preside?

A   Illinois
B   New Jersey
C   California
D   New York

Black Firsts, page 379

378 Who was the first black man to be appointed to the United States Supreme Court?

A   Thurgood Marshall
B   Clarence Thomas
C   Charles Houston
D   John Rock

Civil Rights Chronicle, page 123

379 Who was the first black licensed attorney in the United States?

A John Rock
B Charles Houston
C James Healy
D Macon Allen

Black Firsts, page 249

380 Who was the first black lawyer to practice before the US Supreme Court?

A Thurgood Marshall
B John Rock
C John Menard
D Samuel R. Lowery

Black Firsts, page 330

381 Who was the first black female federal judge?

A Jane Bolin
B Constance Baker Motley
C Madam C. J. Walker
D Patricia Roberts Harris

Almanac of African American Heritage, page 217

382 Who was the first black child born in the colonies?

A   Deborah Sampson
B   William Tucker
C   Graweere
D   Quaco Walker

Black Saga, page 8

383 Who was the first black female lawyer in the United States?

A   Charlotte Ray
B   Jane Bolin
C   Phyllis Mae Dailey
D   Violette Anderson

African American Firsts, page 132

384 Thurgood Marshall was the first black appointed to the US Supreme Court. In what year was he appointed?

A   1968
B   1964
C   1959
D   1967

Black Saga, page 436

385 Who was the first black female admitted to practice before the US Supreme Court?

A   Jane Bolin
B   Charlotte Ray
C   Phyllis Mae Dailey
D   Violette Anderson

Almanac of African American Heritage, page 217

386 In what year did Macon Allen become a licensed attorney?

A   1844
B   1492
C   1894
D   1961

Black Saga, page 135

387 Who was the first black female president of the American Bar Association?

A   Marcia Anderson
B   Paulette Brown
C   Michelle Howard
D   Jill Brown

Boston Globe, September 7, 2014

388 Who was the first black female president of the National Bar Association?

A   Barbara Sizemore
B   Arnette Hubbard
C   Gloria Randle Scott
D   Roselyn Payne Epps

Black Firsts, page 499

389 Who was the first black female surgeon general?

A   Jocelyn Elders
B   Dorothy Brown
C   Effie Ellis
D   Condoleezza Rice

African American Lives, page 271

390 Who was the first black physician in the United States?

A   James Pierpoint Comer
B   James McCune Smith
C   James Durham
D   William Augustus Hinton

Black Firsts, page 600

391 Who was the first black female dentist license to practice in the United States?

A   Dorothy Brown
B   Betty Pullem
C   Ida Gray
D   Fannie Elliott

African American Firsts, page 295

392 Who was the first black in the United States to publish written material advocating the use of violence for equality and self-defense?

A   Booker T. Washington
B   Nat Turner
C   David Walker
D   Malcolm X

Black Saga, page 98

393 Who was the first black director of the Centers for Disease Control?

A   Ben Carson
B   Louis Sullivan
C   Jocelyn Elders
D   David Satcher

Black Firsts, page 598

394 Who was the first black female US Army nurse?

A   Mary Mahoney
B   Susie King Taylor
C   Jocelyn Elders
D   Jane Cooke

Black Firsts, page 616

395 Who was the first black president of the American Nursing Association?

A   Dorothy Brown
B   Barbara Lorraine Nichols
C   Effie Ellis
D   Jocelyn Elders

Almanac of African American Heritage, page 162

396 Which of the following received a patent for disposal panties?

A   Augusta Jackson
B   Marjorie Joyner
C   Ruane Sharon Jeter
D   Tanya Allen

Almanac of African American Heritage, page 166

397 Who was the first black woman elected to the US Congress from Florida?

A   Irene McCoy Gaines
B   Shirley Chisholm
C   Georgia Powers
D   Carrie Meek

Black Firsts, page 324

398 Who was the first black student at the University of Alabama?

A   Autherine Lucy
B   Vivian Malone
C   Hamilton Holmes
D   James Meredith

Black Firsts, page 199

399 Who was the first black female to receive a PhD from MIT?

A   Mildred Smith
B   Patricia Bath
C   Valerie Thomas
D   Shirley Jackson

"Miracles" poster no. 51

400 Who was the first black female president of a major white university?

A   Marguerite Ross Barnett
B   Johnetta Cole
C   Mary Francis Berry
D   Sarah Jane Early

Black Firsts, page 147

401 Who were the first blacks to graduate from a United States medical school?

A   Prince Estabrook and Caesar Brown
B   Fleeta Drumgo, John Cluchette, and George Jackson
C   Thomas and John White
D   Ellen and William Craft

The Timetables of African American History, page 124

402 Who was the first black female principal in the United States?

A   Mary McLeod Bethune
B   Mary Burnett Talbert
C   Fannie Jackson Coppin
D   Mary Peake

Black Firsts, page 208

403 What year did the University of West Point admit its first black student?

A   1870
B   1945
C   1892
D   1954

African American Firsts, page 211

404 In what city was the first black-owned television station established?

A   New York
B   Detroit
C   Washington, DC
D   Philadelphia

Black Firsts, page 70

405 In what year did the University of South Carolina admit its first black student?

A   1951
B   1873
C   1954
D   1959

Black Saga, page 243

406 In what year did the University of North Carolina admit its first black student?

A   1947
B   1951
C   1954
D   1959

Black Saga, page 383

407 Who was the first black woman to earn a college degree in the United States?

A   Philippa Schuyler
B   Rebecca Crumpler
C   Mary Jane Patterson
D   Lucy Stanton Session

Black Firsts, page 160

408 Who was the first black to receive a doctorate degree in the United States?

A   John Merrick
B   George Ruffin
C   John Knowles Paine
D   Edward Bouchet

Black Firsts, page 162

409 Who was the first black president of Howard University?

A   John Hope
B   Fiorello La Guardia
C   Mordecai Johnson
D   Booker T. Washington

Chronology of African American History, 2nd ed., page 169

410 Who was the first black student at Ole Miss?

A   Autherine Lucy
B   Hamilton Holmes
C   James Meredith
D   Vivian Malone

Black Firsts, page 198

411 Who was the first black to graduate from a United States college?

A   Alexander Twilight
B   Charles Reason
C   George Ruffin
D   Robert Purvis

Chronology of African American History, 2nd ed., page 45

412 Who was the first black female school superintendent of a major city?

A   Barbara Sizemore
B   Marguerite Ross Barnett
C   Mary Francis Berry
D   Sarah Jane Early

The Timetables of African American History, page 322

413 Who was the first black professor at a white college?

A   Robert Purvis
B   Julian Bond
C   George Ruffin
D   Charles Reason

Black Firsts, page 182

414 Who was the first black to graduate from the University of Alabama?

A   James Meredith
B   Hamilton Holmes
C   Vivian Malone
D   Mark Ingram

Black Firsts, page 199

415 Who was an educator and civil rights leader who was born a slave and died in 1964?

A   Anna Haywood Cooper
B   Bessye Bearden
C   Millie Hale
D   Nannie Burroughs

African American Almanac, page 101

416 Wilberforce was the first black-owned college in the United States. It also was the first to have a black president. What was this president's name?

A   Booker T. Washington
B   Daniel Payne
C   John Hope
D   Benjamin Mays

Afromation, October 10

417 Who was the second black woman to obtain a medical degree in the United States?

A   Mae Chinn
B   Rebecca Crumpler
C   Effie Ellis
D   Rebecca Cole

Great African-American Women, page 279

418 Who was the first black woman to graduate from Yale Law School?

A   Eunice Rivers
B   Jane Bolin
C   Mary Ann Shadd Cary
D   Johnetta Cole

Great African-American Women, page 25

419 Who was the first black president of Atlanta Baptist College?

A   John Hope
B   Fiorello La Guardia
C   Andrew Young
D   Mordecai Johnson

African American Lives, page 411

420 Who was the first black Harvard graduate?

A   John Hope
B   Howard Long
C   Richard Greener
D   W. E. B. DuBois

African American Firsts, page 29

421 Which college had the first black nursing school?

A   Grambling State University
B   Spelman Seminary
C   Virginia State University
D   Clark Atlanta University

Black Firsts, page 617

422 Who was the first black to earn a law degree in the United States?

A   Charles Reason
B   George Ruffin
C   W. E. B. DuBois
D   Robert Purvis

Almanac of African American Heritage, page 235

423 Who sent federal troops to protect James Meredith when he integrated Ole Miss?

A   President Kennedy
B   President Johnson
C   President Truman
D   President Eisenhower

African American Lives, page 586

424 Who was the first black director of the Peace Corps?

A   Carolyn Robertson Payton
B   Charlotte Ray
C   Phyllis Mae Dailey
D   Violette Anderson

African American Firsts, page 159

425 Who was the first black president of the Southern Baptist Convention?

A   Martin Luther King Jr.
B   Fred Luter
C   T. D. Jakes
D   Fred Shuttlesworth

And Still I Rise, page 260

426 Who was the first black to win the Nobel Peace Prize?

A   Ralph Bunche
B   Desmond Tutu
C   Martin Luther King Jr.
D   Nelson Mandela

African American Almanac, page 69

427 Who was the first black president of the Girl Scouts?

A   Barbara Lorraine Nichols
B   Arnette Hubbard
C   Gloria Randle Scott
D   Roselyn Payne Epps

Black Firsts, page 517

428 Who was the first black woman to earn a BA degree in the United States?

A   Philippa Schuyler
B   Lucy Stanton Session
C   Rebecca Crumpler
D   Mary Jane Patterson

African American Firsts, page 26

429 Who was the first black president of the National Organization of Women?

A   Arnette Hubbard
B   Aileen Hernandez
C   Gloria Randle Scott
D   Roselyn Payne Epps

The Timetables of African American History, page 316

430 Who was the first black Texas Ranger?

A   Milton Olive
B   Nat Love
C   Lee Roy Young
D   Samuel Gravely

Black Firsts, page 270

431 Which of the following black men shot down four Japanese planes at Pearl Harbor?

A   Dorie Miller
B   Jesse Brown
C   Charles Hall
D   Leonard Harmon

Black Saga, page 362

432 In what year did the Port Chicago mutiny occur when sailors refused to handle munitions after unsafe conditions continued following an explosion that killed hundreds of people?

A   1938
B   1952
C   1940
D   1944

Black Saga, page 372

433 Who was the first black to receive the Medal of Honor in the Vietnam War after he dove on a live grenade to save fellow soldiers?

A   William Reed
B   Dennis Bell
C   James Armistead
D   Milton Olive

The Timetables of African American History, page 296

434 In what year did President Truman order that all military personnel be treated equally?

A   1944
B   1946
C   1948
D   1950

The Timetables of African American History, page 260

435 In what year did the first black graduate from the United States Naval Academy?

A   1969
B   1877
C   1949
D   1977

Black Firsts, page 452

436 Who was the first black four-star general in the United States Air Force?

A   Daniel "Chappie" James
B   Colin Powell
C   Ossie Davis
D   Benjamin Davis

The African American Soldier, page 278

437 Who was the first black admiral in the US Navy?

A   Dorie Miller
B   Samuel Gravely
C   Jesse Brown
D   Henry Flipper

Black Firsts, page 455

438 In what state is Port Chicago, where a mutiny occurred in 1944 after an explosion killed three hundred people (two hundred of them blacks), located?

A   California
B   Florida
C   Illinois
D   Virginia

Black Saga, page 372

439 Who received France's highest bravery award for fighting two dozen Germans in World War I to save a wounded soldier?

A   Benjamin Davis Sr.
B   Chappie James
C   Henry Johnson
D   Dorie Miller

African American National Biography, vol. 4, page 578

440 Who was the first black US Air Force general?

A   Benjamin Davis Sr.
B   Benjamin Davis Jr.
C   Roscoe Robinson Jr.
D   Colin Powell

Black Saga, page 386

441 Which of the following people was lost at sea during World War II?

A   Charles Drew
B   Dorie Miller
C   Jill Brown
D   Samuel Gravely

African American Desk Reference, page 304

442 Who was the first black female US Air Force general?

A   Marcelite Harris
B   Eva Jones Dulan
C   Marcella Hayes
D   Vivian McFadden

African American Firsts, page 224

443 What was the name of the ship that Dorie Miller was assigned to at Pearl Harbor?

A   USS *California*
B   USS *Falgout*
C   USS *Harmon*
D   USS *West Virginia*

African American National Biography, vol. 5, page 604

444 What year did the US Air Force end its ban on applicants with sickle cell trait?

A   1963
B   1975
C   1951
D   1981

The Timetables of African American History, page 336

445 In what year did John Green retire, leaving Benjamin Davis Sr. as the only black officer in the US Army?

A   1918
B   1947
C   1929
D   1897

African American Lives, page 212

446 Who was the first black to graduate from the US Naval Academy?

A   Henry Flipper
B   Wesley Brown
C   James W. Smith
D   Primus Hall

Black Firsts, page 452

447 Henry O. Flipper was the first black to graduate from West Point. In what state was he born?

A   Maryland
B   Georgia
C   Mississippi
D   South Carolina

African American Almanac, page 463

448 Who was the first black admitted to West Point?

A   Wesley Brown
B   Henry Flipper
C   Ossie Davis
D   James W. Smith

African American Firsts, page 211

449 In what year did the United States begin a training program for black pilots in Alabama?

A   1619
B   1941
C   1945
D   1951

Black Saga, page 363

450 Who was the first black female US Army two-star general?

A   Marcella Harris
B   Jill Brown
C   Marcia Anderson
D   Willa Brown

The Root, "17 Top Blacks in the Military," November 11, 2014

451 Who was the first black fighter pilot?

A   Ossie Davis
B   Eugene Bullard
C   Percy Sutton
D   Roscoe Brown

Black Firsts, page 460

452 Who was kicked out of West Point for breaking a coconut dipper over the head of another cadet?

A   James W. Smith
B   Henry Flipper
C   William Carney
D   Primus Hall

Black Saga, page 233

453 Who was the first black fighter pilot to shoot down a German airplane during World War II?

A   Leonard Harmon
B   Jesse Brown
C   Charles Hall
D   Dorie Miller

Black Firsts, page 438

454 Who was the first black general in the United States Marines?

A   Edward Gourdin
B   Benjamin Davis Jr.
C   Frank Petersen
D   Colin Powell

Black Firsts, page 449

455 In what year did Henry O. Flipper graduate from the United States Military Academy at West Point?

A   1877
B   1891
C   1856
D   1950

Black Firsts, page 450

456 Who was the first black naval aviator?

A   Samuel Gravely
B   Henry Flipper
C   Frederick Gregory
D   Jesse Brown

African American Firsts, page 218

457 Who was the first black to be admitted to the US Naval Academy?

A   Samuel Massie
B   James Henry Conyers
C   Robert Smalls
D   William Baldwin

Black Firsts, page 452

458 Which of the following is the first United States military ship to be commanded by a black man?

A USS *Rainbow*
B USS *Creole*
C USS *Waring*
D USS *Falgout*

Black Saga, page 411

459 Who was the first black commander of a US warship?

A Lee Roy Young
B Samuel Gravely
C Milton Olive
D Jesse Brown

African American Almanac, page 464

460 Who was the first black American to orbit the earth?

A Bernard Harris
B Frederick Gregory
C Guion Bluford
D Ron McNair

The Timetables of African American History, page 341

461 Who was the first black female air force pilot?

A   Jill Brown
B   Marcella Hayes
C   Marcelite Harris
D   Willa Brown

Almanac of African American Heritage, page 356

462 Who was the first black to graduate from the United States Military Academy at West Point?

A   James Smith
B   Henry Flipper
C   Benjamin Davis Sr.
D   Benjamin Davis Jr.

Black Saga, page 253

463 Who was the first black female four-star admiral?

A   Marcia Anderson
B   Michelle Howard
C   Paulette Brown
D   Marcella Harris

The Root, "17 Top Blacks in the Military," November 11, 2014

464 Who was the first black chairman of the Joint Chiefs of Staff?

A   Allen West
B   Colin Powell
C   Benjamin Davis
D   Ron Brown

Black Saga, page 512

465 Who was the first black four-star general in the US Army?

A   Benjamin Davis
B   Sammy Davis Jr.
C   Roscoe Robinson Jr.
D   Benjamin Davis Jr.

Black Firsts, page 441

466 Who was the first black female US Navy pilot?

A   Jill Brown
B   Marcelite Harris
C   Marcella Hayes
D   Willa Brown

Almanac of African American Heritage, page 354

467 How many Medals Of Honor were awarded to Buffalo Soldiers for their heroic acts in the Indian Wars and the Spanish American War?

A   0
B   9
C   23
D   30

Africana, page 326

468 Whose middle name is Ossian?

A   Daniel James
B   James Smith
C   Colin Powell
D   Henry Flipper

Black Firsts, page 450

469 Who was the first settler of Chicago?

A   Chief John Horse
B   Caesar Hendricks
C   Jean-Baptiste DuSable
D   Walter Payton

African American Lives, page 260

470 Which of the following flew over the North Pole in an open-cockpit plane?

A   Bessie Coleman
B   Gustavus McLeod
C   Ossie Davis
D   Willa Brown

Black Firsts, page 465

471 In what year did Jean-Baptiste DuSable settle the area that is now known as Chicago?

A   1773
B   1842
C   1733
D   1799

Black Saga, page 45

472 In what year did Matthew Henson become the first black American explorer to reach the North Pole?

A   1924
B   1909
C   1888
D   1937

Afromation, June 4

473 Which of the following men came to the New World with Columbus in 1492?

A   Ocho Cinco
B   Onesimus
C   Pedro Nino
D   Pompey Lamb

African American Desk Reference, page 2

474 Wewoka was a Mexican city where runaway slaves would go to live. Who founded Wewoka?

A   John Horse
B   Caesar Hendricks
C   Jose Columbus
D   Jean-Baptiste DuSable

The Timetables of African American History, page 124

475 Which is the only decade before 2000 that had two black members of the United States Senate?

A   1980s
B   1870s
C   1960s
D   1990s

African American Lives, page 937

476 In the history of the United States, how many black women have been US senators?

A   Zero
B   Fourteen
C   Eleven
D   Two

477 In which state was Blanche Bruce, the second black member of the United States Senate, born?

A   Louisiana
B   Mississippi
C   Virginia
D   Georgia

Afromation, March 16

478 Andrew Young is a civil rights activist, politician, and preacher. In what city was he born?

A   Washington, DC
B   Baltimore
C   Philadelphia
D   New Orleans

Encyclopedia of Black America, page 872

479 Which president appointed Thurgood Marshall to the United States Supreme Court?

A   John Kennedy
B   Lyndon Johnson
C   Dwight Eisenhower
D   Richard Nixon

African American Lives, page 565

480 P. B. S. Pinchback served as acting governor of what US state from December 9, 1872, to January 13, 1873?

A   New York
B   Texas
C   Mississippi
D   Louisiana

African American Lives, page 672

481 Thurgood Marshall was the first black appointed to the US Supreme Court. In what city was he born?

A   Washington, DC
B   New Orleans
C   Philadelphia
D   Baltimore

Afromation, July 21

482 Who was killed in a plane crash in Ethiopia taking supplies to famine victims?

A   Secretary of Commerce Ron Brown
B   Baseball star Roberto Clemente
C   Congressman Mickey Leland
D   Singer Otis Redding

Black Saga, page 475

483 In what year was Ron Brown killed in a plane crash?

A   2001
B   1994
C   1996
D   1998

African American Almanac, page 68

484 What year was Mickey Leland, Texas congressman and advocate for the poor, killed in a plane crash?

A   1977
B   1989
C   1991
D   1992

Chronology of African American History, 2nd ed., page 413

485 Whose wife had twins after he was killed in a plane crash?

A   Secretary of Commerce Ron Brown
B   Baseball star Roberto Clemente
C   Congressman Mickey Leland
D   Singer Otis Redding

University of Houston

486 Who was the first black US congressman after Reconstruction?

A   Macon Allen
B   James Healy
C   Oscar DePriest
D   Arthur Mitchell

African American Firsts, page 136

487 Kamala Harris is the second black female US senator. In what state was she elected?

A   California
B   Texas
C   New York
D   Illinois

488 Which black politician sued Barack Obama because he did not think Obama was born in the United States?

A   Ben Carson
B   Herman Cain
C   Alan Keyes
D   Clarence Thomas

And Still I Rise, page 238

489 In what state was President Barack Obama born?

A   Hawaii
B   Kenya
C   Mississippi
D   Illinois

African American Almanac, page 80

490 What is the only city in the United States where residents do not have representatives in the US Senate?

A   Birmingham, Alabama
B   Philadelphia, Mississippi
C   Richmond, Virginia
D   Washington, DC

491 Which president appointed Alexis Herman to the position of United States secretary of labor?

A   Bill Clinton
B   Barack Obama
C   George Bush
D   George W. Bush

African American Almanac, page 76

492 In what country was Barack Obama's father born?

A   Nigeria
B   Kenya
C   Congo
D   Sudan

493 What is the name of the security guard who discovered the break-in at Watergate Hotel?

A   Willis Frank
B   Frank Wills
C   Willis Drummond
D   Wilson Franklin

African American Firsts, page 152

494 Who became the first black chairman of the Republican National Committee in 2009?

A   Colin Powell
B   Tim Scott
C   Michael Steele
D   Herman Cain

And Still I Rise, page 242

495 In 1967 Carl Stokes became the first black mayor of a major US city. Of what city did he become mayor?

A   Akron, Ohio
B   Cleveland
C   Detroit
D   Atlanta

African American Firsts, page 148

496 Which of the following colleges did Jesse Jackson attend?

A Howard
B Morehouse
C North Carolina A&T
D Tuskegee

African American Lives, page 433

497 Whom did President Barack Obama marry?

A Michelle Johnson
B Michelle Robinson
C Michelle Brown
D Michelle Carter

498 Douglas Wilder was the first elected black governor. In what state was he elected?

A Virginia
B New Jersey
C New York
D Vermont

African American Desk Reference, page 22

499 Which president appointed the first black to his cabinet?

A   Franklin Roosevelt
B   Lyndon Johnson
C   John Kennedy
D   George Washington

The Timetables of African American History, page 296

500 What state did Oscar DePriest, first black US congressperson after Reconstruction, represent?

A   Iowa
B   Michigan
C   Illinois
D   Indiana

African American Firsts, page 136

501 Who was the second black member of the US Senate?

A   Blanche Bruce
B   Ebenezer Bassett
C   Hiram Revels
D   P. B. S. Pinchback

The Timetables of African American History, page 174

502 Which president appointed Clarence Thomas to the Supreme Court?

A   Gerald Ford
B   George Bush
C   Richard Nixon
D   Ronald Reagan

African American Lives, page 808

503 Who was the first black woman in the United States cabinet?

A   Patricia Roberts Harris
B   Condoleezza Rice
C   Jocelyn Elders
D   Shirley Chisholm

Great African-American Women, page 286

504 Who was the president when Elizabeth Keckly was a household assistant for his family?

A   Thomas Jefferson
B   Ulysses Grant
C   Woodrow Wilson
D   Abraham Lincoln

The Timetables of African American History, page 159

505 Who was the first black Democrat elected to the US Congress?

A   Arthur Mitchell
B   Oscar DePriest
C   Charles Rangel
D   John Conyers Jr.

Black Firsts, page 319

506 Who was the first black woman elected to the US Congress?

A   Jane Bolin
B   Charlotta Bass
C   Maxine Waters
D   Shirley Chisholm

Great African-American Women, page 38

507 Who was the first black mayor of Atlanta?

A   Bill Campbell
B   Maynard Jackson
C   Shirley Franklin
D   Andrew Young

African American Desk Reference, page 83

508 In what year was Mayor Richard Arrington, the first black mayor of Birmingham, Alabama, elected?

A   2006
B   1984
C   1997
D   1979

Civil Rights Chronicle, page 392

509 President Obama appointed the first black female attorney general. Who was she?

A   Loretta Lynch
B   Michelle Rice-Krispies
C   Susan Rice
D   Condoleezza Rice

And Still I Rise, page 277

510 Who was the secretary of health and human services under George Bush?

A   Condoleezza Rice
B   Louis Sullivan
C   David Satcher
D   Rod Paige

Almanac of African American Heritage, page 219

511 In what year was the first black female Republican elected to the United States Congress?

A   2014
B   2000
C   1996
D   2002

And Still I Rise, page 277

512 Who was the first black to be appointed to the cabinet by a president?

A   Vernon Jordan
B   Franklin Thomas
C   Ron Brown
D   Robert Weaver

Chronology of African American History, 2nd ed., page 189

513 Who ran for the Democratic presidential nomination in 1984 and 1988?

A   Al Sharpton
B   Jesse Jackson
C   Marion Barry
D   Ron Brown

Civil Rights Chronicle, page 403

514 Who ran for vice president in 1980 and 1984 with the Communist Party?

A   Jesse Jackson
B   Angela Davis
C   Lelia Smith Foley
D   Shirley Chisholm

Africana, page 564

515 Who was the first black elected to the United States Senate?

A   Edward Brooke
B   Barack Obama
C   Robert Smalls
D   Douglas Wilder

Black Saga, page 431

516 Rod Paige was the first black secretary of education. Which president appointed him to this cabinet position?

A   Bill Clinton
B   Ronald Reagan
C   George W. Bush
D   Jimmy Carter

Black Firsts, page 302

517 Whom did Barack Obama defeat in the 2004 United States Senate election?

A   Alan Keyes
B   Jesse Jackson Jr.
C   John McCain
D   Michael Steele

African American Almanac, page 81

518 In what state was Jesse Jackson born?

A   North Carolina
B   Mississippi
C   South Carolina
D   Illinois

African American Almanac, page 43

519 Who was the first female and first black secretary of energy?

A   Susan Rice
B   Irene Duhart Long
C   Hazel O'Leary
D   Patricia Roberts Harris

Black Firsts, page 293

520 President Obama appointed the first black attorney general. Who was it?

A   Jeh Johnson
B   Mike Espy
C   Loretta Lynch
D   Eric Holder

African American Almanac, page 76

521 Which president appointed Patricia Roberts Harris to the US cabinet?

A   Ronald Reagan
B   Jimmy Carter
C   George Bush
D   Bill Clinton

African American Almanac, page 75

522 Who was the first black female United States senator?

A   Carol Moseley Braun
B   Cynthia McKinney
C   Maxine Waters
D   Shelia Jackson Lee

African American Almanac, page 67

523 Whom did Barack Obama defeat to win the 2008 presidential election?

A   Thomas Jefferson
B   John McCain
C   Mitt Romney
D   George Bush

524 Monroe Baker became the first black mayor in 1867. In which town was he elected?

A   Gary, Indiana
B   Saint Martin, Louisiana
C   New Orleans, Louisiana
D   Richmond, Virginia

Black Saga, page 219

525 Who was the first black to be elected to a political office in the United States?

A   John Mercer Langston
B   Francis Cardozo
C   John Menard
D   Marion Barry

Black Firsts, page 259

526 In what year did the first black female elected mayor in the United States take office?

A   1977
B   1958
C   1976
D   1972

Black Firsts, page 387

527 Who was the first black to give a speech at the US Capitol?

A   Henry Garnet
B   Booker T. Washington
C   Frederick Douglass
D   Joseph Jenkins Roberts

Afromation, January 7

528 What state elected Mia Love as the first black female Republican to the US Congress?

A   Montana
B   Utah
C   Idaho
D   Illinois

And Still I Rise, page 277

529 Cory Booker became the mayor of what city in 2006?

A   Camden, New Jersey
B   Jersey City, New Jersey
C   Newark, New Jersey
D   Buffalo, New York

And Still I Rise, page 228

530 Who was the national security advisor for George W. Bush?

A   Condoleezza Rice
B   Susan Rice
C   Louis Sullivan
D   Rod Paige

African American Almanac, page 85

531 Which president had a group of advisors called the Black Cabinet?

A   Jimmy Carter
B   Bill Clinton
C   George W. Bush
D   Franklin Roosevelt

Black Saga, page 355

532 Of what city was Coleman Young the mayor?

A   Milwaukee
B   Columbus, Ohio
C   Cleveland
D   Detroit

African American Almanac, page 89

533 Which civil rights leader endorsed former Klansman David Duke for governor of Louisiana?

A   James Meredith
B   Ralph Abernathy
C   John Lewis
D   Julian Bond

African American Lives, page 586

534 Who was the first black US ambassador to a European country?

A   John Mercer Langston
B   Francis Cardozo
C   John Menard
D   Clifton Wharton Sr.

Black Saga, page 398

535 Who was the first black woman to run for vice president?

A   Charlotta Bass
B   Barbara Jordan
C   Maxine Waters
D   Shirley Chisholm

Black Firsts, page 314

536 From what state was Barack Obama elected to the United States Senate?

A   Illinois
B   Hawaii
C   Pennsylvania
D   Ohio

537 In what state was Willie Brown, member of the California legislature for thirty-one years and mayor of Oakland, born?

A   Ohio
B   California
C   Texas
D   New York

Africana, page 323

538 Which of the following presidents of the United States was not a slave owner?

A   James Buchanan
B   James Madison
C   James Monroe
D   James K. Polk

Civil War Chronicle, page 34

539 Strom Thurmond, who ran for president as a segregationist, was the father of a black daughter. What was her name?

A   Essie Mae Washington-Williams
B   Mammy Thurmond
C   Bessie Johnson-Wilson
D   Strometta Gilliingham

And Still I Rise, page 214

540 In what state was the first black Democratic congressional member elected?

A   Illinois
B   Maine
C   Michigan
D   New York

Black Firsts, page 319

541 In what year did Henry Garnet give his speech at the United States House of Representatives?

A   1875
B   1865
C   1855
D   1885

African American Almanac, page 26

542 What was the actual name of President Roosevelt's "Black Cabinet"?

A   Board of Negro Folks
B   Negro Presidential Helpers
C   Federal Council of Negro Affairs
D   Negro Organization for Equal Rights

Africana, page 230

543 Who was the second black US cabinet member?

A   Arthur Mitchell
B   William Coleman
C   Ralph Bunche
D   Condoleezza Rice

African American Lives, page 186

544 Ernest Morial was the first black mayor of New Orleans. What was his nickname?

A   Dutch
B   The Big E
C   The Little E
D   E. M.

African American Almanac, page 56

545 Which of the following was US ambassador to the United Nations under President Obama?

A   Colin Powell
B   Susan Rice
C   Michelle Rice Krispies
D   Condoleezza Rice

African American Almanac, page 85

546 Who was the first black mayor of New York?

A   David Paterson
B   David Alan Grier
C   Dave Justice
D   David Dinkins

And Still I Rise, page 149

547 Whom did Barack Obama defeat to win the 2012 presidential election?

A   John McCain
B   Mitt Romney
C   George Bush
D   George Washington

548 In what year was the first black elected to a political office in the United States?

A   1946
B   1907
C   1866
D   1855

Black Saga, page 160

549 Who was the first black US ambassador to the United Nations?

A   Ronald Dellums
B   David Satcher
C   John Conyers Jr.
D   Andrew Young

Black Firsts, page 323

550 In what year did Robert Weaver become the secretary of Housing and Urban Development?

A   1966
B   1971
C   1962
D   1958

African American Firsts, page 146

551 Lionel Wilson was the black mayor of what city?

A   Oakland
B   Los Angeles
C   Las Vegas
D   San Diego

African American Desk Reference, 64

552 Who was the first black secretary of labor?

A   Jeanette Brown
B   Alexis Herman
C   Shirley Jackson
D   Edith Sampson

African American Almanac, page 76

553 Which of the following was once secretary of Housing and Urban Development?

A   Patricia Roberts Harris
B   Hazel O'Leary
C   Jocelyn Elders
D   Condoleezza Rice

African American Almanac, page 75

554 What was Barack Obama's father's name?

A   Elwick Obama
B   Sharrok Obama
C   Obama Obini
D   Barack Obama

African American Almanac, page 80

555 In what year did Barack Obama become the first black president of the United States?

A   2007
B   2011
C   2009
D   2013

556 Who was the mayor of New Orleans when it was devastated by Hurricane Katrina?

A   Coleman Young
B   Louis Armstrong
C   Ray Nagin
D   Sidney Barthelemy

557 Of what city did Kasim Reed become the mayor in 2010?

A   Los Angeles
B   Houston
C   Atlanta
D   New York

558 Who was the first American president of Liberia?

A   Joseph Jenkins Roberts
B   Booker T. Washington
C   Henry Garnet
D   W. E. B. DuBois

The Timetables of African American History, page 114

559 Who was the first black US senator?

A   Hiram Revels
B   Ebenezer Bassett
C   Douglas Wilder
D   P. B. S. Pinchback

The Timetables of African American History, page 164

560 Who was the first secretary of state for George W. Bush?

A   Condoleezza Rice
B   Colin Powell
C   Louis Sullivan
D   Rod Paige

African American Almanac, page 466

561 Which state did Senator Edward Brooke represent?

A   Illinois
B   New Jersey
C   New York
D   Massachusetts

African American Lives, page 100

562 Of which city was Tom Bradley the mayor?

A   Los Angeles
B   Atlanta
C   New York
D   Philadelphia

Black Saga, page 465

563 Harvey Gantt was the mayor of what city?

A   Charlotte
B   Greensboro
C   Norfolk
D   Richmond

And Still I Rise, page 106

564 Kamala Harris is the second black female US senator. In what year did she take office?

A   2015
B   2013
C   1999
D   2017

565 Who was the first black to be elected (but not seated) to the US Congress?

A   John Mercer Langston
B   Francis Cardozo
C   Hiram Revels
D   John Menard

Black Firsts, page 317

566 In what year did the United States Senate get its first black member?

A   1960
B   1870
C   1962
D   1964

Black Saga, page 234

567 Who was the first black female mayor?

A   Shirley Chisholm
B   Maxine Waters
C   Sharon Pratt Kelley
D   Ellen Walker Craig-Jones

Black Firsts, page 389

568 Where was the first black elected to a political office in the United States?

A   Columbus, Ohio
B   Cleveland, Ohio
C   Brownhelm, Ohio
D   Dayton, Ohio

Black Firsts, page 319

569 Who was Barack Obama's main competitor for the Democratic Party's nominee for president in 2008?

A   Hillary Clinton
B   Joe Biden
C   John Kerry
D   John Edwards

570 Of which city was Wilson Goode the mayor?

A   New York
B   Los Angeles
C   Philadelphia
D   Atlanta

571 Of what city was Kurt Schmoke the mayor?

A   Washington, DC
B   Newark
C   Philadelphia
D   Baltimore

Black Saga, page 510

572 What year did Mississippi get its second black US senator?

A   1986
B   1874
C   1980
D   1960

Black Saga, page 246

573 How many blacks have been members of the United States Senate?

A   Twenty-one
B   Seven
C   Thirty-four
D   Ten

574 How old was Maynard Jackson when he graduated from Morehouse College?

A   Fifteen
B   Sixteen
C   Eighteen
D   Thirty-three

African American National Biography, vol. 4, page 457

575 Which state does Maxine Waters represent in Congress?

A   California
B   New Jersey
C   New York
D   Texas

African American Almanac, page 88

576 Which state did Shirley Chisholm represent in Congress?

A   New York
B   Florida
C   New Jersey
D   Texas

African American Almanac, page 70

577 Who was the mayor of Atlanta from 1982 to 1989?

A   Harold Washington
B   Bill Campbell
C   Andrew Young
D   Maynard Jackson

Africana, page 2037

578 Ron Brown was the first black chairman of the National Democratic Party. In what city was he born?

A   Washington, DC
B   New Orleans
C   Philadelphia
D   Detroit

African American Almanac, page 68

579 Hiram Revels became president of what college in 1872?

A   Florida A&M
B   Tuskegee
C   Virginia State
D   Alcorn

Afromation, March 28

580 In what year did Ralph Bunche win the Nobel Peace Prize?

A   1950
B   1946
C   1948
D   1963

The Timetables of African American History, page 262

581 In what city was Ralph Bunche, Nobel Peace Prize winner, born?

A   New Orleans
B   Detroit
C   Philadelphia
D   Washington, DC

African American Almanac, page 69

582 Which of the following won a Nobel Peace Prize for work on the Arab-Israeli conflict?

A   Thurgood Marshall
B   Martin Luther King Jr.
C   Nelson Mandela
D   Ralph Bunche

African American Almanac, page 69

583 Who was the winner of the 2009 Nobel Peace Prize?

A   Condoleezza Rice
B   Michelle Obama
C   Barack Obama
D   Colin Powell

And Still I Rise, page 246

584 Whose middle name is Shepilov?

A   Vernon Jordan
B   Marcus Garvey
C   Spike Lee
D   Marion Barry

Africana, page 190

585 Whose birth name was Frizzell Gray?

A   Kweisi Mfume
B   Eddie Murphy
C   Elijah Muhammad
D   Louis Farrakhan

Africana, page 1298

586 The last name of which of the following men was Walcott at birth?

A   Maulana Karenga
B   Louis Farrakhan
C   Mumia Abu-Jamal
D   Rap Brown

Africana, page 732

587 Whose middle name is Mosiah?

A   Jesse Jackson
B   Andrew Young
C   Marcus Garvey
D   Denzel Washington

Africana, page 818

588 Whose middle name is Eulion?

A   Vernon Jordan
B   Marion Barry
C   Andrew Young
D   W. E. B. DuBois

African American Almanac, page 55

589 Which of the following had multiple sclerosis and leukemia?

A   Maxine Waters
B   Condoleezza Rice
C   Shirley Chisholm
D   Barbara Jordan

African American Almanac, page 78

590 What was the first major city to have a black female police chief?

A   Detroit
B   Atlanta
C   Los Angeles
D   Philadelphia

African American Firsts, page 178

591 Of what city was Clarence Bradford the police chief?

A   San Antonio
B   Fort Worth
C   Dallas
D   Houston

Almanac of African American Heritage, page 245

592 Which police chief played a major role during the Washington-area sniper attacks?

A   Charles Moose
B   Beverly Harvard
C   Maynard Jackson
D   Willie Williams

593 Of what city was Emmett Turner the police chief?

A   Nashville
B   Memphis
C   Baltimore
D   New Orleans

Almanac of African American Heritage, page 245

594 Who was the first black female police chief of a major US city?

A   Violette Anderson
B   Charlotte Ray
C   Phyllis Mae Dailey
D   Beverly Harvard

African American Firsts, page 178

595 In what city was Walter Winfrey the police chief?

A   New Orleans
B   Houston
C   Nashville
D   Memphis

Almanac of African American Heritage, page 245

596 Who is the "Father of Black History"?

A   Charles Woodson
B   Woody Carter
C   Carter Woodson
D   Clarence Carter

Afromation, May 30

597 What is the name of the 1915 film that portrayed Klansmen as heroes?

A   *The Good Old Boys*
B   *The Hanging Tree*
C   *The Birth of a Nation*
D   *The White Knights*

Civil Rights Chronicle, page 52

598 What was the worst city in the United States for a black to live in, according to the 1948 *Negro Digest?*

A   Richmond, Virginia
B   Birmingham, Alabama
C   Jackson, Mississippi
D   Columbia, South Carolina

Black Saga, page 377

599 What is the name of the TV miniseries that traced the history of a black family from Africa into twentieth-century America?

A *The Family Tree*
B *Stems*
C *Roots*
D *Branches*

Civil Rights Chronicle, page 390

600 Who is the founder of Radio One and TV One?

A Robert Johnson
B Oprah Winfrey
C Ursula Burns
D Cathy Hughes

African American Almanac, page 184

601 Which of the following was a regular news correspondent on the long-running CBS television show *60 Minutes*?

A Greg Gumbel
B Bryant Gumbel
C Al Roker
D Ed Bradley

African American Almanac, page 180

602 What city is the birthplace of news reporter and *60 Minutes* correspondent Ed Bradley?

A Atlanta
B New Orleans
C Philadelphia
D Washington, DC

African American Almanac, page 180

603 Who founded the *Chicago Defender* (a black newspaper)?

A Jesse Jackson
B Robert Abbott
C Richard Allen
D T. Thomas Fortune

African American Desk Reference, page 503

604 Who founded the *New York Freemen* newspaper?

A Muhammad Ali
B T. Thomas Fortune
C Ossie Davis
D Robert Abbott

Afromation, June 21

605 Who founded the Negro Associated Press, which supplied news to black papers?

A   Jesse Jackson
B   Claude Barnett
C   Richard Allen
D   Robert Abbott

African American Firsts, page 77

606 Who was *Time*'s Person of the Year for 2008?

A   Barack Obama
B   John Lewis
C   O. J. Simpson
D   Michael Jordan

607 In what year was the first issue of *Ebony* magazine published?

A   1961
B   1952
C   1945
D   1963

African American Lives, page 458

608 Who was the first black *Time* magazine Man of the Year?

A   Joe Louis
B   Jesse Jackson
C   Martin Luther King Jr.
D   Muhammad Ali

African American Lives, page 503

609 Who was the first black owner of a major newspaper (the *Oakland Tribune*)?

A   T. Thomas Fortune
B   Robert Maynard
C   Robert Johnson
D   Robert Church

African American Firsts, page 122

610 *In My Place* is about the first black woman to attend which of the following colleges?

A   Mississippi State
B   Florida
C   Mississippi
D   Georgia

African American National Biography, vol. 4, page 391

611 Whose autobiography is titled *The Good Fight*?

A   James Farmer
B   Shirley Chisholm
C   Colin Powell
D   Muhammad Ali

Africana, page 424

612 Who wrote *Before the Mayflower: A History of the Negro in America?*

A   Carter Woodson
B   Frederick Douglass
C   Lerone Bennett
D   William Nell

African American Almanac, page 98

613 Who was the first black anchor of a major network morning news show?

A   Ed Bradley
B   Bryant Gumbel
C   Mal Goode
D   Greg Gumbel

African American National Biography, vol. 3, page 670

614 Which magazine published a caricature of President Barack Obama on its cover wearing Muslim attire and his wife, Michelle, with an afro and assault rifle?

A   *Time*
B   *The New Yorker*
C   *Life*
D   *Newsweek*

615 Who joined Charlayne Hunter as one of the first two black students at the University of Georgia?

A   James Meredith
B   John Lewis
C   Hamilton Holmes
D   Vivian Malone

African American Firsts, page 117

616 What national news network did Max Robinson, the first black anchorman, work for?

A   NBC
B   Fox
C   CBS
D   ABC

African American Desk Reference, page 20

617 In what state was Harriet Jacobs born?

A   Virginia
B   Tennessee
C   South Carolina
D   North Carolina

African American Lives, page 441

618 Samuel Cornish and John Russwurm were the founders of the first black newspaper in the United States. What was its name?

A *Emancipator*
B *Freedom's Journal*
C *Crisis*
D *Mirror of Liberty*

Almanac of African American Heritage, pages 30–32

619 Whose autobiography is titled *My American Journal*?

A Colin Powell
B Condoleezza Rice
C Don King
D Thurgood Marshall

620 Who published the first magazine intended for a black audience?

A Frederick Douglass
B David Ruggles
C Lerone Bennett
D William Nell

Black Saga, page 126

621 Mary Ann Shadd Cary was the first female editor of a North American newspaper. What was the name of the publication?

A *Justice for All*
B *Provincial Freedom*
C *Justice for Us*
D *Freedom's Journal*

Afromation, June 19

622 Which of the following was a reporter on the *MacNeil/Lehrer News Hour* (a news show on the Public Broadcasting Service)?

A   Oprah Winfrey
B   Max Robinson
C   Ed Bradley
D   Charlayne Hunter Gault

African American Almanac, page 185

623 Who was the first black network news commentator?

A   Max Robinson
B   Ed Bradley
C   Mal Goode
D   Bryant Gumbel

African American Firsts, page 119

624 Which of the following is a *Good Morning America* cohost and breast cancer survivor?

A   Gayle King
B   Robin Roberts
C   Melissa Harris Perry
D   Tamron Hall

625 Whose autobiography is titled *Incidents in the Life of a Slave Girl*?

A   Jane Pittman's
B   Harriet Tubman's
C   Harriet Jacobs's
D   Sojourner Truth's

Great African-American Women, page 288

626 Who was the first black to have a book of poetry published in the United States?

A   Langston Hughes
B   Katherine Dunham
C   Rita Dove
D   Phillis Wheatley

Black Firsts, page 740

627 What was the name of David Walker's publication advocating the use of violence for equality and self-defense?

A   *Freedom's Journal*
B   *Crisis*
C   *Appeal*
D   *Fight Back*

African American Desk Reference, page 56

628 Who was the first black on the cover of *Vogue* magazine?

A   Beverly Johnson
B   Naomi Campbell
C   Naomi Sims
D   Vanessa Williams

The Timetables of African American History, page 322

629 What was the name of the first black magazine?

A *Emancipator*
B *Mirror of Liberty*
C *Crisis*
D *Appeal*

African American Firsts, page 112

630 How old was Ed Bradley, prominent black journalist on CBS's *60 Minutes*, when he died in 2006 of leukemia?

A Sixty-five
B Forty-three
C Sixty-nine
D Ninety-six

CBS.com

631 Phillis Wheatley was a great poet and the first black to have a book of poetry published in the United States. What is the name of the ship that brought her to North America?

A *Rainbow*
B *Golconda*
C *Sea Horse*
D *Phillis*

African American Lives, page 872

632 Harriet Jacob's autobiography *Incidents in the Life of a Slave Girl* is a detailed account of the suffering slaves had to endure. After Jacobs was willed to her master's niece, how old was her new master?

A   Three
B   Ten
C   Twenty
D   Sixty

Africana, page 1023

633 "The Slave Auction" is a gripping poem detailing the horrors of slavery. Who is the author?

A   Mary Prince
B   Lucy Bagby Johnson
C   Madame Bernard Couvent
D   Frances Harper

Black Saga, page 156

634 James Weldon Johnson was a poet, lawyer, novelist, and civil rights leader. In which state was he born?

A   Maryland
B   Georgia
C   Florida
D   Virginia

Afromation, March 7

635 Who was the first African American to play the lead role in Shakespeare's *Othello*?

A   Ira Aldridge
B   Sidney Poitier
C   Harry Belafonte
D   Paul Robeson

The Timetables of African American History, page 253

636 Who is the founder of *Encore* magazine?

A   Ida Elizabeth Lewis
B   John Johnson
C   Mari Evans
D   Oprah Winfrey

Great African-American Women, page 291

637 Which of the following poets died at the age of thirty-three after battling tuberculosis?

A   Langston Hughes
B   Paul Laurence Dunbar
C   Rita Dove
D   Phillis Wheatley

African American Lives, page 252

638 The life of which person is portrayed in the book *Uncle Tom's Cabin?*

A   David Clarke
B   Kayne West
C   Paris Dennard
D   Josiah Henson

Black Saga, page 94

639 What year was the miniseries *Roots* first broadcast on television?

A   1977
B   1970
C   1979
D   1980

African American Desk Reference, page 340

640 Harriet Adams Wilson wrote the first novel published by a black woman in the United States. What is the name of her novel?

A   *So Many Mountains to Climb*
B   *The Worst of Times*
C   *Our Nig*
D   *Why Do They Hate Us?*

African American Firsts, page 186

641 Whose child is *The President's Daughter* about?

A   Thomas Jefferson's
B   Franklin Roosevelt's
C   Lyndon Johnson's
D   George Washington's

African American Lives, page 120

642 Who is the author of *If They Come in the Morning*?

A   Angela Davis
B   Benjamin Chavis
C   Bobby Seale
D   Stokely Carmichael

African American Almanac, page 40

643 Who is the first black woman to have won a Pulitzer Prize for Drama?

A   Alice Walker
B   Suzan-Lori Parks
C   Lonette McKee
D   Toni Morrison

And Still I Rise, page 212

644 Who is the author of the poem "If We Must Die"?

A   Claude McKay
B   Martin Luther King Jr.
C   E. Franklin Frazier
D   Henry Garnet

African American Almanac, page 152

645 Who is the author of the first short story published in the United States by a black woman?

A   Sarah Parker Remond
B   Mary Burnett Talbert
C   Frances Watkins Harper
D   Willie Barrow

Black Firsts, page 743

646 Who is the author of *Autobiography of an Ex-Colored Man*?

A   Ben Carson
B   James Weldon Johnson
C   Clarence Thomas
D   Herman Cain

African American Lives, page 457

647 Who is the author of *The Negro Family in the United States*?

A   Henry Garnet
B   Charles McKay
C   Carter Woodson
D   E. Franklin Frazier

African American Almanac, page 104

648 Who was the first black male author to have a poem published in the United States?

A   Paul Dunbar
B   Langston Hughes
C   Jupiter Hammon
D   James Weldon Johnson

African American Firsts, 183

649 Who is the author of *Immunological Studies in Sickle Cell Anemia*?

A   William Cardozo
B   Louis Sullivan
C   Louis Wright
D   Charles Drew

African American Desk Reference, page 232

650 Who is the author of the book *April 4, 1968: Martin Luther King Jr.'s Death and How It Changed America*?

A   Coretta Scott King
B   John Lewis
C   Michael Eric Dyson
D   Jesse Jackson

651 Who authored the first slave narrative written by a female?

A   Harriet Tubman
B   Lucy Bagby Johnson
C   Madame Bernard Couvent
D   Mary Prince

Black Saga, page 108

652 Who is the author of *The Underground Railroad*?

A   George Schuyler
B   William Still
C   Mumia Abu Jamal
D   Harriet Tubman

Africana, page 1780

653 Who is the author of *Blues for Mr. Charlie*?

A   Wallace Thurmond
B   Lewis Allen
C   Richard Wright
D   James Baldwin

African American Lives, page 43

654 Which of the following wrote the first novel published by a black woman in the United States?

A   Elizabeth Jennings
B   Ann Plato
C   Harriet Adams Wilson
D   Margaret Garner

Black Saga, page 169

655 What pseudonym did author Harriet Jacobs use in her autobiography, *Incidents in the Life of a Slave Girl*, which details the suffering slaves endured?

A   Elizabeth Keckley
B   Harriet Tubman
C   Linda Brent
D   Harry Jacobs

Africana, page 1023

656 Who is the author of *Why Blacks Kill Blacks*?

A   James Porter
B   Alvin Poussaint
C   Lofton Mitchell
D   Robert Franklin Williams

657 Who was the first black to publish an almanac?

A   Benjamin Banneker
B   Samuel Ringgold Ward
C   A. Phillip Randolph
D   Frederick Douglass

African American Firsts, page 288

658 Who is the author of *Black Women in White*?

A   Estelle Osborne
B   Darlene Hine
C   Mary Elizabeth Mahoney
D   Susie King Taylor

Great African-American Women, page 286

659 Who is the author of *The President's Daughter*?

A   Richard Wright
B   Ralph Ellison
C   William Wells Brown
D   August Wilson

African American Lives, page 120

660 Frances Harper was a women's rights advocate, antislavery advocate, and author. In what city was she born?

A   Washington, DC
B   Memphis
C   Philadelphia
D   Baltimore

Africana, page 938

661 Who is the author of *Behind the Scenes: Or, Thirty Years a Slave and Four Years in the White House*?

A   Elizabeth Keckley
B   Solomon Northrup
C   Jocelyn Elders
D   Sally Hemmings

The Timetables of African American History, page 159

662 Who is the author of *The Negro's Church*?

A   Walter White
B   James Baldwin
C   Richard Wright
D   Benjamin Mays

Afromation, April 12

663 Which of the following white women is the author of *Uncle Tom's Cabin?*

A   Nancy Reagan
B   Harriet Beecher Stowe
C   Mary Todd
D   Susan B. Anthony

The Timetables of African American History, page 125

664 Lerone Bennett is an author, editor, and historian. What state was he born in?

A   North Carolina
B   Mississippi
C   South Carolina
D   Tennessee

African American Almanac, page 98

665 Who is the first known black to write a poem in English?

A   Frances Harper
B   Lucy Terry
C   Rita Dove
D   Harriet Jacobs

African American Lives, page 806

666 What is the fruit in the Billie Holiday song "Strange Fruit"?

A   lynched men
B   pomegranates
C   pineapples
D   coconuts

667 What is the name of the book that listed names and addresses of locations black travelers could dine or stay at during segregated times?

A   The Green Book
B   The Blue Book
C   The Colored Book
D   The Black Book

668 Who is the author of *Black No More*?

A   Jimmy Walker
B   Clarence Thomas
C   George Schuyler
D   Ken Hamblin

Africana, page 1678

669 When is Black History Month?

A   July
B   February
C   January
D   June

670 In which state is Alcorn State University located?

A Mississippi
B Louisiana
C Georgia
D Texas

671 In which state is Elizabeth City State University located?

A North Carolina
B Louisiana
C Virginia
D South Carolina

672 In which state is Shaw University located?

A South Carolina
B North Carolina
C Virginia
D West Virginia

673 In which state is Bowie State University located?

A Virginia
B Bowie
C Pennsylvania
D Maryland

674 In which state is Fayetteville State University located?

A   South Carolina
B   Louisiana
C   Maryland
D   North Carolina

675 In what city is Johnson C. Smith University located?

A   Atlanta
B   Charlotte
C   Durham
D   Raleigh

676 In what city is Morgan State University located?

A   Morgantown, West Virginia
B   Atlanta
C   Baltimore
D   Washington, DC

677 In which state is Bluefield State College located?

A   Texas
B   South Carolina
C   Virginia
D   West Virginia

678 Who was the first black president of Fisk University?

A Charles Spurgeon Johnson
B John Hope
C Benjamin Hooks
D Mordecai Johnson

Black Saga, page 332

679 In which state is Albany State located?

A Mississippi
B Florida
C South Carolina
D Georgia

680 In what state was John Hope, first black president of Atlanta Baptist College (now Morehouse), born?

A South Carolina
B North Carolina
C Georgia
D Tennessee

Africana, page 964

681 Mary Bethune was a civil rights leader and educator. In what state was she born?

A Maryland
B South Carolina
C Massachusetts
D North Carolina

African American Almanac, page 98

682 Of which college was Benjamin Mays the president from 1940 to 1967?

A   Morehouse
B   Howard
C   North Carolina A&T
D   Tuskegee

Afromation, April 12

683 In which state is Coppin State College located?

A   Coppin
B   Pennsylvania
C   Virginia
D   Maryland

684 In what city is Morehouse College located?

A   Philadelphia
B   Memphis
C   Atlanta
D   Washington, DC

685 In which state is Grambling located?

A   Florida
B   Georgia
C   Louisiana
D   Texas

686 In what year was Kappa Alpha Psi, a predominately black fraternity, founded?

A   1904
B   1917
C   1907
D   1911

Black Saga, page 303

687 In which state is Knoxville College located?

A   Tennessee
B   North Carolina
C   Kentucky
D   Virginia

688 In which state is Prairie View A&M University located?

A   Louisiana
B   Georgia
C   Texas
D   Florida

689 In what city is Howard University located?

A   Washington, DC
B   Charlotte
C   Nashville
D   Atlanta

690 In which state is Jackson State University located?

A   Mississippi
B   Louisiana
C   Jackson
D   Texas

691 In what city is Fisk University located?

A   Atlanta
B   Memphis
C   Nashville
D   Washington, DC

692 In which state is Saint Paul's College located?

A   West Virginia
B   South Carolina
C   Kentucky
D   Virginia

693 Where is Spelman College located?

A   Charlotte
B   Atlanta
C   Spelman City
D   Houston

694 In which state is Fort Valley State College located?

A Georgia
B Florida
C Fort Valley
D Mississippi

695 In what city is North Carolina A and T located?

A Durham
B Charlotte
C Raleigh
D Greensboro

696 At what university was Kappa Alpha Psi, a predominately black fraternity, founded?

A Harvard
B Howard
C Indiana
D Tuskegee

Black Saga, page 303

697 In what year was the first black sorority, Alpha Kappa Alpha, founded?

A 1937
B 1902
C 1897
D 1908

Black Saga, page 296

698 Who was the first black woman president of Spelman College?

A   Fannie Coppin
B   Eunice Rivers
C   Jane Bolin
D   Johnetta Cole

African American Desk Reference, page 206

699 In which state is Hampton University located?

A   West Virginia
B   South Carolina
C   North Carolina
D   Virginia

700 Which college was once known as Atlanta Baptist?

A   Howard
B   Clark
C   Morehouse
D   Morris Brown

Encyclopedia of Black America, page 566

701 Which of the following men was named Michael at birth?

A   Martin Luther King Jr.
B   Spike Lee
C   Malcolm X
D   Magic Johnson

Afromation, March 8

702 Which civil rights icon died in 2005?

A   Fannie Hamer
B   John Lewis
C   Julian Bond
D   Rosa Parks

And Still I Rise, page 227

703 Which civil rights icon died in 2006?

A   John Lewis
B   Julian Bond
C   Fannie Hamer
D   Coretta Scott King

African American Almanac, page 45

704 Which of the following men was never married?

A   George Washington Carver
B   Medgar Evers
C   Frederick Douglass
D   Booker T. Washington

African American Lives, page 147

705 How old was Nelson Mandela when he died?

A   One hundred
B   Eighty-one
C   Fifty-two
D   Ninety-five

And Still I Rise, page 270

706 In what South African massacre were sixty-nine blacks killed by police?

A   Orangeburg
B   Central
C   M Street
D   Sharpeville

Africana, page 1701

707 Which of the following speaks Japanese, Russian, and Swahili?

A   Oprah Winfrey
B   Condoleezza Rice
C   Susan Rice
D   Mae Jemison

NASA biography data

708 What states is Gullah, a language and culture of West Africa and the Caribbean, most often associated with?

A   Florida and Alabama
B   Texas and Louisiana
C   South Carolina and Georgia
D   Virginia and West Virginia

Africana, page 895

709 What country had a major earthquake in 2010?

A   Nigeria
B   Haiti
C   Sudan
D   Jamaica

And Still I Rise, page 251

710 What is the last name of the couple in the Supreme Court case that resulted in the legalization of interracial marriage in the United States?

A   Brown
B   Loving
C   Hate
D   White

Civil Rights Chronicle, page 335

711 What was the name of the man who filibustered for over twenty-four hours against a civil rights bill?

A   Strom Thurmond
B   Clarence Thomas
C   Jesse Helms
D   Trent Lott

Black Saga, page 397

712 Two females had been on the Supreme Court in the first 233 years of the United States. How many women did Barack Obama appoint in his eight years as US president?

A Three
B Zero
C One
D Two

713 Which of the following was convicted (by an all-black jury) in Georgia for killing two law enforcement officers?

A Todd Bridges
B Tupac Shakur
C Stokely Carmichael
D Rap Brown

African American Lives, page 107

714 In what year did lawyer Johnnie Cochran die?

A 2009
B 2005
C 2012
D 2002

African American National Biography, vol. 2, page 341

715 In what state was Anita Hill, who accused Clarence Thomas of sexual harassment, born?

A   Arkansas
B   Florida
C   Oklahoma
D   Texas

African American Almanac, page 42

716 Which of the following is Lani Guinier's profession?

A   Police Chief
B   FBI Agent
C   Professor and lawyer
D   Judge

African American Desk Reference, page 330

717 Which of the following scored 101 points in a high school basketball game that ended at halftime because the opponent quit?

A   Michael Jordan
B   Wilt Chamberlain
C   Lisa Leslie
D   Cheryl Miller

Los Angeles Times, February 8, 1990

718 Who is the first black female to win the all-around gold medal in gymnastics?

A   Simone Biles
B   Dominique Dawes
C   Diane Durham
D   Gabby Douglas

And Still I Rise, page 261

719 Who was the founder of the Negro Baseball League?

A   Josh Gibson
B   Satchel Paige
C   Rube Foster
D   Buck O'Neil

The Timetables of African American History, page 223

720 What congressman was a star quarterback at the University of Oklahoma?

A   J. C. Watts
B   Charles Rangel
C   John Conyers
D   Kweisi Mfume

African American National Biography, vol. 8, page 176

721 Who became the first black in Major League Baseball in 1947?

A   Josh Gibson
B   Hank Aaron
C   Willie Mays
D   Jackie Robinson

722 Which college did Jackie Robinson attend?

A   Michigan
B   Southern California
C   Illinois
D   UCLA

Afromation, November 27

723 Who was the first black golfer to qualify to play in the Masters Tournament in Augusta, Georgia?

A   Calvin Peete
B   Lee Elder
C   Tiger Woods
D   Charlie Sifford

Black Saga, page 465

724 Who was the first black jockey to ride a winning horse in the Kentucky Derby?

A   Willie Sims
B   Oliver Lewis
C   Jimmy Winkfield
D   Isaac Murphy

The Timetables of African American History, page 175

725 Boxer Jack Johnson was arrested for taking his white girlfriend (and future wife) across state lines. What law forbade taking women across state lines for "immoral purposes"?

A   The Skeezer Act
B   The Snow White Act
C   The Purity Act
D   The Mann Act

African American Lives, page 455

726 Don Imus made racist and sexist comments on his radio program about which of the following basketball teams?

A   Tennessee
B   LA Sparks
C   Detroit Pistons
D   Rutgers

And Still I Rise, page 231

727 Which Football Hall of Fame member became a supreme court justice in Minnesota?

A   Alan Page
B   Carl Eller
C   Chuck Foreman
D   Jim Marshall

Any Given Number, page 189

728 Who was the coach of Rutgers when Don Imus, radio host, made racist and sexist remarks about the team's basketball players?

A   Dawn Staley
B   Vivian Springer
C   Nikki Caldwell
D   Carolyn Peck

And Still I Rise, page 231

729 Which of the following was once a football coach at Morgan College?

A   Jesse Jackson
B   Charles Drew
C   Marion Barry
D   Ron McNair

Africana, page 632

730 Bill Pickett was a legendary black cowboy and rodeo star. In what state was he born?

A   Louisiana
B   Georgia
C   Oklahoma
D   Texas

African American Firsts, page 326

731 Which of the following was a black cowboy?

A   Redd Foxx
B   Deadeye Dick
C   Deadwood Dick
D   Brown Foxx

Black Firsts, page 710

732 Bill Pickett was a famous cowboy and rodeo star. What killed him?

A   Being shot in a gunfight
B   Malaria
C   A gunshot from a Native American
D   A horse kick to the head

Africana, page 1524

733 Which of the following had polio and scarlet fever as a child?

A   Gymnast Simone Biles
B   Track star Wilma Rudolph
C   Track star Florence Griffith Joyner
D   Basketball star Cheryl Miller

African American Almanac, page 440

734 What July 4, 1910 event led to race riots that resulted in the killings of thirteen blacks?

A   Jack Johnson defeating former heavyweight champion Jim Jeffries
B   New York July 4th celebration
C   The election of a black vice-president
D   Las Vegas July 4th celebration

African American National Biography, vol. 4, page 582

735 Which of the following events did white Virginia Governor Ralph Northam not remember if it happened?

A   if he played in the NBA
B   if he was ever president
C   if he kissed a porcupine
D   if he was in blackface, if he was in klan hood

736 Which of the following was the first southern city to integrate lunch counters?

A   Dallas
B   Fort Worth
C   Houston
D   San Antonio

The Timetables of African American History, page 278

737 Otis Redding was a famous rhythm and blues singer. In what year was he killed in a plane crash?

A   1970
B   1963
C   1971
D   1967

African American Desk Reference, page 395

738 Who was the first black woman nominated for an Oscar for Best Actress in a Leading Role?

A   Halle Berry
B   Whoopi Goldberg
C   Dorothy Dandridge
D   Hattie McDaniel

African American Almanac, page 222

739 In 1970, the first African American woman entered the Miss America Pageant as a contestant. Who was she?

A   Cheryl Brown
B   Vanessa Williams
C   Dorothy Dandridge
D   Beverly Johnson

The Timetables of African American History, page 310

740 What song asks the antiwar question "How you gonna make me kill somebody I don't even know"?

A   War's "The World Is a Ghetto"
B   Edwin Starr's "War"
C   Stevie Wonder's "Heaven Help Us All"
D   Prince's "Party Up"

741 What is legendary dancer Bill Robinson's nickname?

A   Rockin' Robin
B   Wild Bill
C   Bojangles
D   Smoothie

742 Who was the first black to sing before the Queen of England?

A   Marian Anderson
B   Diana Ross
C   Tina Turner
D   Elizabeth Greenfield

Great African American Women, page 285

743 Which state is the birthplace of Oprah Winfrey?

A   Alabama
B   Mississippi
C   New York
D   Tennessee

African American Almanac, page 194

744 Which ship did Stephen Spielberg make a movie about?

A *Amistad*
B *Clothide*
C *Golconda*
D *W. S. Waring*

And Still I Rise, page 193

745 Who played Mammy in *Gone with the Wind*?

A Hattie McDaniel
B Butterfly McQueen
C Lena Horne
D Ruby Dee

African American Firsts, page 80

746 Who was the first black to produce and direct a major Hollywood film?

A Melvin Van Peebles
B John Singleton
C Mario Van Peebles
D Gordon Parks Sr.

African American Firsts, page 83

747 Who was the first black woman to have her work performed on Broadway?

A   Maya Angelou
B   Alice Walker
C   Lorraine Hansberry
D   Alice Childress

Black Firsts, page 17

748 Which of the following radio stations became the first black-owned radio station in the United States?

A   BIRD
B   WERD
C   WILD
D   WORD

Black Firsts, page 62

749 For what movie did John Singleton receive the Best Director Oscar nomination?

A   *Straight Out of Compton*
B   *New Jack City*
C   *Boyz n the Hood*
D   *Juice*

Black Saga, page 547

750 Which of the following was the first black film?

A *Stormy Weather*
B *Body and Soul*
C *The Railroad Porter*
D *School Daze*

751 Who is the first black princess in a Disney movie?

A Tiana
B Snow White
C Ebony
D Cinderella

And Still I Rise, page 247

752 Who portrayed the character Jane Pittman in a movie?

A Dorothy Dandridge
B Cicely Tyson
C Hattie McDaniel
D Whoopi Goldberg

African American Almanac, page 252

753 Who composed "Lift Every Voice and Sing" with James Weldon Johnson?

A Scott Joplin
B Stevie Wonder
C John Rosamond Johnson
D Thomas Turpin

African American Lives, page 458

754 Who was the second black Miss America?

A   Vanessa Williams
B   Helen Ford
C   Kimberly Allen
D   Suzette Charles

Almanac of African American Heritage, page 81

755 Who was the first black person to appear regularly on a television soap opera?

A   Cicely Tyson
B   Ellen Holly
C   Holly Evans
D   Louise Beavers

Black Saga, page 442

756 Who was the first black female sculpture to exhibit her work in Rome?

A   Edmonia Lewis
B   Nancy Prophet
C   Phoebe Beasley
D   Meta Fuller

Black Firsts, page 64

757 Who was *Glamour* magazine's 1991 Woman of the Year?

A   Iman
B   Anita Hill
C   Naomi Campbell
D   Vanessa Williams

Great African-American Women, page 115

758 What was the name of the first winner of the Miss Black America Pageant?

A   Suzette Charles
B   Saundra Williams
C   Dorothy Dandridge
D   Beverly Johnson

Black Saga, page 442

759 Which of the following men was a nineteenth-century Shakespearean actor?

A   Ira Aldridge
B   Joshua Johnson
C   Nathaniel Whiting
D   Stepin Fetchit

Black Saga, page 95

760 What man's life is the movie *The Great White Hope* based on?

A   Joe Frazier
B   Jack Johnson
C   James Earl Jones
D   Muhammad Ali

African American Lives, page 454

761 What city is the birthplace of comedian and social activist Dick Gregory?

A   Chicago
B   Memphis
C   New Orleans
D   Saint Louis

762 In what year was the first Miss Black America Pageant held?

A   1972
B   1944
C   1968
D   1956

Black Saga, page 442

763 In what year was the Dance Theatre of Harlem School founded?

A   1943
B   1969
C   1974
D   1956

Black Saga, page 445

764 Which state did the first black contestant in the Miss America Pageant represent?

A   Massachusetts
B   Iowa
C   New Jersey
D   New York

The Timetables of African American History, page 310

765 Which man was a famous portrait painter in the late 1700s and early 1800s?

A   Joshua Johnson
B   Canada Lee
C   Jamie Killicks
D   Paul Dunbar

Black Saga, page 74

766 Which of the following is Marian Anderson's profession?

A   Playwright
B   Sculptor
C   Pianist
D   Opera singer

Afromation, December 3

767 Which of the following died of cancer at the age of thirty-four?

A   Lorraine Hansberry
B   Billie Holiday
C   Dorothy Dandridge
D   Lena Horne

Black Saga, page 400

768 Which of the following died of an epileptic seizure?

A   Track star Florence Griffith Joyner
B   Singer Billie Holiday
C   Congresswoman Barbara Jordan
D   Track star Wilma Rudolph

African American National Biography, vol. 3, page 647

769 Which of the following is Josephine Baker's profession?

A   Director
B   Pianist
C   Dancer and singer
D   Newscaster

Afromation, April 17

770 Who was the "Wonder-Boy Preacher"?

A   Louis Farrakhan
B   Charles Emanuel Grace
C   Al Sharpton
D   Martin Luther King Jr.

Africana, page 1702

771 Who is the pastor of the Potter's House in Dallas, Texas?

A   Father Divine
B   Eddie Long
C   T. D. Jakes
D   Creflo Dollar

African American Almanac, page 125

772 In what state was Richard Allen, founder of the AME (African Methodist Episcopal) Church, born?

A   Virginia
B   North Carolina
C   Maryland
D   Pennsylvania

Afromation, October 1

773 How old was Al Sharpton when he began preaching?

A   Seven
B   Four
C   Fifteen
D   Twenty-one

Africana, page 1702

774 Which member of the Nation of Islam was born with the last name Poole?

A   Louis Farrakhan
B   Elijah Muhammad
C   Malcolm X
D   Muhammad Ali

African American Almanac, page 28

775 Which of the following was a white wife of Father Divine?

A   The Divine Mother
B   Helen Reddy
C   Sweet Thing
D   Sweet Angel

African American Lives, page 291

776 In what year did the Mormon Church rule that a single drop of black blood made a person unfit to become a priest?

A   1876
B   1865
C   1866
D   1855

Black Saga, page 160

777 In what year did South African archbishop Desmond Tutu win the Nobel Peace Prize?

A   1986
B   1980
C   1984
D   1987

Chronology of African American History, 2nd ed., page 371

778 Father Divine was a religious leader and advocate for equality. In what state was he born?

A   South Carolina
B   Virginia
C   Missouri
D   Maryland

African American Lives, page 290

779 Who founded the African Methodist Episcopal Church?

A   Jesse Jackson
B   Richard Allen
C   Claude Barnett
D   Robert Abbott

Afromation, October 1

780 T. D. Jakes founded the Greater Emmanuel Temple of Faith in 1979. Where was it located?

A Houston
B Montgomery, West Virginia
C Natchez, Mississippi
D Dallas

African American Almanac, page 125

781 In what year was the Nation of Islam founded?

A 1960
B 1940
C 1950
D 1930

The Timetables of African American History, page 236

782 Who founded the Nation of Islam?

A Elijah Muhammad
B Louis Farrakhan
C Malcolm X
D Wallace Fard

Africana, page 1399

783 In what city was the Nation of Islam founded?

A   Chicago
B   Dallas
C   Detroit
D   New York

The Timetables of African American History, page 236

784 Which member of the Nation of Islam was born with the last name Clay?

A   Louis Farrakhan
B   Muhammad Ali
C   Malcolm X
D   Elijah Muhammad

African American Almanac, page 420

785 What is the title of the *New Yorker* magazine cover that depicted President Obama and Mrs. Obama as radical Muslims?

A   "The Politics of Hatred"
B   "The Politics of Racism"
C   "The Politics of Fear"
D   "The Politics of Scum"

786 National Negro Doll was a company that made black dolls. What year was it founded?

A   1951
B   1921
C   1931
D   1911

The Timetables of African American History, page 210

787 Who was the founder of North Carolina Mutual Insurance Company?

A   John Merrick
B   Edward Bouchet
C   John Knowles Paine
D   Tony Brown

African American Desk Reference, page 11

788 Who was the first black female CEO of a Fortune 500 company?

A   Ursula Burns
B   Oprah Winfrey
C   Madam C. J. Walker
D   Beyoncé

And Still I Rise, page 245

789 Who was the first black woman to become a billionaire?

A   Aretha Franklin
B   Shelia Rice Johnson
C   Beyoncé
D   Oprah Winfrey

790 Which black man owned a variety of businesses in Memphis and was nicknamed "the Boss of Beale Street"?

A   Earl Graves
B   Kenneth Clark
C   Reginald Lewis
D   Robert Church Sr.

Africana, page 435

791 Who was the first self-made female millionaire in the United States?

A   Patricia Roberts Harris
B   Jane Bolin
C   Oprah Winfrey
D   Madam C. J. Walker

Black Saga, page 302

792 Which company did John W. Thompson become chairman of in 2014?

A   Twitter
B   Microsoft
C   Exxon
D   Facebook

And Still I Rise, page 272

793 Which woman's parents were a twelve-year-old black girl and a white rapist?

A   Dorothy Dandridge
B   Ethel Waters
C   Mahalia Jackson
D   Lena Horne

African American Lives, page 858

794 What colony made a 1729 law stipulating that cutting a slave into four pieces and displaying the pieces in public was legal for some crimes?

A   Virginia
B   Georgia
C   South Carolina
D   Maryland

Black Saga, page 33

795 Which colony enacted a 1740 law that made it illegal to castrate, cut out the tongue of, put out an eye of, or scald a slave?

A   Rhode Island
B   South Carolina
C   North Carolina
D   Virginia

Black Saga, page 36

796 In what year was Abner Louima sodomized by a policeman with a stick?

A   1963
B   1997
C   1993
D   2001

And Still I Rise, page 191

797 For what crime did a 1712 South Carolina law make it legal to castrate a slave?

A   Being a three-time runaway
B   Being a four-time thief
C   Being a four-time runaway
D   Being a two-time runaway

Black Saga, page 27

798 Where was Abner Louima sodomized with a stick by a policeman?

A   In a restaurant
B   In a nightclub
C   In the woods
D   At a police precinct

And Still I Rise, page 191

799 Which woman was impregnated twice as a result of rapes (one by a black man and one by a white sheriff)?

A   Moms Mabley
B   Maya Angelou
C   Billie Holiday
D   Oprah Winfrey

Africana, page 1214

800 Which of the following women was raped as a seven-year-old?

A   Oprah Winfrey
B   Billie Holiday
C   Moms Mabley
D   Maya Angelou

Africana, page 103

Music

801 According to the Wilson Pickett song, who needs to slow his or her Mustang down?

A   Susie
B   Maybelline
C   Papa
D   Sally

802 What is the destination of the midnight train in the Gladys Knight song?

A   Georgia
B   Kansas City
C   Los Angeles
D   Virginia

803 What was Ben E. King's first solo hit after he left the Drifters?

A   "Don't Play That Song"
B   "It's All Over"
C   "Spanish Harlem"
D   "I Had a Love"

804 Which artist(s) recorded "I Stand Accused"?

A   Otis Redding
B   Sam and Dave
C   Marvin Gaye
D   Isaac Hayes

805 Which artist recorded "Sweet Soul Music"?

A   Arthur Conley
B   Bill Withers
C   Bobby Womack
D   Clarence Carter

806 According to an Isaac Hayes song, who is "a bad mother (shut your mouth)"?

A   Superfly
B   Moms Mabley
C   Truck Turner
D   Shaft

807 What is legendary performer Tina Turner's birth name?

A   Willie Mae Thornton
B   Cora Walton
C   Lillie Mae Jones
D   Anna Mae Bullock

808 In his song, what does Joe Tex say he will not do with a big fat woman?

A   Make love with her
B   Let her sit on his bed
C   Bump no more
D   Take her to dinner

809 Who was the first female artist inducted into the Rock and Roll Hall of Fame?

A   Tina Turner
B   Gladys Knight
C   Aretha Franklin
D   Diana Ross

810 Which artist(s) recorded "Teardrops from My Eyes"?

A   Ruth Brown
B   Lena Horne
C   Mahalia Jackson
D   The Platters

811 What kind of music is legendary performer Gary Davis best known for?

A   Jazz
B   Rap
C   Gospel
D   R&B (soul)

812 Which of the following jumps the fence in the Rufus Thomas song "Walking the Dog"?

A   A dog
B   An elephant
C   A kangaroo
D   A man

813 What kind of music is legendary performer Nat King Cole best known for?

A   Rap
B   Gospel
C   Jazz
D   Reggae

814 Which of the following released a 2017 album titled *Freedom Highway*?

A   Stevie Wonder
B   Common
C   Rhiannon Giddens
D   John Legend

815 The group Arrested Development had a song with a state's name as the title. What is the name of the song?

A   "Georgia"
B   "Tennessee"
C   "Mississippi"
D   "New York"

816 What kind of music is legendary performer Sam Lightnin' Hopkins best known for?

A   Blues
B   Country
C   Jazz
D   R&B (soul)

817 According to the Whodini song, when do the freaks come out?

A   At noon
B   During full moons
C   At dusk
D   At night

818 Which artist(s) recorded *They Call Me the Fat Man*?

A   Heavy D
B   Big Pun
C   Fats Domino
D   Barry White

819 Which of the following groups did Jerry Butler sing with?

A   The O'Jays
B   The Impressions
C   The Spinners
D   The Temptations

820 What city is the birthplace of legendary singer James Cleveland?

A   Chicago
B   Cleveland
C   Detroit
D   New York

821 How old was Michael Jackson when he died?

A   Fifty
B   Fourteen
C   Forty-three
D   Fifty-seven

822 Which artist recorded "Ain't Got No Home"?

A   Z. Z. Hill
B   Fats Domino
C   Sonny Boy Williamson
D   Clarence Henry

823 In the Stevie Wonder song "Superstition," how old is the baby that breaks the looking glass?

A   Thirteen months
B   Thirteen days
C   Seven months
D   Seven days

824 Which artist recorded the hit song "Whatever You Like"?

A   T-Pain
B   Ice Milk
C   T.I.
D   Ice Cube

825 What kind of music is legendary performer Chuck Berry best known for?

A   Jazz
B   Rock and roll
C   Rap
D   Blues

826 What is the number of the cloud in the Temptations song?

A   Nine
B   Twelve
C   One
D   Seven

827 From where does the midnight train depart in the Gladys Knight song?

A   Georgia
B   Chicago
C   New York
D   Los Angeles

828 Which of the following is not a title of a Notorious B.I.G. album?

A   *Born Again*
B   *Life After Death*
C   *Will Live Till I Die*
D   *Ready to Die*

829 In the O'Jays song "Brandy," the title character is a _____.

A   Girlfriend
B   Dog
C   Cat
D   Ex-girlfriend

830 What kind of music is legendary performer Sidney Bechet best known for?

A   Gospel
B   Jazz
C   Funk
D   Rap

831 What city is the birthplace of rapper Luther Campbell?

A   Orlando
B   Atlanta
C   Myrtle Beach, South Carolina
D   Miami

832 Which artist recorded "What's Love Got to Do with It"?

A   Tina Turner
B   Roberta Flack
C   Diana Ross
D   Whitney Houston

833 Edwin Starr had a hit song titled "War." According to the song, what is war good for?

A   Absolutely nothing
B   Keeping the population small
C   Killing communists
D   Stopping terrorism

834 Which artist recorded the 2001 hit song "Family Affair"?

A   Mariah Carey
B   Mary J. Blige
C   Brandy
D   Monica

835 What kind of music is legendary performer Freddie King best known for?

A   Blues
B   Classical
C   Jazz
D   R&B (soul)

836 Which member of the Jackson Five was named Sigmund?

A   Tito
B   Michael
C   Randy
D   Jackie

837 What is the name of David Ruffin's brother who was also a famous singer?

A   Johnny Ruffin
B   Donnie Ruffin
C   Ronnie Ruffin
D   Jimmy Ruffin

838 What kind of music is legendary performer André Watts best known for?

A   Gospel
B   Classical
C   Rap
D   Reggae

839 Which artist recorded the album *Modern Sounds in Country and Western Music*?

A   Roy C
B   Blind Lemon Jefferson
C   Charley Pride
D   Ray Charles

840 According to the Platters song, what gets in your eyes?

A   Smog
B   Smoke
C   Eye drops
D   Tears

841 R&B singer Marvin Gaye was murdered. Who was the murderer?

A   His father
B   A Klansman
C   A jealous husband
D   His wife

842 According to the Beyoncé song, "If you like it, then you ought to ____it."

A   Bite it
B   Kiss it
C   Put a ring on it
D   Pay for it

843 Which artist(s) recorded "Do It till You're Satisfied"?

A   The Sex Machines
B   Digital Underground
C   The Satisfactions
D   B. T. Express

844 Which Jackson recorded *Rhythm Nation*?

A   Michael
B   Jermaine
C   LaToya
D   Janet

845 How old was blues legend Blind Lemon Jefferson when he died?

A   Thirty-two
B   Thirty-eight
C   Forty
D   Forty-two

846 Who was nicknamed Peg Leg because he lost his leg at the age of twelve in a sawmill accident?

A   Clayton Bates
B   Maurice Hines
C   Bert Williams
D   George Walker

African American Desk Reference, page 425

847 Which artist recorded "Don't Answer the Door"?

A   Little Milton
B   Z. Z. Hill
C   Jimmy Reed
D   B.B. King

848 What city is the birthplace of singer Tracy Chapman?

A   Columbus, Ohio
B   Columbia, South Carolina
C   Cleveland
D   Dayton, Ohio

849 What place is Dionne Warwick looking for when she asks, "Do you know the way?"

A Kansas City
B San Jose
C Georgia
D Virginia

850 Afrika Bambaataa recorded a song titled "The Renegades of_____."

A Soul
B Freedom
C Funk
D Rap

851 Which artist(s) recorded an album titled *Fear of a Black Planet*?

A Ice-T
B Ice Cube
C N.W.A.
D Public Enemy

852 Which of the following artists recorded "Hound Dog"?

A Billie Holiday
B Big Mama Thornton
C Koko Taylor
D Mitty Collier

853 DJ Yella and MC Ren were members of which group?

A 2 Live Crew
B N.W.A.
C The Four Tops
D The Treacherous Three

854 What kind of music is legendary performer Natalie Hinderas best known for?

A R&B (soul)
B Funk
C Jazz
D Classical

855 How old was Jimi Hendrix when he died?

A Seventeen
B Twenty-seven
C Twenty-nine
D Thirty-one

856 Which artist recorded "Pannonica"?

A Thelonious Monk
B Nat King Cole
C Stevie Wonder
D W. C. Handy

857 Which artist recorded "Function at the Junction"?

A   Shorty Long
B   George Clinton
C   Kurtis Blow
D   Too Short

858 Which of the following groups did Philippe Wynne join after leaving the Spinners?

A   The Four Tops
B   Funkadelic
C   The Rolling Stones
D   The Temptations

859 Mos Def and Talib Kweli are members of which of the following groups?

A   Black Star
B   Blackstreet
C   Whitesnake
D   Public Enemy

860 What musical instrument is legendary performer Dizzy Gillespie best known for playing?

A   Guitar
B   Piano
C   Saxophone
D   Trumpet

861 Which artists recorded "On Broadway"?

A   The Drifters
B   The Temptations
C   The Four Tops
D   New York City

862 What city is the birthplace of legendary singer Stevie Wonder?

A   Gary, Indiana
B   Saginaw, Michigan
C   Macon, Georgia
D   Los Angeles

863 Which of the following is Dorothy Donegan's profession?

A   Jazz singer and pianist
B   Playwright
C   Poet
D   Sculptor

864 According to the Fats Domino song, where did he find his thrill?

A   Cherry Hill
B   Blackberry Hill
C   Blueberry Hill
D   Strawberry Hill

865 According to the title of the Charley Pride song, what do you do to an angel in the morning?

A   Kiss her
B   Pray to her
C   Love her like the devil
D   Give her breakfast

866 Complete the Roberta Flack song title: "First Time Ever I Saw Your _____."

A   Eyes
B   Face
C   Love
D   Heart

867 What kind of music is legendary performer Uhuru Black best known for?

A   Jazz
B   Reggae
C   R&B (soul)
D   Rap

868 "_____ Minutes of Funk" is the title of a Whodini song.

A   Five
B   Ten
C   Thirty
D   Sixty

869 Which Tennessee city or town is the birthplace of Tina Turner?

A   Nutbush
B   Nashville
C   Memphis
D   Knoxville

870 Which artist(s) recorded "The Humpty Dance"?

A   B. T. Express
B   Digital Underground
C   Arrested Development
D   The Spinners

871 Which artist(s) recorded the hit song "Hey Ya"?

A   Ne-Yo
B   Outkast
C   Public Enemy
D   De La Soul

872 Otis Redding was a famous rhythm and blues singer. How old was he when he died?

A   Forty-four
B   Thirty-four
C   Forty-two
D   Twenty-six

873 Which artist recorded *Bags & Trane*?

A   Milt Jackson
B   Louis Armstrong
C   Miles Davis
D   Wynton Marsalis

874 Which artist recorded "The Harder They Come"?

A   Bob Marley
B   Burning Spear
C   Charles Brown
D   Jimmy Cliff

875 Which artist(s) recorded "Dirty Mind"?

A   2 Live Crew
B   Prince
C   The Ohio Players
D   N.W.A.

876 Billy Ocean's song "When The Going Gets Tough, The Tough Gets Going" is on the soundtrack of which movie?

A   Tough Enough
B   Jewel Of The Nile
C   Romancing The Stone
D   Tough Guys

877 Who is the most famous black country-and-western singer?

A   Son House
B   Chuck Berry
C   Little Richard
D   Charley Pride

878 Which artist recorded "Down Home Blues"?

A   Ike Turner
B   Clarence Henry
C   Sonny Boy Williamson
D   Z. Z. Hill

879 What is Kurtis Blow's birth name?

A   Little Walter
B   Walker Smith
C   Kurtis Walker
D   Curtis Jackson

880 What musical instrument is legendary performer Bo Diddley best known for?

A   Piano
B   Guitar
C   Saxophone
D   Trumpet

881 Which artist(s) recorded *First Take*?

A   Take 6
B   Betty Wright
C   Donna Summer
D   Roberta Flack

882 Which group did Jeffrey Osborne sing with?

A   SOS
B   The Delphonics
C   LTD
D   The Platters

883 Which artist(s) recorded "Everybody Is a Star"?

A   Sister Sledge
B   The Pointer Sisters
C   Sly and the Family Stone
D   The Spinners

884 How many Grammy awards did Michael Jackson's album *Thriller* win?

A   Five
B   Two
C   Eight
D   Ten

885 Which artist recorded the hit song "Big Poppa"?

A   Lil Wayne
B   The Notorious B.I.G.
C   Tupac Shakur
D   50 Cent

886 What can the Weekend not feel in his song?

A   His heart
B   His feet
C   His face
D   His legs

887 Which of the following is legendary performer Billie Holiday's nickname?

A   Holly
B   Lady Day
C   Wild Bill
D   The Blues Queen

888 Which artist recorded "I'll Play the Blues for You"?

A   Jimmy Reed
B   B.B. King
C   Albert King
D   Little Milton

889 Which of the following is the title of a song by Outkast?

A "Ms. Jordan"
B "Me and Mrs. Jones"
C "Ms. Johnson"
D "Ms. Jackson"

890 Which of the following music is legendary performer Tina Turner best known for?

A Rap
B Country
C Gospel
D R&B (soul)

891 Which of the following is the title of a Snoop Dogg song?

A "Vodka on Ice"
B "Gin and Juice"
C "Beer and Weed"
D "Rum and Coke"

892 According to a Chuck Berry song, who is asked, "Why can't you be true?"

A Renee
B Miss Molly
C Papa
D Maybelline

893 Which artist(s) recorded "Hold On, I'm Coming"?

A   Sam Cooke
B   Isaac Hayes
C   Sam and Dave
D   The Temptations

894 Which artist recorded "Limbo Rock"?

A   Chuck Berry
B   Chubby Checker
C   Fats Domino
D   Little Richard

895 Which artist recorded "Maple Leaf Rag"?

A   Duke Ellington
B   Count Basie
C   Scott Joplin
D   W. C. Handy

896 Which artist(s) recorded the hit song "Paid in Full"?

A   Wu Tang Clan
B   Eric B. and Rakim
C   Black-Eyed Peas
D   Rob Base and DJ E-Z Rock

897 Which artist recorded "Boogaloo Down Broadway"?

A Fats Domino
B Chubby Checker
C Johnny C
D Roy C

898 What was singer Melba Moore's birth name?

A Judith Moore
B Beatrice Hill
C Melba Lynn Smith
D Melvina Scott

899 What kind of music is Rob Base best known for?

A Classical
B Jazz
C R&B (soul)
D Rap

900 Which artist(s) recorded "Jimmy Mack"?

A Jimmy Mack
B The Supremes
C The Marvalettes
D Martha and the Vandellas

901 T-Bone Walker was a great blues man. What was his real name?

A   Joseph Walker
B   Eddie Walker
C   Aaron Walker
D   Walker Smith

902 Which artist recorded "Little Walter"?

A   Timmi Tymmi Tommi
B   Little Walter
C   Terri Terry Turri
D   Tony Toni Tone

903 Which artist(s) recorded "Mercy"?

A   Robert Cray
B   Miles Davis
C   Andraé Crouch
D   Take 6

904 Which artist recorded "Ghostbusters"?

A   Van McCoy
B   George McCrae
C   Prince
D   Ray Parker Jr.

905 Which artist(s) recorded "Sittin' on the Dock of the Bay"?

A   Jerry Butler
B   Otis Redding
C   Isaac Hayes
D   Percy Sledge

906 In the Tupac song, he sings about love in which state?

A   California
B   New York
C   Florida
D   Texas

907 Which artist(s) recorded the hit song "C.R.E.A.M."?

A   Wu Tang Clan
B   The Treacherous Three
C   The Cream Puffs
D   Public Enemy

908 Which of the following artist(s) recorded "Get Your Kicks on Route 66"?

A   Jimmy Cliff
B   Burning Spear
C   James Brown
D   The King Cole Trio

909 Which artist(s) recorded "The Breaks"?

A   Tupac Shakur
B   B. T. Express
C   Shorty Long
D   Kurtis Blow

910 According to a James Brown song, who has a brand-new bag?

A   Mama
B   Miss Molly
C   Papa
D   Renee

911 What kind of music is legendary performer Benny Carter best known for?

A   Jazz
B   Country
C   Rap
D   R&B (soul)

912 What kind of music is legendary performer W. C. Handy best known for?

A   Blues
B   Jazz
C   R&B (soul)
D   Rap

913 Which of the following did LL Cool J say he could not live without in a song title?

A   His women
B   His Corvette
C   His boom box
D   His radio

914 Which of the following is Ma Rainey's profession?

A   Blues singer
B   Opera singer
C   Preacher
D   Rapper

915 What musical instruments is legendary performer Herbie Hancock best known for playing?

A   Trumpet and trombone
B   Guitar and bass
C   Fiddle and banjo
D   Piano and keyboard

916 Which member of the Jackson family had the hit song "Daddy's Home"?

A   Jermaine
B   Joseph
C   Michael
D   Randy

917 Which of the following was actress and singer Brandy's last name at birth?

A Jackson
B Norwood
C Johnson
D DeBarge

918 In the Roberta Flack song "Killing Me Softly," she is being softly killed by his _____.

A Song
B Feathers
C Knife
D Love

919 Who is nicknamed "the Crown Prince of Gospel"?

A Edwin Hawkins
B James Cleveland
C Pop Staples
D Thomas Dorsey

920 Which of the following was the host of the nationally syndicated television show *Soul Train*?

A Samuel L. Jackson
B Tom Joyner
C Morgan Freeman
D Don Cornelius

921 Who is nicknamed "the Father of Soul"?

A   Percy Sledge
B   James Brown
C   Ray Charles
D   Clarence Carter

922 What was Ike Turner's first name at birth?

A   Izear
B   Isiah
C   Luster
D   Isaac

The Encyclopedia of Jazz and Blues, page 656

923 Which artist(s) recorded "My Guy"?

A   Diana Ross
B   Martha and the Vandellas
C   The Marvalettes
D   Mary Wells

924 According to the Ray Parker song, who you gonna call when something strange is going on?

A   The police
B   Ghostbusters
C   9/1/2001
D   Casper

925 Which artist recorded "Wang Dang Doodle"?

A   Mitty Collier
B   Billie Holiday
C   Memphis Minnie
D   Koko Taylor

926 Which artist recorded "Memphis Blues"?

A   Muddy Waters
B   Count Basie
C   Memphis Minnie
D   W. C. Handy

927 Which of the following groups did Eddie Levert sing with?

A   The O'Jays
B   The Four Tops
C   The Spinners
D   The Temptations

928 Who was the second youngest member of the Jackson Five?

A   Tito
B   Marlon
C   Michael
D   Randy

929 According to the song title, how many problems does Jay-Z have?

A   Too many
B   Thirteen
C   Sixty-nine
D   Ninety-nine

930 What is the name of the woman who steals love in the Betty Wright song?

A   Heart Snatcher
B   Love Thief
C   Clean-Up Woman
D   The Master of Love

931 What color are the lines in the title of a Grandmaster Flash song?

A   Red
B   Black
C   White
D   Blue

932 What city is the birthplace of Prince?

A   Detroit
B   Minneapolis
C   Los Angeles
D   Chicago

933 Which of the following is a song by The Time?

A Jungle Fever
B Welcome To The Jungle
C Jungle Love
D Jungle Boogie

934 Which artist recorded "Sexual Healing"?

A Otis Redding
B Isaac Hayes
C Prince
D Marvin Gaye

935 What city is the birthplace of legendary singer and musician Louis Armstrong?

A New Orleans
B Houston
C Memphis
D Los Angeles

936 Which artist(s) recorded "Kiss from a Rose"?

A Roberta Flack
B Seal
C Sly and the Family Stone
D Wynton Marsalis

937 What relation is Valerie Simpson to Nicholas Ashford?

A   She is his daughter
B   She is his mother
C   She is his sister
D   She is his wife

938 Which of the following is Ida Cox's profession?

A   Opera singer
B   Blues singer
C   Rapper
D   Sculptor

939 Which artist recorded "The Sweetest Taboo"?

A   Tracy Chapman
B   Billie Holiday
C   Tina Turner
D   Sade

940 Which artist recorded "I Had a Talk with My Man"?

A   Billie Holiday
B   Mitty Collier
C   Koko Taylor
D   Big Mama Thornton

941 Who is "Dirty" in the Michael Jackson song?

A   Billie Jean
B   Debbie
C   Donna
D   Diana

942 Which artist(s) recorded "Got My Mojo Working"?

A   Jimmy Reed
B   Muddy Waters
C   John Lee Hooker
D   Howlin' Wolf

943 What is the name of the father of the Jackson Five members?

A   Michael Sr.
B   Marlon
C   Joseph
D   Steven

944 Whom did Aaliyah, Grammy-nominated singer, model, and actress, marry when she was just fifteen?

A   Prince
B   R. Kelley
C   Chris Brown
D   Jaheim

945 Which of the following women married Bobby Brown?

A   Mary J. Blige
B   Janet Jackson
C   Mariah Carey
D   Whitney Houston

946 Which artist recorded "Boogie Chillun"?

A   Muddy Waters
B   Sonny Boy Williamson
C   John Lee Hooker
D   Robert Johnson

947 In the Public Enemy song "Night of the Living Baseheads," why did the man strip his jeep?

A   To get romance
B   To fill his pipe
C   To get a gun
D   To buy food

948 Who was "the Mother of Gospel Music"?

A   Sallie Martin
B   Ella Fitzgerald
C   Mahalia Jackson
D   Roberta Flack

949 Which artist starred in the movie *The Bodyguard*?

A   Whitney Houston
B   Janet Jackson
C   Mariah Carey
D   Jennifer Hudson

950 What is the name of the mother of the Jackson Five?

A   Janelle
B   Josephine
C   Katherine
D   Rebbie

951 Which artist(s) recorded "Soul Makossa"?

A   Bob Marley
B   Manu Dibango
C   Soul II Soul
D   Thelonious Monk

952 Which artist recorded "Quiet Storm"?

A   Quincy Jones
B   Lionel Richie
C   Smokey Robinson
D   Barry White

953 Which artist recorded "Fattening Frogs for Snakes"?

A   John Lee Hooker
B   Clarence Henry
C   Sonny Boy Williamson
D   Z. Z. Hill

954 What is the last name of Johnny B. in the Chuck Berry song?

A   Goode
B   Crazy
C   Badd
D   Wild

955 Which Jackson stayed with Motown in 1975 as a solo singer?

A   Randy
B   Michael
C   Jermaine
D   Tito

956 What group are André 3000 and Big Boi are known as?

A   The Fat Boys
B   André and Big Boy
C   Outkast
D   3000 and One

957 According to the title of a song by the Charles Brown Trio, you should get yourself another _____.

A man
B fool
C job
D woman

958 Which artist(s) recorded "My Ding-A-Ling"?

A The Ding-a-Lings
B Chuck Berry
C Fats Domino
D Little Richard

959 What kind of music are Salt N Pepa best known for?

A Rap
B Jazz
C R&B (soul)
D Blues

960 Which white singer bought a tombstone for Bessie Smith (who died in 1937) in 1970?

A David Bowie
B Dolly Parton
C Janis Joplin
D Olivia Newton John

History Channel, October 4

961 According to the title of a Brook Benton song, where is the rainy night?

A   Florida
B   Georgia
C   Southern California
D   Pittsburgh

962 According to a Curtis Mayfield song, everybody used him, ripped him off, and abused him. Who was he?

A   Stagger Lee
B   Shaft
C   Freddie
D   Superfly

963 Which of the following groups had a song titled "Mr. Wendell"?

A   Digital Underground
B   Arrested Development
C   Public Enemy
D   The Wendells

964 What first name was music legend Miles Davis given at birth?

A   Michael
B   Marvin
C   Maxwell
D   Miles

965 Which of the following is the title of a song by Outkast?

A   "Fannie Hamer"
B   "MLK"
C   "Rosa Parks"
D   "Harriet Tubman"

966 Which of the following groups did Curtis Mayfield sing with?

A   The Four Tops
B   The Impressions
C   The Spinners
D   The Temptations

967 In the song title by Aaliyah, what gets rocked?

A   The boat
B   The bells
C   The house
D   The party

968 Billie Holiday was a legendary jazz singer. How old was she when died?

A   Fifty-two
B   Thirty-eight
C   Ninety-one
D   Forty-four

969 Which member of the Jackson Five married Elvis Presley's daughter?

A   Randy
B   Jermaine
C   Michael
D   Tito

970 According to the song title, how many questions are there for 50 Cent?

A   Twenty-one
B   Ninety-nine
C   Fifty
D   Three

971 What is Quincy Jones's middle name?

A   Thurgood
B   Reginald
C   Samuel
D   Delight

972 Which artist recorded "Stagger Lee"?

A   Harry Belafonte
B   Fats Waller
C   Lloyd Price
D   Otis Redding

973 What city is nicknamed Motown?

A   Philadelphia
B   Detroit
C   Atlanta
D   Chicago

974 Which artist recorded "T'ain't Nobody's Business if I Do"?

A   Koko Taylor
B   Robert Johnson
C   Billie Holiday
D   Mitty Collier

975 Which artist recorded "This Masquerade"?

A   Michael Jackson
B   Herbie Hancock
C   Grover Washington Jr.
D   George Benson

976 According to the Commodores song, a woman with a great body is a(n) _____?

A   penthouse
B   outhouse
C   hottie body
D   brick house

977 Which artist recorded "You're The First, the Last, My Everything"?

A   Fats Domino
B   Barry White
C   Heavy D
D   Isaac Hayes

978 Who was the leader of Jimmy James and the Blue Flames?

A   Jimmy Ruffin
B   James Brown
C   Jimi Hendrix
D   Rick James

979 What kind of music is N.W.A. best known for?

A   Blues
B   Jazz
C   R&B (soul)
D   Rap

980 Which artist(s) recorded "Say It Loud, I'm Black and I'm Proud"?

A   Tupac Shakur
B   Prince
C   Sam and Dave
D   James Brown

981 In the song "Sittin' on the Dock of the Bay," how many miles does Otis Redding say he roamed?

A One thousand
B Two thousand
C Five thousand
D Five hundred

982 What musical instrument is legendary performer John Coltrane best known for playing?

A Saxophone
B Piano
C Guitar
D Trumpet

983 What is the nickname of Michael Jackson's youngest child (Prince Michael II)?

A Baby Mike
B Lil Mikey
C Blanket
D Pillow

984 Which song is commonly known as the "Black National Anthem"?

A "Oh Happy Day"
B "We Shall Overcome"
C "Lift Every Voice and Sing"
D "Say It Loud, I'm Black and I'm Proud"

985 Which artist recorded "Superfly"?

A   Prince
B   Isaac Hayes
C   MC Hammer
D   Curtis Mayfield

986 Which of the following is the title of a Beyoncé album?

A   *Hennessy*
B   *Gatorade*
C   *Buttermilk*
D   *Lemonade*

987 What color is the rooster in the Howlin' Wolf song?

A   Black
B   Brown
C   Red
D   White

988 Which of the following is the title of a song by Common?

A   "To Be"
B   "Bumblebee"
C   "Be"
D   "Not to Be"

989 Which of the following is the name of Beyoncé and Jay-Z's first child?

A   Blue Ivy
B   Northwest
C   Ebony
D   Bee-Z

990 Who is nicknamed "the Father of Gospel Music"?

A   James Cleveland
B   Thomas Dorsey
C   T. D. Jakes
D   Edwin Hawkins

991 Which artist recorded "When a Man Loves a Woman"?

A   Otis Redding
B   Jerry Butler
C   Percy Sledge
D   Ben E. King

992 Which artist recorded "Sitting in the Park"?

A   Donna Summer
B   Billy Stewart
C   Jackie Wilson
D   Johnny Ace

993 Which group recorded an album titled *As Nasty As They Wanna Be*?

A   The Fat Boys
B   N.W.A.
C   Salt N Pepa
D   2 Live Crew

994 Which artist recorded "Minnie the Moocher"?

A   Duke Ellington
B   Count Basie
C   Cab Calloway
D   Louis Armstrong

995 Which artist recorded "Only the Strong Survive"?

A   Percy Sledge
B   Big Mama Thornton
C   Otis Redding
D   Jerry Butler

996 According to the Chairman of the Board song, whom do you pay if you dance to the music?

A   The singers
B   The deejay
C   The band
D   The piper

997 Which of the following types of music is legendary performer Fats Domino best known for?

A   Jazz
B   Gospel
C   R&B (soul)
D   Reggae

998 What city is the birthplace of legendary singer Curtis Mayfield?

A   Philadelphia
B   Detroit
C   New York
D   Chicago

999 The duet "I'll Be Missing You" by Puff Daddy and Faith Evans is a tribute to what rapper?

A   Eazy-E
B   The Notorious B.I.G.
C   Tupac Shakur
D   Jason Mizell

1000   Which artist(s) recorded "You Dropped a Bomb on Me"?

A   Jackson Five
B   The Gap Band
C   The Ohio Players
D   Sly and the Family Stone

1001   What kind of music is legendary performer Billie Holiday best known for?

A   Rock and pop
B   Classical
C   Gospel
D   Blues and jazz

1002   What is music legend Duke Ellington's first name?

A   David
B   Donald
C   Edward
D   Eugene

1003   Michael Jackson recorded a hit titled "Ben." What is Ben?

A   A monkey
B   A cat
C   A rat
D   A llama

1004   Which artist recorded "Nobody Knows You When You're Down and Out"?

A   Count Basie
B   Bessie Smith
C   Scott Joplin
D   W. C. Handy

1005   Which artist recorded the hit song "Mad"?

A   Ice-T
B   Ike Turner
C   Ne-Yo
D   Ice Cube

1006   Which of the following groups did Dennis Edwards sing with?

A   The Four Tops
B   The O'Jays
C   The Spinners
D   The Temptations

1007   Which of the following singers did the Commodores pay tribute to in the song "Nightshift"?

A   James Brown
B   The Notorious B.I.G.
C   Marvin Gaye
D   Tupac Shakur

1008   Which artist(s) recorded the hit album *Amerikkka's Most Wanted*?

A   T.I.
B   Ice-T
C   Ice Cube
D   T-Pain

1009   Rapper Tupac Shakur was shot to death. How old was he when he died?

A   Twenty-two
B   Twenty-five
C   Twenty-nine
D   Twenty-eight

1010   Of which of the following music groups was Lauryn Hill a member?

A   Outkast
B   SWV
C   The Fugees
D   The Hill Sisters

1011   What kind of music is legendary performer Earl Hines best known for?

A   Jazz
B   Country
C   Gospel
D   Rap

1012   Which actress married singer Bill Withers?

A   Marla Gibbs
B   Denise Nicholas
C   Phylicia Allen
D   Roxie Roker

1013 Jay-Z, head of Def Jam, a hip-hop record label, created what line of clothing that sold for more than $200 million?

A Jaywear
B Rocawear
C FUBU
D Z Wear B Wear

1014 Which artist recorded the hit song "Doo Wop (That Thing)"?

A Mariah Carey
B Brandy
C Monica
D Lauryn Hill

1015 Which artist recorded the hit song "It Was a Good Day"?

A Ice Cube
B The Notorious B.I.G.
C Ne-Yo
D T.I.

1016 Bill Withers recorded a song titled "_____'s Hands."

A Grandma's
B Grandpa's
C Momma's
D Papa's

1017   What kind of music is legendary performer Little Walter best known for?

A   R&B (soul)
B   Funk
C   Blues
D   Rap

1018   In the song title by Hues Corporation, what gets rocked?

A   The boat
B   The bells
C   The house
D   The party

1019   What is music legend Jelly Roll Morton's birth name?

A   Fred Jellystone
B   Mark Morton
C   Ferdinand Lementhe
D   Leroy Morton

1020   Which artist recorded "Midnight Stroll"?

A   Andraé Crouch
B   Milt Jackson
C   Robert Cray
D   Seal

1021   According to the Dr. Dre song, "It's nothin' but a _____."

A   G thang
B   P thang
C   D thang
D   B thang

1022   Which of the following musical instruments is legendary performer Benny Carter best known for playing?

A   Piano
B   Guitar
C   Saxophone
D   Fiddle

1023   Which artist recorded "Let's Stay Together"?

A   Percy Sledge
B   Jerry Butler
C   Otis Redding
D   Al Green

1024   In the title of a Lionel Richie song, where are they dancing?

A   On Broadway
B   Up on the roof
C   In the streets
D   On the ceiling

1025 Which state is the birthplace of blues legend Blind Willie Johnson?

A Arkansas
B Texas
C Mississippi
D Louisiana

1026 Who wrote the song "Never Can Say Goodbye"?

A Smokey Robinson
B Isaac Hayes
C Michael Jackson
D Clifton Davis

1027 There is an Atlanta hip-hop group called Lil Jon and the _____.

A South Side Boyz
B West Side Boyz
C North Side Boyz
D East Side Boyz

1028 What kind of music is legendary performer Grace Bumbry best known for?

A Jazz
B Gospel
C Classical
D R&B (soul)

1029   What fictitious woman did the Jimmy Castor Bunch name a boogie after?

A   Brenda Butt
B   Betty Booty
C   Bonnie Booty
D   Bertha Butt

1030   Which artist recorded "Shaft"?

A   MC Hammer
B   John Shaft
C   Isaac Hayes
D   Prince

1031   Which artist recorded the hit song "How Ya Like Me Now?"

A   Big Daddy Kane
B   Kool Moe Dee
C   Kanye West
D   LL Cool J

1032   How many little birds are there in the title of a Bob Marley song?

A   Twelve
B   Five
C   Three
D   Nine

1033   In the song by the Brothers Johnson, what is the number of the strawberry letter?

A   Sixty-six
B   Thirty-two
C   Fifty-five
D   Twenty-three

1034   Which artist(s) recorded "Macho Man"?

A   The Ohio Players
B   The Village People
C   RuPaul
D   The Chi-Lites

1035   Which artist(s) recorded "Oh Girl" (the original)?

A   The Spinners
B   Isaac Hayes
C   The Chi-Lites
D   The Temptations

1036   Who was the first black female choreographer at New York's Metropolitan Opera?

A   Rita Dove
B   Vanessa Williams
C   Moneta Sleet
D   Katherine Dunham

African American Desk Reference, page 428

1037   Which artist(s) recorded "Please, Mr. Postman"?

A   The Marvalettes
B   Martha and the Vandellas
C   Chuck Berry
D   Mary Wells

1038   Which artist recorded "Banana Boat Song (Day-O)"?

A   Duke Ellington
B   Harry Belafonte
C   Bob Marley
D   Louis Armstrong

1039   Which artist(s) recorded *Bitches Brew*?

A   Robert Cray
B   Wynton Marsalis
C   Miles Davis
D   Take 6

1040   Which artist recorded "Crossroads"?

A   Otis Redding
B   John Lee Hooker
C   Muddy Waters
D   Robert Johnson

1041   Which Jackson recorded the *Off The Wall* album?

A   Janet
B   Jermaine
C   Michael
D   Rebbie

1042   Which member of the Jackson family is named Maureen?

A   Janet
B   Katherine
C   LaToya
D   Rebbie

1043   Which member of the Jackson family is known for wearing one glove?

A   LaToya
B   Jermaine
C   Michael
D   Janet

1044   Which of the following was a hit song by the Sugar Hill Gang?

A   "Navajo"
B   "Cheyenne"
C   "Blackfoot"
D   "Apache"

1045   Which artist recorded the hit song "Testify"?

A   Mahalia Jackson
B   Kirk Franklin
C   Prince
D   Common

1046   What kind of music is legendary performer Fletcher Henderson best known for?

A   Country
B   Jazz
C   R&B (soul)
D   Rap

1047   T-Pain has a song titled_____.

A   "5 o'Clock"
B   "10 o'Clock"
C   "6 o'Clock"
D   "7 o'Clock"

1048   Which member of the Jackson Five married Berry Gordy's daughter?

A   Tito
B   Michael
C   Randy
D   Jermaine

1049 What kind of music is legendary performer Christian McBride best known for?

A Jazz
B Country
C Gospel
D R&B (soul)

1050 Where is the meeting in the Klymaxx song?

A In the ladies' room
B In the nightclub
C In the men's room
D In the hot tub

1051 Which member of the Jackson family is named Toriano?

A LaToya
B Tito
C Randy
D Joseph

1052 Which artist recorded "Hey Mister, Your Wife Is Cheating"?

A Lightnin' Hopkins
B Little Milton
C B.B. King
D Little Walter

1053   According to a song, where are the crazy little women?

A   Virginia
B   San Francisco
C   San Jose
D   Kansas City

1054   Who was the youngest member of the Jackson Five?

A   Marlon
B   Michael
C   Jermaine
D   Randy

1055   In the song title by Benzino, what gets rocked?

A   The house
B   The boat
C   The bells
D   The party

1056   According to his song, where is DMX going to act a fool?

A   Down in there
B   Way outside
C   At the liquor store
D   Up in here

1057   In the song title by LL Cool J, what gets rocked?

A   Your world
B   The boat
C   The bells
D   The party

1058   What is legendary blues singer Koko Taylor's birth name?

A   Cora Walton
B   Ellie Clampett
C   Lille Mae Jones
D   Willie Mae Thornton

1059   According to the Four Tops song, who might walk away?

A   Maybelline
B   Miss Molly
C   Papa
D   Renee

1060   What city is the birthplace of Michael Jackson?

A   Indianapolis
B   Gary, Indiana
C   Macon, Georgia
D   Saginaw, Michigan

1061   What kind of music is Manu DiBango best known for?

A   Blues
B   Jazz
C   Makossa
D   Reggae

1062   Lucille is B.B. King's _____.

A   Wife
B   Twin sister
C   Guitar
D   Mother

1063   Which artist(s) recorded "Strokin'"?

A   Clarence Carter
B   N.W.A.
C   Roy C
D   Rufus Thomas

1064   Which artist(s) recorded the hit song "Shoop"?

A   Missy Elliot
B   Lil' Kim
C   Salt N Pepa
D   Queen Latifah

1065　What kind of music is legendary performer Betty Carter best known for?

A　Jazz
B　Country
C　Gospel
D　R&B (soul)

1066　Which state is the birthplace of blues legend Blind Lemon Jefferson?

A　Louisiana
B　Mississippi
C　Tennessee
D　Texas

1067　Which artist(s) recorded "I Don't Want to Fight"?

A　Tina Turner
B　Ike Turner
C　Stevie Wonder
D　Rihanna

1068　Rapper the Notorious B.I.G. was shot to death. How old was he when he died?

A　Twenty-eight
B　Thirty-seven
C　Twenty-four
D　Thirty-two

1069   Which artist recorded "Just a Friend"?

A   Biz Markie
B   George Clinton
C   Kurtis Blow
D   Shorty Long

1070   What musical instrument is Fats Domino most famous for playing?

A   Piano
B   Trombone
C   Saxophone
D   Drums

1071   Which state is the birthplace of blues legend Bobby Bland?

A   Mississippi
B   Tennessee
C   Alabama
D   Texas

1072   Which artist(s) recorded "Deep As The River"?

A   Harry Belafonte
B   Fats Waller
C   The Supremes
D   Lloyd Price

1073 Which artist(s) recorded "We Are Family"?

A Sister Sledge
B The Pointer Sisters
C The Brothers Johnson
D Sly and the Family Stone

1074 Which of the following music is legendary performer King Curtis best known for?

A Reggae
B Jazz
C Rap
D R&B (soul)

1075 Which of the following was named Calvin Cordozar Broadus at birth?

A Prince
B Snoop Dogg
C Professor Longhair
D Clarence Carter

1076 What color are the little apples in the O. C. Smith song?

A Red
B Purple
C Green
D Yellow

1077   Which artist(s) recorded "The Great Pretender"?

A   Muddy Waters
B   The Platters
C   The Impressions
D   The Pretenders

1078   How old was Charlie Parker when he died?

A   Fifty
B   Fifty-four
C   Forty-four
D   Thirty-four

1079   Which artist(s) recorded "So Much to Say"?

A   Miles Davis
B   Take 6
C   Robert Cray
D   Richard Sherman

1080   Which artist recorded "Dear Mama"?

A   LL Cool J
B   Ice-T
C   Tupac Shakur
D   Big Daddy Kane

1081   Which artist(s) recorded a country song titled "Fairytale"?

A   Lionel Richie
B   Charley Pride
C   The Pointer Sisters
D   Ray Charles

1082   Which artist(s) recorded "That's What Love Will Make You Do"?

A   Little Walter
B   B.B. King
C   Jimmy Reed
D   Little Milton

1083   What musical instrument is legendary performer Duke Ellington best known for?

A   Piano
B   Guitar
C   Saxophone
D   Trumpet

1084   What kind of music is Take 6 best known for?

A   Gospel
B   Jazz
C   Rap
D   Rock

1085 What city is the birthplace of singer Rick James?

A Philadelphia
B Minneapolis
C Buffalo
D Pittsburgh

1086 Who taught legend T-Bone Walker the blues?

A Leadbelly
B Memphis Minnie
C John Lee Hooker
D Blind Lemon Jefferson

1087 In a Sam Cooke song, she was too young to fall in love and he was too young to know. What is the title of the song?

A "Only Sixteen"
B "Only Fifteen"
C "Only Thirteen"
D "Only Eighteen"

1088 Which artist recorded "Love to Love You, Baby"?

A Tina Turner
B Diana Ross
C Millie Jackson
D Donna Summer

1089   Which artist recorded "Johannesburg"?

A   Jali Musa Jawara
B   Gil Scott Heron
C   Manu Dibango
D   Salif Keita

1090   Who is dead in the Curtis Mayfield song?

A   Martin
B   Freddie
C   Superfly
D   Tupac

1091   Chuck D, Flavor Flav, and Professor Griff were members of which group?

A   Public Enemy
B   The Sugar Hill Gang
C   The Jersey Boys
D   Wu Tang Clan

1092   Which artist(s) recorded *Bad Influence*?

A   Tupac Shakur
B   Miles Davis
C   Robert Cray
D   Take 6

1093   Who is the composer of *Treemonisha*?

A   Paul Dunbar
B   Richard Wright
C   Scott Joplin
D   Wallace Thurmond

1094   What city is the birthplace of legendary singer Fats Domino?

A   Los Angeles
B   Kansas City
C   Little Rock, Arkansas
D   New Orleans

1095   Which of the following is the title of a Run-DMC song?

A   "King of Rap"
B   "King of Soul"
C   "King of Pop"
D   "King of Rock"

1096   According to the Temptations song, who was a rolling stone?

A   Mama
B   Little Sister
C   Papa
D   Baby Brother

1097   What musical instrument is legendary performer Miles Davis best known for playing?

A   Piano
B   Trumpet
C   Saxophone
D   Guitar

1098   Which artist recorded *Black Codes*?

A   James Brown
B   Louis Armstrong
C   Milt Jackson
D   Wynton Marsalis

1099   Which of the following groups did Phillipe Wynne sing with?

A   The Temptations
B   The Four Tops
C   The O'Jays
D   The Spinners

1100   Which artist(s) recorded "Unforgettable" (the original)?

A   Louis Armstrong
B   Harry Belafonte
C   Nat King Cole
D   Sly and the Family Stone

1101   Which artist(s) recorded the hit song "No Diggity"?

A   Blackstreet
B   Whitesnake
C   Black Heat
D   Snoop Dogg

1102   Which artist(s) recorded "Proud Mary"?

A   Marvin Gaye and Tammi Terrell
B   Mary J. Blige
C   Ike and Tina Turner
D   Mary Wells

1103   Which artist(s) recorded "Gonna Make You Sweat"?

A   James Brown
B   The Gap Band
C   C+C Music Factory
D   Sly and the Family Stone

1104   Kenny Edmunds is a popular singer, songwriter, and producer. What is his nickname?

A   Kenny G
B   Grandmaster
C   Kay Jay
D   Baby Face

1105   Which group did Bobby Brown sing with?

A   Jodeci
B   The Platters
C   New Edition
D   De La Soul

1106   What kind of music is legendary performer Teddy Pendergrass best known for?

A   Rap
B   Jazz
C   R&B (soul)
D   Reggae

1107   What kind of music are Boyz II Men best known for?

A   R&B (soul)
B   Classical
C   Jazz
D   Rap

1108   Which artist recorded "Fast Car"?

A   Tracy Chapman
B   Natalie Cole
C   Sade
D   Donna Summer

1109   Which artist(s) recorded "Yes We Can Can"?

A   Sly and the Family Stone
B   The Jackson Five
C   Sister Sledge
D   The Pointer Sisters

1110   Who was the founder of Motown?

A   Gordon Parks Sr.
B   Berry Gordy
C   Gordon Parks Jr.
D   William Robinson

1111   How old was blues legend Robert Johnson when he died?

A   Thirty-three
B   Twenty-seven
C   Thirty-eight
D   Forty-five

1112   Which artist recorded "Hush Hush"?

A   Jimmy Reed
B   B.B. King
C   Lightnin' Hopkins
D   Little Milton

1113   Which of the following is Adelaide Hall's profession?

A   Pianist
B   Rapper
C   Jazz singer
D   Playwright

1114   Which artist recorded "Smokestack Lightnin'"?

A   John Lee Hooker
B   Jimmy Reed
C   Howlin' Wolf
D   Muddy Waters

1115   What kind of music are legendary performers Soul Stirrers best known for?

A   Country
B   Gospel
C   Jazz
D   R&B (soul)

1116   Which artist recorded "Evil"?

A   Little Walter
B   Lightnin' Hopkins
C   Little Milton
D   Howlin' Wolf

1117   Which artist recorded "The Hustle"?

A   Van McCoy
B   George McCrae
C   Ray Parker Jr.
D   Donna Summer

1118   What city is the birthplace of singer Lou Rawls?

A   Los Angeles
B   Chicago
C   New Orleans
D   New York

1119   Which of the following groups did David Ruffin sing with?

A   The Temptations
B   The Four Tops
C   The Spinners
D   The Drifters

1120   Who said "knock you out" in the LL Cool J song?

A   Mama
B   Lil Jon
C   Papa
D   Tyson

1121 Which of the following recorded an album titled *The Infamous*?

A DMX
B Mobb Deep
C T.I.
D Ice Cube

1122 What song did Lil' Kim do a remake of with Christine Aguilera, Maya, and Pink?

A "Lady Marmalade"
B "Respect"
C "Baby Love"
D "Midnight Train to Georgia"

1123 Who was once James Brown's manager?

A Jesse Jackson
B Benjamin Hooks
C Al Sharpton
D Vernon Jordan

1124 Which artist recorded the hit song "Best of Me"?

A Kem
B Jay-Z
C Anthony Hamilton
D Maxwell

1125   Which artist recorded the hit song "The Cookbook"?

A   Lil' Kim
B   Missy Elliott
C   Little Caesar
D   Big Pun

1126   Which artist recorded "King of the Country Blues"?

A   Ray Charles
B   Roy C
C   Charley Pride
D   Blind Lemon Jefferson

1127   Which of the following is legendary performer Sarah Vaughn's nickname?

A   The Perfect One
B   Super Sarah
C   Mrs. V
D   The Divine One

1128   Which artist(s) recorded the hit song "I Tried"?

A   Bone Thugs-N-Harmony
B   Blackstreet
C   Wu Tang Clan
D   A Tribe Called Quest

1129   Which of the following won a Tony Award for *Dreamgirls*?

A   Mary Alice
B   Diahann Carroll
C   Jennifer Holliday
D   Nell Carter

1130   What kind of music is Eric Wright best known for?

A   Gospel
B   Jazz
C   R&B (soul)
D   Rap

1131   What city is the birthplace of Spike Lee?

A   Newark
B   Hartford
C   New York
D   Atlanta

1132   Which artist recorded "Sophisticated Lady"?

A   Duke Ellington
B   Count Basie
C   Diana Ross
D   Louis Armstrong

1133　Which artist recorded "Red Bank Boogie"?

A　Lloyd Price
B　Fats Waller
C　Harry Belafonte
D　Count Basie

1134　What city is the birthplace of legendary musician Jimi Hendrix?

A　Portland, Oregon
B　Seattle
C　San Diego
D　Portland, Maine

1135　Which artist(s) recorded *Songs in A Minor*?

A　Destiny's Child
B　Janet Jackson
C　Alicia Keys
D　Mary J. Blige

1136　DJ Joseph Sadler is also known as _____.

A　Grandmaster Flash
B　Luke Skywalker
C　Flavor Flav
D　Snoop Dogg

1137   Which artist(s) recorded the hit song "Happy"?

A   The Weekend
B   Prince
C   Pharrell Williams
D   Chris Brown

1138   According to a song, who threw a seven and Billy swore he threw an eight?

A   Papa
B   Shaft
C   Stagger Lee
D   Superfly

1139   Jean Knight recorded a hit song titled "Mr. Big _____."

A   Love
B   Stuff
C   Mouth
D   Nose

1140   Which of the following Michael Jackson songs is not on the *Thriller* album?

A   "Billie Jean"
B   "The Way You Make Me Feel"
C   "Human Nature"
D   "Beat It"

1141   What is music legend Dizzy Gillespie's first name?

A   Grant
B   Rufus
C   John
D   Harold

1142   Which artist recorded "Peace in the Valley"?

A   Andraé Crouch
B   James Bland
C   Nat King Cole
D   Tommy Dorsey

1143   What is the name of Joseph Jackson's oldest son?

A   Marlon
B   Jermaine
C   Jackie
D   Tito

1144   According to the song by Three 6 Mafia, it is "hard out here for a _____."

A   hooker
B   pimp
C   homeless child
D   wino

1145   Which artist recorded the hit song "Hot in Herre"?

A   The Notorious B.I.G.
B   Tupac Shakur
C   Nelly
D   Jaheim

1146   What kind of music is legendary performer Simon Estes best known for?

A   R&B (soul)
B   Rap
C   Country
D   Classical

1147   Which artist recorded "Lean on Me" (the original)?

A   Percy Sledge
B   Bill Withers
C   Jerry Butler
D   Otis Redding

1148   Who wrote the song "Lady," which was a big hit for country singer Kenny Rogers?

A   Smokey Robinson
B   Charley Pride
C   Quincy Jones
D   Lionel Richie

1149 Who once went by the name of Luke Skywalker?

A Michael Jordan
B Morris Day
C Luther Campbell
D Tupac Shakur

1150 What musical instrument is legendary performer Jimi Hendrix best known for playing?

A Guitar
B Piano
C Trombone
D Trumpet

1151 What city is the birthplace of rapper Queen Latifah?

A New York City
B Hartford, Connecticut
C Newark, New Jersey
D Philadelphia

1152 Which artist(s) recorded the hit song "All of Me"?

A John Legend
B Jaheim
C The O'Jays
D Luther Vandross

1153   What is music legend Fats Waller's first name?

A   Thomas
B   Wally
C   Walter
D   Willie

1154   What is Busta Rhymes's birth name?

A   Kurtis Blowout
B   Trevor Smith Jr.
C   James Rhymes
D   Buster Fluster

1155   Which state is the birthplace of blues legend T-Bone Walker?

A   Florida
B   Mississippi
C   Tennessee
D   Texas

1156   Which artist was nicknamed Satchmo?

A   Louis Armstrong
B   Harry Belafonte
C   Jackie Wilson
D   Fats Domino

1157   What is blues legend Bobby Bland's nickname?

A   The Candy Man
B   The Bland Man
C   Blue
D   The Sandman

1158   Who recorded albums titled *The Carter I*, *The Carter II*, *The Carter III*, and *The Carter IV*?

A   The Carter Brothers
B   Clarence Carter
C   Benny Carter
D   Lil Wayne

1159   Which artist recorded "Big Boss Man"?

A   John Lee Hooker
B   Fats Domino
C   Jimmy Reed
D   Muddy Waters

1160   What musical instrument is legendary performer Charlie Parker best known for?

A   Piano
B   Saxophone
C   Guitar
D   Trumpet

1161   What city is the birthplace of singer MC Hammer?

A   Los Angeles
B   Oakland
C   San Diego
D   San Francisco

1162   Which artist recorded "Ain't Misbehavin'"?

A   Harry Belafonte
B   Fats Domino
C   Fats Waller
D   Lloyd Price

1163   Which artist recorded "I'm Not Perfect, but I'm Perfect for You"?

A   Grace Jones
B   Donna Summer
C   Janet Jackson
D   Jean Knight

1164   What kind of music are legendary performers the Winans best known for?

A   Jazz
B   Classical
C   Rap
D   Gospel

1165   What is Fats Domino's first name?

A   Freddy
B   Fats
C   Andre
D   Antoine

1166   Which artist recorded "Patches"?

A   Clarence Carter
B   Bill Withers
C   Bobby Womack
D   Otis Redding

1167   What is the phone number title of a song by the Time?

A   "222-6900"
B   "555-6000"
C   "634-5789"
D   "777-9311"

1168   What kind of music is legendary performer Louis Armstrong best known for?

A   R&B (soul)
B   Gospel
C   Rap
D   Jazz

1169   Which artist recorded "What a Wonderful World"?

A   Duke Ellington
B   Count Basie
C   Louis Armstrong
D   Whitney Houston

1170   What kind of music is legendary performer Muddy Waters best known for?

A   Gospel
B   Blues
C   Rap
D   R&B (soul)

1171   Which artist recorded an album titled *All Hail the Queen*?

A   Koko Taylor
B   Aretha Franklin
C   Mahalia Jackson
D   Queen Latifah

1172   Who was nicknamed "the Godfather of Soul"?

A   Sam Cooke
B   Al Green
C   James Brown
D   Otis Redding

1173 Which artist recorded the hit song "Hypnotize"?

A   Tupac Shakur
B   P. Diddy
C   The Notorious B.I.G.
D   Biz Markie

1174 Which of the following groups did Teddy Pendergrass sing with?

A   Harold Melvin and the Blue Notes
B   The Impressions
C   The O'Jays
D   The Temptations

1175 Which artist(s) recorded the hit album *The Low End Theory*?

A   Johnny Quest
B   A Tribe Called Quest
C   The Low Downs
D   Loose Ends

1176 Which artist(s) recorded the hit song "Weak"?

A   TLC
B   En Vogue
C   SWV
D   STP

1177   Which artist recorded "Harder Than the Best"?

A   Burning Spear
B   Bob Marley
C   Charles Brown
D   Jimmy Cliff

1178   Della Reese is a famous actress and singer. What was her last name at birth?

A   Early
B   Fieldreese
C   Reesefield
D   Young

1179   Which artist recorded "Carry Me Back to Old Virginny"?

A   Nat King Cole
B   Whitney Houston
C   James Bland
D   Tommy Dorsey

1180   How old was reggae legend Bob Marley when he died?

A   Thirty-six
B   Thirty-four
C   Forty-one
D   Forty-two

1181   Which of the following artists recorded "My Babe"?

A   Little Walter
B   Little Richard
C   The Notorious B.I.G.
D   Smokey Robinson

1182   Which of the following is the title of an Aretha Franklin song?

A   "Ship of Fools"
B   "Chain of Men"
C   "Chain of Fools"
D   "Chain of Lovers"

1183   What is the phone number title of a Wilson Pickett song?

A   "777-9311"
B   "540-0623"
C   "634-5789"
D   "777-7777"

1184   Which of the following is a Jennifer Hudson song?

A   "Red Light"
B   "Green Light"
C   "Stoplight"
D   "Spotlight"

1185   What kind of music is legendary performer Jimi Hendrix best known for?

A   Jazz
B   Rock
C   Rap
D   R&B (soul)

1186   Who replaced an older member in the Jackson Five and then the group became the Jacksons?

A   Randy
B   Marlon
C   Michael
D   Tito

Africana, page 1021

1187   Which artist recorded "One O'Clock Jump"?

A   Harry Belafonte
B   Count Basie
C   Scott Joplin
D   W. C. Handy

1188   Which artist recorded the hit song "On the Block"?

A   Scarface
B   50 Cent
C   Busta Rhymes
D   Lil Wayne

1189   Which artist(s) recorded "There's a Riot Going On"?

A   Prince
B   Louis Armstrong
C   Milt Jackson
D   Sly and the Family Stone

1190   Which of the following is legendary performer Diana Ross's nickname?

A   The Supreme One
B   Lady Di
C   The Queen of Soul
D   The Boss

1191   What was music legend Cab Calloway's first name at birth?

A   James
B   John
C   Cabell
D   Cornelius

1192   Which member of the Jackson family acted on the television show *Good Times*?

A   LaToya
B   Jermaine
C   Janet
D   Michael

1193   Which artist recorded "Kung Fu Fighting"?

A   Carl Douglas
B   George McCrae
C   Ray Parker Jr.
D   Van McCoy

1194   Which of the following recorded an album titled *The Miseducation of [her name]*?

A   MC Lyte
B   Lauryn Hill
C   Janet Jackson
D   Whitney Houston

1195   Which group was Kool Moe Dee a member of?

A   The Treacherous Three
B   The Sugar Hill Gang
C   Black Star
D   Salt N Pepa

1196   Which of the following women married James DeBarge?

A   Whitney Houston
B   Mariah Carey
C   Mary J. Blige
D   Janet Jackson

1197   Legendary singer Sam Cooke died at what age?

A   Thirty-eight
B   Thirty-three
C   Thirty-six
D   Forty

1198   Who was the first hip-hop group to be inducted into the Rock and Roll Hall of Fame?

A   Run-DMC
B   The Sugar Hill Gang
C   Grandmaster Flash and the Furious Five
D   Outkast

1199   According to a song by War, who was "a friend of mine"?

A   Cisco Kid
B   Frisco Kid
C   Low Rider
D   Stagger Lee

1200   How many Grammy awards did hip-hop Fugees member Lauryn Hill win in 1999?

A   Five
B   Seven
C   Two
D   Three

Sports

1201   Who had forty-two points, fifteen rebounds, and seven assists in the last game of a NBA Finals as a rookie while playing center?

A   Charles Barkley
B   Magic Johnson
C   Michael Jordan
D   Julius Erving

1202   Which college was the first to have five black starters in the NCAA basketball championship game?

A   University of Nevada, Las Vegas
B   UCLA
C   Texas Western
D   Marquette

1203   Which Heisman Trophy winner died of leukemia (never played in the NFL)?

A   O. J. Simpson
B   Ernie Davis
C   Mike Garrett
D   Mike Rozier

1204   Who holds the NFL record with seven sacks in one game?

A   Lawrence Taylor
B   Bruce Smith
C   Reggie White
D   Derrick Thomas

New York Times, November 12, 1990

1205   Basketball star Walter Davis's nickname was the name of a breed of dog. What was his nickname?

A   Pit Bull
B   Greyhound
C   Poodle
D   Terrier

1206   Who was the first boxer to hold titles in three different weight classes at the same time?

A   Sugar Ray Leonard
B   Sugar Ray Robinson
C   Thomas Hearns
D   Henry Armstrong

Encyclopedia of Black America, page 116

1207   Who was the first man to average a triple double (ten points, ten rebounds, and ten assists) for a season in the NBA?

A   Julius Erving
B   Oscar Robertson
C   Russell Westbrook
D   Michael Jordan

1208   Which of the following was the first man to have one hundred stolen bases in a season?

A   Lou Brock
B   Maury Wills
C   Jackie Robinson
D   Rickey Henderson

1209   Which track star set three world records and tied one world record on the same day?

A   Jesse Owens
B   Jackie Joyner-Kersee
C   Carl Lewis
D   Michael Johnson

1210   Which college did legendary track star Edwin Moses attend?

A   Ohio State
B   Morehouse
C   UCLA
D   Tennessee State

1211   Who was the first woman to play professional baseball in the Negro Leagues?

A   Toni Stone
B   Althea Gibson
C   Connie Morgan
D   Peanut Johnson

African American Lives, page 795

1212   Who holds the NBA record for the most playoff points in his career?

A   Michael Jordan
B   Karl Malone
C   LeBron James
D   Kareem Abdul-Jabbar

1213   How many home runs did Ernie Banks hit in his career?

A   512
B   501
C   504
D   499

1214   Who played Mars Blackmon in the Nike commercials?

A   Michael Jordan
B   Spike Lee
C   Magic Johnson
D   Tiger Woods

1215   What college did basketball star Wayman Tisdale attend?

A   Oklahoma
B   Oklahoma State
C   Kansas
D   Missouri

1216   Which of the following did Rafer Johnson win in the 1960 Olympics?

A   Hundred-meter run
B   Decathlon
C   High jump
D   Pole vault

1217   Which of the following was once married to Mike Tyson?

A   Robin Roberts
B   Nicole Brown
C   Robin Givens
D   Robin Williams

1218   In what year did Muhammad Ali win the heavyweight boxing championship, taking it from Sonny Liston?

A   1960
B   1961
C   1964
D   1970

1219   What is the nickname of baseball star and Hall of Fame member John Henry Lloyd of the Negro League?

A   Pop
B   Cannonball
C   Little John
D   Big John

1220   Which of the following was the National League MVP in 1975 and 1976?

A   Joe Morgan
B   George Foster
C   Bill Madlock
D   Bobby Bonds

1221   Which of the following hit fifty-six home runs in 1997 and 1998?

A   Reggie Jackson
B   Barry Bonds
C   Frank Thomas
D   Ken Griffey Jr.

1222   Which of the following men was nicknamed the Refrigerator?

A   William Perry
B   Tyler Perry
C   Manute Bol
D   Charles Barkley

1223   What college did legendary track star Jesse Owens attend?

A   Southern California
B   UCLA
C   Ohio State
D   Michigan

1224   Which of the following was a track, football, and basketball star in college?

A   Bo Jackson
B   Jackie Robinson
C   LeBron James
D   Deion Sanders

Africana, page 1628

1225   What college did Heisman Trophy winner Troy Smith attend?

A   Oklahoma
B   Ohio State
C   Florida State
D   Florida

1226   Who was the first female to be the winning pitcher in a Little League World Series game?

A   Monie Love
B   Monique Johnson
C   Mo'Ne Davis
D   Michelle Davis

1227   How many home runs did Hank Aaron hit in his career?

A   660
B   586
C   755
D   801

1228   Which of the following was the 2013 National League MVP?

A   Andrew McCutchen
B   Jayson Heyward
C   Curtis Granderson
D   Matt Kemp

1229   How long did it take Mike Tyson to knock out Michael Spinks in the heavyweight title bout?

A   Four hours
B   Twenty-seven seconds
C   Ninety-one seconds
D   Thirty-five minutes

1230   What college did basketball star Wes Unseld attend?

A   Louisville
B   Memphis State
C   Maryland
D   Kentucky

1231   Which of the following had a .388 batting average in 1977?

A   Rickey Henderson
B   Willie Wilson
C   Rod Carew
D   Tony Gwynn

1232   What number did Baseball Hall of Fame member Willie Mays wear?

A   24
B   34
C   25
D   44

1233   What number did Football Hall of Fame member Buck Buchanan wear in the pros?

A   98
B   65
C   86
D   99

1234   What position did baseball star and Hall of Fame member Willie McCovey play?

A   Second base
B   Outfield
C   Pitcher
D   First base

1235   What number did Baseball Hall of Fame member Rod Carew wear?

A   25
B   21
C   26
D   29

1236   What was baseball pitcher John Odom's nickname?

A   Blue Moon
B   Jay O
C   Little John
D   The Big O

1237   What number did Baseball Hall of Fame member Ozzie Smith wear?

A   6
B   3
C   1
D   8

1238   What position did football star John Hicks play in college?

A   Offensive lineman
B   Linebacker
C   Defensive lineman
D   Tight end

1239   Which of the following was the 1984 National League Rookie of the Year?

A   Chili Davis
B   Doc Gooden
C   Willie McGee
D   Darryl Strawberry

1240   Bill Russell played thirteen seasons with the Boston Celtics. How many championships did he win during his career?

A   Eight
B   Four
C   Seven
D   Eleven

1241   What number did football star Mike Singletary wear in college?

A   63
B   51
C   62
D   55

1242   What number did Heisman Trophy–winning running back Barry Sanders wear in college?

A   22
B   25
C   21
D   32

1243   Who made the game-winning basket when North Carolina State defeated Houston in the 1983 NCAA championship game?

A   Lorenzo Charles
B   Dereck Whittenburg
C   David Thompson
D   Sidney Lowe

1244   What position did basketball star Jim McDaniel play in college?

A   Guard
B   Forward
C   Center
D   Point guard

1245 What is the most points Michael Jordan scored in a 1986 playoff loss to the Boston Celtics?

A Sixty-three
B Thirty-seven
C Forty-six
D Fifty-one

1246 Which of the following was the American League MVP in 1995?

A Frank Thomas
B Reggie Jackson
C Mo Vaughn
D Ken Griffey Jr.

1247 What college did basketball star Patrick Ewing attend?

A Maryland
B Louisville
C North Carolina
D Georgetown

1248 How is basketball star Reggie Miller related to basketball star Cheryl Miller?

A He is her brother
B He is her father
C He is her husband
D He is her son

1249   Who is the only NBA player to average thirty points and twenty rebounds per game in a season—and he did it seven times?

A   Kareem Abdul-Jabbar
B   Michael Jordan
C   Shaquille O'Neal
D   Wilt Chamberlain

1250   What team did baseball star and Hall of Fame member Kirby Puckett play for?

A   Saint Louis Cardinals
B   New York Yankees
C   Pittsburgh Pirates
D   Minnesota Twins

1251   Which Olympian was a female basketball star at the University of North Carolina?

A   Florence Griffith Joyner
B   Jackie Joyner-Kersee
C   Marion Jones
D   Wilma Rudolph

1252   What college did Heisman Trophy winner Ricky Williams attend?

A   Texas
B   Southern California
C   Texas A&M
D   Texas Tech

1253   Which Dallas Cowboy had two interceptions against the Pittsburgh Steelers in Super Bowl XXX?

A   Everson Walls
B   Larry Brown
C   Mel Renfro
D   Deion Sanders

1254   K. C. Jones is a Hall of Fame basketball player. Which team did he play for?

A   Los Angeles Lakers
B   Boston Celtics
C   New York Knicks
D   Seattle Supersonics

1255   Who was the second man to average a triple double (ten points, ten rebounds, and ten assists) for the season in the NBA?

A   Oscar Robertson
B   Julius Erving
C   Russell Westbrook
D   Michael Jordan

1256   Who is the only NBA Finals most valuable player to lead his team in points, rebounds, assists, steals, and blocked shots?

A   Kevin Durant
B   LeBron James
C   Michael Jordan
D   Magic Johnson

1257   Which Negro League team did John Henry Lloyd play for (1911–1915 and 1926–1930)?

A   Pittsburgh
B   Kansas City
C   Newark
D   New York

1258   In what year did Arthur Ashe become the only black male ever to have won the Wimbledon title?

A   1982
B   1937
C   1968
D   1975

1259   Which Negro League team did baseball legend and Hall of Fame member Satchel Paige play for (1939–1948)?

A   Homestead
B   Kansas City
C   Chicago
D   Saint Louis

1260   What position did football star Bubba Smith play in college?

A   Linebacker
B   Defensive lineman
C   Offensive lineman
D   Tight end

1261   How many home runs did Willie Stargell hit in his career?

A   475
B   504
C   512
D   521

1262   Who was the most valuable player of the 2015 NBA Finals?

A   LeBron James
B   Kevin Durant
C   Andre Iguodala
D   Stephen Curry

1263   What number did Baseball Hall of Fame member Elston Howard wear?

A   28
B   24
C   30
D   32

1264   Jim Brown played nine years in the NFL. How many years did he lead the league in rushing?

A   9
B   8
C   5
D   10

1265   Which of the following led the American League in stolen bases in 1987?

A   Harold Reynolds
B   Harold Baines
C   Dee Gordon
D   Tim Raines

1266   Who won the Heisman Trophy in 2015?

A   Deshaun Watson
B   Jameis Winston
C   Derrick Henry
D   Lamar Jackson

1267   Whose nickname is Chocolate Thunder?

A   Jack Johnson
B   Darryl Dawkins
C   Joe Louis
D   Moses Malone

1268   What college did football star George Webster attend?

A   Michigan
B   Michigan State
C   Notre Dame
D   Purdue

1269　How old was George Foreman when he knocked out Michael Moorer to regain the heavyweight title?

A　Twenty-three
B　Thirty-nine
C　Forty-five
D　Forty-eight

1270　What event did Allen Johnson win a gold medal for in the 1996 Olympics?

A　400-meter hurdles
B　Long jump
C　200-meter run
D　110-meter hurdles

1271　What number did football star Art Monk wear in the pros?

A　80
B　81
C　87
D　88

1272　Who was the first basketball player to be a Parade All-American for four consecutive years?

A　Wilt Chamberlain
B　Cheryl Miller
C　Michael Jordan
D　Lisa Leslie

1273   What is the nickname of teams at Alcorn State?

A   Chiefs
B   Warriors
C   Braves
D   Redmen

1274   Which basketball star was nicknamed Mailman?

A   Kobe Bryant
B   Karl Malone
C   Moses Malone
D   Sam Jones

1275   Who led the American League in stolen bases every year from 1980 to 1991 except 1987?

A   Rickey Henderson
B   Kenny Lofton
C   Willie Wilson
D   Harold Reynolds

1276   What college did basketball star James Worthy attend?

A   North Carolina State
B   Wake Forest
C   Duke
D   North Carolina

1277 Which athlete was suspended in 1996 for not standing during the playing of the National Anthem?

A Mahmoud Abdul-Raul
B Kareem Abdul-Jabbar
C Dennis Rodman
D Charles Barkley

1278 Which of the following basketball stars played a season with the Harlem Globetrotters before entering the NBA?

A Oscar Robertson
B Darryl Dawkins
C Wilt Chamberlain
D Bill Russell

1279 Which team (other than the Yankees) did Baseball Hall of Fame member Reggie Jackson play for the most in his career?

A New York Mets
B Oakland A's
C Minnesota Twins
D San Diego Padres

1280 Which of the following was the National League MVP in 1989?

A Kevin Mitchell
B Fred McGriff
C Eric Davis
D Darryl Strawberry

1281 How many wins did legendary Grambling football coach Eddie Robinson have in his career?

A 399
B 452
C 137
D 408

1282 What sport is Dominique Dawes best known for?

A Basketball
B Figure skating
C Gymnastics
D Softball

1283 What number did Baseball Hall of Fame member Roberto Clemente wear?

A 20
B 21
C 25
D 27

1284 Who is the only man to be a unanimous selection for the Most Valuable Player Award in the NBA?

A Wilt Chamberlain
B Stephen Curry
C LeBron James
D Michael Jordan

1285   What is the last name of Curly of the Harlem Globetrotters?

A   Neal
B   Johnson
C   Lemon
D   Haynes

1286   Who is the only NFL player to average one hundred yards rushing per game in his career?

A   Emmitt Smith
B   O. J. Simpson
C   Barry Sanders
D   Jim Brown

1287   Who was the first black to be inducted into the National Football League Hall of Fame?

A   Dick Lane
B   Jim Brown
C   Emlen Tunnell
D   Jim Parker

African American Desk Reference, page 538

1288   What college did Heisman Trophy winner Barry Sanders attend?

A   Oklahoma State
B   Nebraska
C   Colorado
D   Oklahoma

1289 Who was the most valuable player the first two seasons of the WNBA?

A   Lisa Leslie
B   Cynthia Cooper
C   Cheryl Miller
D   Sheryl Swoopes

1290 Which of the following was the National League MVP in 1995?

A   Barry Bonds
B   Darryl Strawberry
C   Barry Larkin
D   Ron Gant

1291 Which team(s) did baseball legend and Hall of Fame member Hank Aaron play for?

A   Atlanta Braves, Milwaukee Braves, and Milwaukee Brewers
B   Chicago Cubs
C   Chicago White Sox
D   Detroit Tigers

1292 Which college did Bill Russell lead to NCAA basketball titles in 1955 and 1956?

A   North Carolina
B   UCLA
C   Boston College
D   San Francisco

1293   How many strokes did Tiger Woods finish ahead of the runner-up in the 2000 US Open?

A   Eleven
B   One
C   Fifteen
D   Nine

1294   Who is the only black driver to have won a NASCAR Winston Cup race?

A   Willy T. Ribbs
B   Wendell Scott
C   Rojo Jack
D   Bill Lester

1295   For what event did Shani Davis win the gold medal in the 2006 and 2010 Olympics?

A   High jump
B   Two-hundred-meter bobsled
C   One-thousand-meter skating
D   Long jump

1296   What college did basketball star Darrell Griffith attend?

A   Kentucky
B   North Carolina
C   Louisville
D   Memphis State

1297 How many points did Willis Reed score in game 7 of the 1970 NBA Finals when he played despite being injured?

A Twenty-seven
B Twenty-two
C Twenty
D Four

1298 Which of the following won the American League Cy Young Award and MVP in 1971?

A Vida Blue
B John Odom
C Jim Grant
D Bob Gibson

1299 What city is the birthplace of Hall of Fame baseball player Ernie Banks?

A Tampa
B Los Angeles
C Oklahoma City
D Dallas

1300 Which team did Doc Gooden play for when he threw his only no-hitter?

A New York Yankees
B Cincinnati Reds
C New York Mets
D Los Angeles Dodgers

1301   Which of the following won the American League Cy Young
Award in 2012?

A   CC Sabathia
B   David Price
C   Marcus Stroman
D   Chris Archer

1302   What is the nickname of the athletic teams at Paine?

A   Lions
B   Cougars
C   Panthers
D   Tigers

1303   Which pro team did football star Roosevelt Brown play for?

A   Dallas Cowboys
B   Green Bay Packers
C   New York Giants
D   Washington Redskins

1304   What college did football legend Lawrence Taylor attend?

A   Grambling
B   Georgia
C   North Carolina
D   Virginia

1305 What number did football star John Mackey wear in the pros?

A 86
B 88
C 87
D 89

1306 How many home runs did Ken Griffey Jr. hit in his career?

A 630
B 547
C 499
D 599

1307 What city were the Blue Birds of the Negro League from?

A Dayton
B Boston
C Baltimore
D Columbus

1308 Which of the following hit fifty home runs for the San Diego Padres in 1998?

A Sammy Sosa
B Greg Vaughn
C Ken Griffey Jr.
D Barry Bonds

1309   Which of the following was the World Series MVP in 2000?

A   Dave Justice
B   Derek Jeter
C   Bernie Williams
D   Ken Griffey Jr.

1310   Which event did a pregnant Serena Williams win in 2017 to give her twenty-three career Grand Slam single titles?

A   Australian Open
B   French Open
C   Wimbledon
D   US Open

1311   In what city were the Tigers (1934–1937) of the Negro League located?

A   Cincinnati
B   Cleveland
C   Columbus
D   Dayton

1312   What is the nickname of boxing legend Joe Louis?

A   Sweet Lou
B   Smoking Joe
C   The Black Bomber
D   The Brown Bomber

1313   What position did basketball star Joe Dumars play in the pros?

A   Center
B   Forward
C   Guard
D   Point guard

1314   What college did basketball star Derrick Coleman attend?

A   Villanova
B   Saint John's
C   North Carolina State
D   Syracuse

1315   What number did Heisman Trophy–winning running back Herschel Walker wear in college?

A   42
B   33
C   34
D   44

1316   Which of the following was the American League MVP in 1997?

A   Derek Jeter
B   Frank Thomas
C   Darryl Strawberry
D   Ken Griffey Jr.

1317   Wilt Chamberlain holds the record for most rebounds in a NBA game. What is the record?

A   Thirty-one
B   Twenty-seven
C   Fifty-five
D   Thirty-four

History Channel, November 24, 1960

1318   What position did football star Jerry Robinson play in college?

A   Linebacker
B   Defensive back
C   Offensive lineman
D   Tight end

1319   Who won the Heisman Trophy in 1985?

A   Tim Brown
B   Charlie Ward
C   Herschel Walker
D   Bo Jackson

1320   What college did basketball star Doc Rivers attend?

A   UCLA
B   Duke
C   Maryland
D   Marquette

1321   What number did baseball star Lou Brock wear?

A   20
B   21
C   26
D   29

1322   What number did Football Hall of Fame member Kellen Winslow Sr. wear in the pros?

A   83
B   81
C   80
D   88

1323   Which Negro League team did Josh Gibson play for the most?

A   Kansas City
B   New York
C   Homestead
D   Saint Louis

1324   Which state is the birthplace of baseball star Bobby Bonds?

A   Texas
B   California
C   Louisiana
D   Maryland

1325　What city were the Black Sox of the Negro League from?

A　Baltimore
B　Boston
C　Chicago
D　Philadelphia

1326　What number did football star Bubba Smith wear in college?

A　95
B　77
C　90
D　99

1327　Who was the first Cy Young Award winner?

A　Bob Gibson
B　Joe Black
C　Vida Blue
D　Don Newcombe

1328　Which of the following led the National League in stolen bases from 1956 to 1959?

A　Hank Aaron
B　Willie Mays
C　Maury Wills
D　Lou Brock

1329   Which Southern California running back won the Heisman Trophy in 1979?

A   Mike Garrett
B   Marcus Allen
C   Charles White
D   Sam Cunningham

1330   What position did baseball star Billy Williams play?

A   Catcher
B   Outfield
C   Pitcher
D   Second base

1331   Which woman won the heptathlon in two Olympics?

A   Gail Devers
B   Evelyn Ashford
C   Florence Griffith Joyner
D   Jackie Joyner-Kersee

1332   What position did baseball star Leon Day play in the Negro Leagues?

A   Pitcher
B   Outfield
C   Catcher
D   Third base

1333 In what city were the Royal Giants of the Negro League located?

A Brooklyn
B Chicago
C Los Angeles
D Philadelphia

1334 What position did baseball star and Hall of Fame member Frank Robinson play?

A Third base
B Outfield
C Pitcher
D Shortstop

1335 Which basketball player is nicknamed the Rifleman?

A Wesley Person
B Henry Bibby
C Lucas McCain
D Chuck Person

1336 In what city were the Buckeyes (1943–1948 and 1950) of the Negro League located?

A Dayton
B Cincinnati
C Columbus
D Cleveland

1337   Which boxer took a bite out of Evander Holyfield's ear?

A   Muhammad Ali
B   George Foreman
C   Lennox Lewis
D   Mike Tyson

1338   Everson Walls and Ron Springs were teammates with the Dallas Cowboys. In later life what did Walls give to Springs?

A   A kidney
B   A liver
C   A heart
D   A house

1339   What college did basketball star Kenny Anderson attend?

A   Georgia Tech
B   North Carolina
C   Kansas
D   Louisville

1340   What is football star Tank Younger's first name?

A   Thomas
B   Dick
C   Frank
D   Paul

1341   What college did basketball legend Julius Erving play for?

A   North Carolina
B   Kansas
C   Massachusetts
D   UNLV

1342   What number did baseball star Harold Baines wear?

A   6
B   9
C   3
D   8

1343   How many gold medals did Carl Lewis win in the 1984 Olympics?

A   Two
B   Four
C   Seven
D   One

1344   Who is the only man to have scored one hundred points in a National Basketball Association game?

A   Kobe Bryant
B   Kareem Abdul-Jabbar
C   Michael Jordan
D   Wilt Chamberlain

1345　In what city did George Foreman win a gold medal in the Olympics?

A　Los Angeles
B　Mexico City, Mexico
C　Montreal, Canada
D　Rome, Italy

1346　Who made the first three-point shot in NCAA basketball?

A　Isaiah Thomas
B　Oscar Robertson
C　Austin Carr
D　Ronnie Carr

1347　What city were the Monarchs of the Negro League from?

A　Chicago
B　Kansas City
C　New York
D　Saint Louis

1348　Which of the following basketball stars was not a member of the "Dream Team"?

A　Isaiah Thomas
B　Scottie Pippen
C　Charles Barkley
D　Clyde Drexler

1349 Who was the first basketball player to go from high school to the pros?

A Moses Malone
B Wilt Chamberlain
C Darryl Dawkins
D Kobe Bryant

1350 What number did football star Cornelius Bennett wear in college?

A 99
B 56
C 90
D 97

1351 What college did football star and Heisman Trophy winner Charlie Ward play for?

A Alabama
B Florida State
C Miami
D Southern California

1352 What Olympic star was known for having extremely long fingernails?

A Jackie Joyner
B Florence Griffith Joyner
C Marion Jones
D Wilma Rudolph

1353   Which of the following won a Gold Glove every year from 1990 to 1999?

A   Rickey Henderson
B   Vince Coleman
C   Ken Griffey Jr.
D   Kenny Lofton

1354   Who won the Heisman Trophy in 2010 and was the first pick in the NFL draft in 2011?

A   Michael Vick
B   Robert Griffin III
C   Cam Newton
D   JaMarcus Russell

1355   Which team did baseball star Frank Thomas play for most of his career?

A   Detroit Tigers
B   Chicago Cubs
C   Chicago White Sox
D   Milwaukee and Atlanta Braves

1356   What number did baseball legend and Hall of Fame member Jackie Robinson wear?

A   44
B   40
C   41
D   42

1357   What position did baseball star Joe Williams play in the Negro Leagues?

A   Pitcher
B   Outfield
C   Catcher
D   Shortstop

1358   Which track-and-field event is Alice Coachman best known for?

A   Shot put
B   Discus
C   Long jump
D   High jump

1359   What position did basketball player Mark Aguirre play in college?

A   Center
B   Forward
C   Guard
D   Point guard

1360   Hawkeye Whitney was a basketball star who played for North Carolina State. What was his first name?

A   William
B   Frederick
C   Tyrone
D   Charles

1361   Which Negro League team did baseball star Oscar Charleston play for (1932–1938)?

A   Philadelphia
B   New York
C   Newark
D   Pittsburgh

1362   How many knockouts did boxer Archie Moore have in his professional career?

A   141
B   52
C   8
D   37

Black Firsts, page 669

1363   Which of the following pro teams did football legend and Hall of Fame member Deacon Jones play for?

A   Chicago Bears
B   Los Angeles Rams
C   New York Giants
D   New York Jets

1364   Which team did Baseball Hall of Fame member Ernie Banks play for?

A   Chicago Cubs
B   New York Mets
C   Chicago White Sox
D   Milwaukee and Atlanta Braves

1365   What number did football legend Lawrence Taylor wear in college?

A   56
B   58
C   98
D   99

1366   What number did Baseball Hall of Fame member Billy Williams wear?

A   44
B   21
C   26
D   29

1367   Which of the following was the American League Rookie of the Year in 1996?

A   Eric Davis
B   Derek Jeter
C   Torii Hunter
D   Ken Griffey Jr.

1368   What college did basketball star Scott May attend?

A   Indiana
B   North Carolina
C   Kentucky
D   UCLA

1369   What is basketball star Bob Love's nickname?

A   Lover Boy
B   Butterbean
C   The Love Doctor
D   The Love Man

1370   What college did basketball star Austin Carr attend?

A   Marquette
B   UCLA
C   Notre Dame
D   Michigan

1371   Which Negro League team did Mule Suttles play for (1936–1940 and 1942–1944)?

A   Kansas City
B   New York
C   Newark
D   Pittsburgh

1372   Which of the following was the National League MVP from 2001 through 2004?

A   Willie Mays
B   Kevin Mitchell
C   Barry Bonds
D   Sammy Sosa

1373   Who was the first black to win an individual gold medal in the Winter Olympics?

A   Debi Thomas
B   Shani Davis
C   Jazmine Fenlator
D   Vonetta Flowers

1374   How many home runs did Willie McCovey hit in his career?

A   600
B   504
C   512
D   521

1375   Who set the NFL record with 149 receptions in a season (2019)?

A   Antonio Brown
B   Larry Fitzgerald
C   Michael Thomas
D   Julius Jones

1376   What number did Heisman Trophy–winning running back O. J. Simpson wear in college?

A   34
B   33
C   32
D   44

1377 What number did football legend and Hall of Fame member Walter Payton wear in the pros?

A 34
B 32
C 33
D 35

1378 Who was the first heavyweight boxer to regain the title?

A Muhammad Ali
B Jack Johnson
C Floyd Patterson
D George Foreman

1379 What event did Joe DeLoach win a gold medal for in the 1988 Olympics?

A High jump
B 110-meter hurdles
C 200-meter run
D 400-meter hurdles

1380 What position did baseball legend and Hall of Fame member Satchel Paige play in the Negro Leagues?

A Pitcher
B Outfield
C Third base
D Shortstop

1381   Which professional basketball team did Bob McAdoo play for first?

A   New York Knicks
B   Boston Celtics
C   Los Angeles Lakers
D   Buffalo Braves

1382   Which team did baseball star Darryl Strawberry play for most of his career?

A   Philadelphia Phillies
B   Montreal Expos
C   New York Mets
D   San Diego Padres

1383   What position did baseball star Lee Smith play?

A   Pitcher
B   Outfield
C   Shortstop
D   Second base

1384   Franco Harris caught a deflected pass and scored a touchdown to put Pittsburgh in the lead ahead of Oakland. What is this play known as?

A   The Pittsburgh Play
B   The Immaculate Reception
C   The Catch
D   The Miracle in Pittsburgh

1385   What number did Football Hall of Fame member Mike Singletary wear in the pros?

A   56
B   50
C   58
D   63

1386   Only three men in baseball history have five hundred home runs and thirty-two hundred hits. Which player is not one of the three?

A   Eddie Murray
B   Hank Aaron
C   Barry Bonds
D   Willie Mays

1387   What number did baseball star Tony Oliva wear?

A   1
B   3
C   8
D   6

1388   What did NBA star Lloyd Free change his name to?

A   Fabulous Free
B   Johnny B. Good
C   World B. Free
D   Muhammad Free

1389   Which team did baseball star Tim Raines play for most of his career?

A   Toronto Blue Jays
B   Montreal Expos
C   New York Mets
D   San Diego Padres

1390   What number did Football Hall of Fame member Charlie Taylor wear in the pros?

A   81
B   49
C   42
D   82

1391   Which of the following was the World Series MVP in 1964 and 1967?

A   Lou Brock
B   Bob Gibson
C   Elston Howard
D   Ernie Banks

1392   Which legendary track star won 122 races in a row?

A   Jesse Owens
B   Carl Lewis
C   Michael Johnson
D   Edwin Moses

1393   What is the nickname of teams at Mississippi Valley State?

A   Blue Devils
B   Delta Devils
C   Little Devils
D   Red Devils

1394   What number did Football Hall of Fame member Gale Sayers wear in the pros?

A   42
B   46
C   40
D   44

1395   What college did basketball star Kobe Bryant play for?

A   Duke
B   None
C   North Carolina
D   UCLA

1396   What is the nickname of teams at Florida A&M?

A   Rattlers
B   Gators
C   Hurricanes
D   Seminoles

1397   What number did football star Hugh Green wear in college?

A   98
B   74
C   99
D   88

1398   Which Olympian was a female basketball star at UCLA?

A   Jackie Joyner
B   Florence Griffith Joyner
C   Marion Jones
D   Wilma Rudolph

1399   What position did football star Jonathan Ogden play in college?

A   Quarterback
B   Linebacker
C   Defensive lineman
D   Offensive lineman

1400   Who was the first black baseball manager in major league history?

A   Rube Foster
B   Willie Randolph
C   Frank Robinson
D   Maury Wills

1401 Who won the Heisman Trophy in 2011?

A Montee Ball
B Cam Newton
C Robert Griffin III
D Trent Richardson

1402 Who was the youngest player to win the Heisman Trophy?

A Rashan Salaam
B Ernie Davis
C Marcus Allen
D Lamar Jackson

1403 Who was the first NFL player to rush for two thousand yards in a season?

A Eric Dickerson
B O. J. Simpson
C Terrell Davis
D Barry Sanders

1404 What position did basketball star Artis Gilmore play in the pros?

A Guard
B Forward
C Center
D Point guard

1405   What is Football Hall of Fame member Buck Buchanan's first name?

A   Junious
B   Dick
C   Lynwood
D   Paul

1406   What number did baseball legend and Hall of Fame member Bob Gibson wear?

A   34
B   45
C   44
D   24

1407   What position did basketball legend and Hall of Fame member Magic Johnson play in the pros?

A   Point guard
B   Forward
C   Guard
D   Center

1408   Which state is the birthplace of golfer Tiger Woods?

A   New York
B   Florida
C   New Jersey
D   California

1409   Which team did Baseball Hall of Fame member Billy Williams play for?

A   Detroit Tigers
B   Houston Astros
C   Cincinnati Reds
D   Chicago Cubs

1410   Who was the first black player for the New York Yankees?

A   Elston Howard
B   Whitey Ford
C   Reggie Jackson
D   Roy White

1411   Which of the following suffered with Parkinson's disease?

A   Joe Frazier
B   Mike Tyson
C   Muhammad Ali
D   Jack Johnson

African American Almanac, page 421

1412   Which player scored forty-one points to lead his team to the NCAA basketball title in 1978?

A   Jack Givens
B   Scott May
C   Danny Manning
D   Michael Jordan

1413   Which of the following was the World Series MVP for the Chicago White Sox in 2005?

A   Frank Thomas
B   Carl Everett
C   Willie Harris
D   Jermaine Dye

1414   What is the last name of the pro basketball star nicknamed Earl the Pearl?

A   Frazier
B   Drexler
C   Monroe
D   Oysters

1415   Who was the first black to win the Heisman Trophy?

A   O. J. Simpson
B   Ernie Davis
C   Mike Garrett
D   Archie Griffin

1416   What position did baseball star Cecil Fielder play?

A   Second base
B   Outfield
C   Pitcher
D   First base

1417   Who was the only player to run for three touchdowns in a Super Bowl game?

A   Franco Harris
B   Terrell Davis
C   Thurman Thomas
D   Emmitt Smith

1418   What events did Michael Johnson win gold medals for in the 1996 Olympics?

A   200-meter run and 400-meter run
B   110- and 400-meter hurdles
C   High jump and pole vault
D   Long jump and triple jump

1419   Who was the first black player in the modern National Football League?

A   Dick Lane
B   Jim Brown
C   Kenny Washington
D   Ollie Matson

African American National Biography, vol. 8, page 140

1420   What is the name of the man who finished second in the 2018 Daytona 500, becoming the first black to have a top-five NASCAR finish in fifty years?

A   Darrell Wallace Jr.
B   Bubba Scott
C   Wally Junior
D   Wendell Wallace

1421   What number did football star Randy Moss wear in college?

A   88
B   86
C   87
D   89

1422   Which outfielder was the 1989 National League Rookie of the Year?

A   Dave Justice
B   Eric Davis
C   Jerome Walton
D   Darryl Strawberry

1423   Which sport is Debi Thomas best known for?

A   Tennis
B   Basketball
C   Figure skating
D   Track and field

1424   What event did Gail Devers win a gold medal for in the 1992 Olympics?

A   100-meter run
B   110-meter hurdles
C   200-meter run
D   Long jump

1425   What event did Jackie Joyner-Kersee win a gold medal for in the 1992 Olympics?

A   Discus
B   Heptathlon
C   High jump
D   Long jump

1426   Who was the first black driver to race in the Indianapolis 500?

A   Charlie Wiggins
B   Willy T. Ribbs
C   Rajo Jack
D   Wendell Scott

1427   What college did football star Byron Leftwich attend?

A   Virginia
B   Marshall
C   Virginia Tech
D   West Virginia

1428   Which NBA star averaged more than fifty points per game for an entire season?

A   Wilt Chamberlain
B   Michael Jordan
C   Kareem Abdul-Jabbar
D   Kobe Bryant

Macmillan Encyclopedia: The African American Experience, page 124

1429   What number did Oklahoma football star Keith Jackson wear in college?

A   80
B   84
C   88
D   89

1430   Which of the following was the National League MVP in 2007?

A   Ryan Howard
B   Jimmy Rollins
C   Kevin Mitchell
D   Sammy Sosa

1431   Who was the first collegiate player to rush for two thousand yards in one season?

A   Barry Sanders
B   O. J. Simpson
C   Herschel Walker
D   Marcus Allen

1432   Which team did baseball star and Hall of Fame member Rod Carew play most of his career with?

A   Saint Louis
B   New York Mets
C   San Francisco
D   Minnesota

1433   How many bases did baseball star Rickey Henderson steal in 1982?

A   99
B   130
C   162
D   121

1434   What college did basketball legend Wilt Chamberlain play for?

A   Kansas
B   Kentucky
C   San Francisco
D   UCLA

1435   What position did football star Bruce Smith play in college?

A   Linebacker
B   Defensive lineman
C   Offensive lineman
D   Tight end

1436   What is the nickname of teams at Alabama A&M?

A   Bulls
B   Bullfrogs
C   Bulldogs
D   Fighting Bulls

1437   What college did Heisman Trophy winner Andre Ware attend?

A   Houston
B   Southern California
C   Texas
D   Florida State

1438   What college did Everson Walls attend?

A   Florida State
B   Howard
C   LSU
D   Grambling

1439   Who was the first man to rush for 250 yards in a NFL game?

A   O. J. Simpson
B   Jim Brown
C   Gale Sayers
D   Ollie Matson

Pro-Football-Reference.com

1440   Which of the following men won baseball's Triple Crown in 1966?

A   Hank Aaron
B   Frank Robinson
C   Willie McCovey
D   Willie Mays

1441   Who was the first black baseball player in the American League?

A   Jackie Robinson
B   Larry Doby
C   Satchel Paige
D   Sam Jethroe

1442   What college did basketball star Penny Hardaway attend?

A   Memphis State
B   Louisville
C   Kansas
D   Kentucky

1443   Who was the first black to play in the National Hockey League?

A   Grant Fuhr
B   Ferguson Jenkins
C   Willie O'Ree
D   Wendell Scott

1444   What is the nickname of Lorenzo Davis of the Negro League?

A   Wild Bill
B   Renzzie
C   The Devil
D   Piper

1445   What number did football star Deion Sanders wear with the Dallas Cowboys?

A   20
B   21
C   1
D   22

1446   What college did basketball legend David Thompson attend?

A   Maryland
B   North Carolina State
C   North Carolina
D   UCLA

1447   Who made the game-winning shot when Indiana defeated Syracuse in the 1987 NCAA title game?

A   Keith Smart
B   Scott May
C   Isaiah Thomas
D   Quinn Buckner

1448   Who was the first Southern California running back to win the Heisman Trophy?

A   Marcus Allen
B   Mike Garrett
C   Ricky Bell
D   O. J. Simpson

1449   What college did football star Rob Woodson attend?

A   Penn State
B   Michigan State
C   Pittsburgh
D   Purdue

1450   What was football legend Walter Payton's nickname?

A   Sweetness
B   Salty Walt
C   Mr. Bear
D   Sweet P

1451   Where did Muhammad Ali win the title from Sonny Liston?

A   Miami
B   Lewiston, Maine
C   Las Vegas
D   Kingston, Jamaica

1452   What college did Heisman Trophy winner Desmond Howard attend?

A   Southern California
B   Ohio State
C   Michigan
D   Notre Dame

1453   What events did Florence Griffith Joyner win a gold medal for in the 1988 Olympics?

A   100-meter, 200-meter, and 400-meter relay
B   110- and 400-meter hurdles
C   200- and 400-meter run
D   200-meter run and high jump

1454   In which city did Carl Lewis win four gold medals in the Olympics?

A   Barcelona, Spain
B   Los Angeles
C   Atlanta
D   Seoul, South Korea

1455   Which of the following was inducted into the Baseball Hall of Fame without the five-year waiting period?

A   Willie Mays
B   Jackie Robinson
C   Roberto Clemente
D   Hank Aaron

1456 Simone Biles won a team gold medal and three individual gold medals at the 2016 Olympics. In which event did she not win the gold medal (she won the bronze)?

A   All-around
B   Floor exercise
C   Vault
D   Balance beam

1457 What number did football star Warren Sapp wear in college?

A   98
B   75
C   76
D   99

1458 What was baseball player Jim Grant's nickname?

A   Jay Gee
B   Catfish
C   Mudcat
D   The Strikeout Kid

1459 What college did football star and Heisman Trophy winner Charles Woodson attend?

A   Southern California
B   Michigan State
C   Purdue
D   Michigan

1460   What college did football star Alan Page attend?

A   Southern California
B   Notre Dame
C   Ohio State
D   Michigan

1461   What position did baseball star Monte Irvin play in the Negro Leagues?

A   Outfield
B   First base
C   Pitcher
D   Shortstop

1462   What number did Heisman Trophy–winning running back Marcus Allen wear in college?

A   34
B   21
C   33
D   44

1463   Who is the only man to win the two-hundred-meter and four-hundred-meter runs in the Olympics?

A   Edwin Moses
B   Michael Johnson
C   Bob Hayes
D   Carl Lewis

1464   What number did Heisman Trophy–winning running back Bo Jackson wear in college?

A   34
B   44
C   32
D   22

1465   What number did Baseball Hall of Fame member Kirby Puckett wear?

A   32
B   34
C   44
D   45

1466   What basketball player was nicknamed the Round Mound of Rebound?

A   William Perry
B   Oliver Miller
C   Robert Traylor
D   Charles Barkley

1467   What event did Charles Austin win a gold medal for in the 1996 Olympics?

A   High jump
B   Long jump
C   Pole vault
D   Triple jump

1468 What was the nickname of the Homestead team in the Negro Leagues?

A Heroes
B Homesteaders
C Homers
D Grays

1469 Which of the following was the 1990 National League Rookie of the Year?

A Ken Griffey Jr.
B Derek Jeter
C Dave Justice
D Barry Bonds

1470 Which college did track star Wilma Rudolph attend?

A Virginia State
B Spelman
C Tennessee State
D Hampton

1471 Which of the following boxers was the heavyweight champion from 1937 to 1949?

A Joe Louis
B Jack Johnson
C Muhammad Ali
D Sugar Ray Robinson

1472   What college did basketball star Bob Lanier attend?

A   Villanova
B   Syracuse
C   Saint Bonaventure
D   Georgetown

1473   In what year did Lee Elder qualify for the Masters Tournament?

A   1981
B   1967
C   1974
D   1994

1474   What event did Carl Lewis win a gold medal for in the 1996 Olympics?

A   Two-hundred-meter run
B   Long jump
C   One-hundred-meter run
D   Triple jump

1475   What college did basketball star Sam Bowie attend?

A   Louisville
B   Georgetown
C   North Carolina
D   Kentucky

1476 The Harlem Globetrotters had a star who was called Meadowlark. What was his last name?

A Lemon
B Haynes
C Neal
D Tatum

1477 How many home runs did Eddie Murray hit in his career?

A 521
B 643
C 512
D 504

1478 Who were the firsts brothers to be chosen in the first round in the National Football League draft in the same year?

A Michael Dean and William Perry
B Ronde and Tiki Barber
C Shannon and Sterling Sharpe
D Tremaine and Terrell Edmunds

1479 Which athlete is nicknamed the Flying Squirrel?

A Gabby Douglas
B David Thompson
C Connie Hawkins
D Jesse Owens

1480   What city were the Black Crackers of the Negro League from?

A   Birmingham
B   Atlanta
C   Chicago
D   Louisville

1481   Who set the long jump record with a leap of twenty-nine feet and two inches in 1968? (This remained the record until 1991.)

A   Bob Beamon
B   Jesse Owens
C   Carl Lewis
D   Rafer Johnson

1482   What number did football star Derrick Thomas wear in the pros?

A   57
B   56
C   58
D   59

1483   What position did basketball star Charles Barkley play?

A   Guard
B   Center
C   Forward
D   Point guard

1484   Which of the following professional football teams did Tony Dorsett play for most of his career?

A   Dallas
B   San Francisco
C   Detroit
D   Pittsburgh

1485   What position did basketball player Dwayne Pearl Washington play in college?

A   Center
B   Forward
C   Guard
D   Point guard

1486   What pro team did football star and Hall of Fame member Joe Greene play for?

A   Dallas
B   Pittsburgh
C   Philadelphia
D   Chicago

1487   Which state is the birthplace of Muhammad Ali?

A   Texas
B   Kentucky
C   New York
D   Tennessee

1488   Which of the following was the National League MVP in 1991?

A   Tony Gwynn
B   Gary Sheffield
C   Terry Pendleton
D   Barry Bonds

1489   Which of the following players shattered two backboards with dunks in 1979?

A   Darryl Dawkins
B   Muggsy Bogues
C   Shaquille O'Neal
D   Wilt Chamberlain

1490   What is the nickname of teams at Fayetteville State?

A   Mustangs
B   Broncos
C   Pintos
D   Ponies

1491   Who was the first player from the Negro Leagues to be inducted into the Baseball Hall of Fame?

A   Mule Suttles
B   Josh Gibson
C   Cool Papa Bell
D   Satchel Paige

1492   What number did Football Hall of Fame member Tony Dorsett wear in the pros?

A   35
B   32
C   33
D   34

1493   How old was Tiger Woods when he played in his first PGA Tour event?

A   Eighteen
B   Fourteen
C   Twenty
D   Sixteen

1494   Which of the following professional football teams did Hall of Fame member Earl Campbell play for most of his career?

A   Houston
B   Dallas
C   Pittsburgh
D   Texas

1495   What is the nickname of teams at Morgan State?

A   Buffaloes
B   Bears
C   Morticians
D   Magicians

1496   What events did Carl Lewis win a gold medal for in the 1988 Olympics?

A   Hundred-meter run and long jump
B   Discus and shot put
C   Long jump and triple jump
D   Long jump and two-hundred-meter run

1497   What number did football legend and Hall of Fame member Lawrence Taylor wear in the pros?

A   56
B   55
C   50
D   58

1498   What number did Baseball Hall of Fame member Joe Morgan wear?

A   3
B   8
C   6
D   9

1499   Prior to a player scoring one hundred points in a NBA game, who held the record with seventy-one?

A   Wilt Chamberlain
B   Elgin Baylor
C   Michael Jordan
D   Oscar Robertson

African American National Biography, vol. 1, page 315

1500   What was the name of the first Major League Baseball team that Frank Robinson managed?

A   Cincinnati Reds
B   Chicago White Sox
C   Cleveland Indians
D   Detroit Tigers

1501   What college did Heisman Trophy winner Ron Dayne attend?

A   Wisconsin
B   Minnesota
C   Michigan
D   Notre Dame

1502   Which of the following hit fifty-eight home runs in 2006?

A   Ryan Howard
B   Barry Bonds
C   Sammy Sosa
D   Sammy Davis Jr.

1503   What position did baseball star Vida Blue play?

A   Second base
B   Outfield
C   Shortstop
D   Pitcher

1504 Which basketball player was nicknamed Honeycomb?

A   Jason Kidd
B   Gus Williams
C   Gus Johnson
D   Jayson Williams

1505 What number did Baseball Hall of Fame member Frank Robinson wear?

A   27
B   21
C   20
D   32

1506 What number did football star Lee Roy Selmon wear in college?

A   93
B   77
C   88
D   99

1507 What basketball star was nicknamed Doctor Dunkenstein?

A   Darrell Griffith
B   Dominique Wilkins
C   Michael Jordan
D   Rodney McCray

1508   Which of the following was the World Series MVP in 1989 for the Oakland A's?

A   Rickey Henderson
B   Reggie Jackson
C   Vida Blue
D   Dave Stewart

1509   What position did Negro League legend and Baseball Hall of Fame member Cool Papa Bell play?

A   Second base
B   Outfield
C   Pitcher
D   Shortstop

1510   What position did baseball star and Hall of Fame member Dave Winfield play?

A   Pitcher
B   Shortstop
C   Outfield
D   Second base

1511   What number did Hall of Fame running back Marion Motley of the Cleveland Browns wear?

A   32
B   44
C   76
D   1

1512   What college did Heisman Trophy winner Mark Ingram attend?

A   Notre Dame
B   Georgia
C   Alabama
D   Florida

1513   Which woman scored forty-seven points in a NCAA basketball championship game?

A   Maya Moore
B   Sheryl Swoopes
C   Lisa Leslie
D   Cheryl Miller

African American National Biography, vol. 7, page 471

1514   What number did Baseball Hall of Fame member Willie McCovey wear?

A   44
B   34
C   32
D   45

1515 Which of the following had a photo taken of him while wearing a white wedding dress?

A   Charles Barkley
B   Allen Iverson
C   Shaquille O'Neal
D   Dennis Rodman

1516   What is basketball star Campy Russell's first name?

A   Campanella
B   Isaiah
C   Michael
D   Robert

1517   What college did basketball star Larry Johnson attend?

A   Houston
B   UNLV
C   UCLA
D   North Carolina State

1518   Which of the following won the National League Cy Young Award and MVP in 1968?

A   Juan Marichal
B   Ferguson Jenkins
C   Vida Blue
D   Bob Gibson

1519   Which of the following was the 1983 National League Rookie of the Year?

A   Andre Dawson
B   Doc Gooden
C   Darryl Strawberry
D   Tim Raines

1520 How many home runs did Willie Mays hit in his career?

A 607
B 586
C 660
D 755

1521 What number did Heisman Trophy–winning running back Earl Campbell wear in college?

A 21
B 20
C 32
D 34

1522 What position did basketball player Corliss Williamson play in college?

A Center
B Forward
C Guard
D Point guard

1523 What position did football star Derrick Thomas play in college?

A Tight end
B Defensive back
C Offensive lineman
D Linebacker

1524   Which National League team did Baseball Hall of Fame member Frank Robinson play for?

A   Houston Astros
B   Chicago Cubs
C   Cincinnati Reds
D   Detroit Tigers

1525   What number did Football Hall of Fame member Franco Harris wear in the pros?

A   32
B   30
C   33
D   34

1526   Which of the following was the World Series MVP in 1973 for the Oakland A's?

A   John Odom
B   Reggie Jackson
C   Bert Campaneris
D   Vida Blue

1527   Which of the following was a star pitcher at Vanderbilt University?

A   Bob Gibson
B   Doc Gooden
C   David Price
D   J. R. Richard

1528   What is Negro League star and Hall of Fame member Buck O'Neill's first name?

A   Buckaroo
B   John
C   Larry
D   Walter

1529   Who was the first black quarterback to win the Heisman Trophy?

A   Donovan McNabb
B   Charlie Ward
C   Andre Ware
D   Doug Williams

1530   What position did football star Reggie Roby play in college?

A   Quarterback
B   Linebacker
C   Offensive lineman
D   Punter

1531   Who was the youngest pitcher to win the Cy Young Award?

A   Bob Gibson
B   Vida Blue
C   Ferguson Jenkins
D   Doc Gooden

1532   What is basketball star Allen Iverson's nickname?

A   The Little A
B   Mr. Practice
C   The Answer
D   The Question

1533   What college did basketball star Larry Finch attend?

A   UCLA
B   Georgetown
C   Memphis State
D   Houston

1534   How old was Muhammad Ali when he lit the flame at the Atlanta Olympics?

A   Sixty-four
B   Sixty-one
C   Seventy-nine
D   Fifty-four

1535   What number did baseball star Frank White wear?

A   32
B   24
C   30
D   20

1536   What number did football star George Webster wear in college?

A   90
B   52
C   60
D   70

1537   Which man is nicknamed the Glove?

A   Basketball star Kobe Bryant
B   Basketball star Gary Payton
C   Basketball star Sean Kemp
D   Football Hall of Famer O. J. Simpson

1538   What college did basketball star Sean May attend?

A   Kentucky
B   Maryland
C   North Carolina
D   North Carolina State

1539   What position did baseball star and Hall of Fame member Ferguson Jenkins play?

A   Pitcher
B   Outfield
C   Third base
D   Shortstop

1540   In what year did the first black jockey ride the winner of the Kentucky Derby?

A   1993
B   1875
C   1881
D   2001

1541   What event did Dan O'Brien win a gold medal for in the 1996 Olympics?

A   Javelin
B   Discus
C   Decathlon
D   Shot put

1542   How many voters did not vote for Hank Aaron as a first-ballot Hall of Famer?

A   2
B   9
C   23
D   15

New York Times, January 13, 1982

1543   What position did basketball player Sean Elliott play in the pros?

A   Forward
B   Center
C   Guard
D   Point guard

1544   What number did football star Derrick Thomas wear in college?

A   57
B   56
C   55
D   58

1545   Which of the following positions did baseball star and Hall of Fame member Willie Stargell play most of his career?

A   Outfield
B   Catcher
C   Pitcher
D   Third base

1546   Which quarterback threw four touchdowns in one quarter in a Super Bowl?

A   Russell Wilson
B   Steve McNair
C   Warren Moon
D   Doug Williams

1547   What number did baseball legend and Hall of Fame member Hank Aaron wear?

A   42
B   40
C   44
D   24

1548 Which team did Baseball Hall of Fame member Joe Morgan win a World Series with?

A Cincinnati
B Houston
C San Francisco
D Saint Louis

1549 What is Football Hall of Famer Deacon Jones's first name?

A Dick
B Duke
C David
D Don

1550 Buck Williams was a basketball star at Maryland. What was his first name?

A Charles
B William
C Isaiah
D Wallace

1551 Which Southern California running back won the Heisman Trophy in 1968?

A Marcus Allen
B O. J. Simpson
C Mike Garrett
D Ricky Bell

1552   What college did Heisman Trophy winner Ernie Davis attend?

A   Southern California
B   Syracuse
C   Notre Dame
D   Ohio State

1553   Which city was the location of the rematch between Muhammad Ali and Sonny Liston?

A   New York
B   Miami
C   Lewiston, Maine
D   Las Vegas

1554   What was the name of the horse ridden by Oliver Lewis that won the first Kentucky Derby?

A   Lucky Lady
B   Secretariat
C   Aristides
D   Big Red

Black Saga, page 248

1555   What college did track and football star Bob Hayes attend?

A   Ohio State
B   Florida A&M
C   Southern California
D   UCLA

1556   What is Negro League legend and Hall of Fame member Satchel Paige's first name?

A   William
B   Satchmo
C   Samuel
D   Leroy

1557   Which pro team did football star and Hall of Fame member Willie Brown play for?

A   Seattle Seahawks
B   Dallas Cowboys
C   Pittsburgh Steelers
D   Oakland Raiders

1558   What number did football star Corey Moore wear in college?

A   56
B   52
C   7
D   66

1559   What is the nickname of teams at Tuskegee?

A   Fighting Airmen
B   Experiments
C   Golden Tigers
D   Red Tails

1560   What college did basketball star Danny Manning attend?

A   UCLA
B   Georgetown
C   North Carolina
D   Kansas

1561   What position did football star Cornelius Bennett play in college?

A   Linebacker
B   Defensive back
C   Offensive lineman
D   Punter

1562   Which Negro League team did Smokey Joe Williams play for (1911–1923)?

A   New York
B   Chicago
C   Homestead
D   Pittsburgh

1563   What number did baseball star Ken Griffey Jr. wear for Seattle?

A   30
B   27
C   24
D   32

1564   What college did basketball star John Shumate attend?

A   Oregon State
B   Purdue
C   Oregon
D   Notre Dame

1565   Where did an NBA player score one hundred points in a single game?

A   Los Angeles
B   Hershey, Pennsylvania
C   New York
D   Philadelphia

1566   Who was the first black pitcher to win a game in the World Series?

A   Joe Greene
B   Don Newcombe
C   Joe Black
D   Joe White

1567   Which of the following was the American League MVP in 1993 and 1994?

A   Mo Vaughn
B   Frank Thomas
C   Ryan Howard
D   Ken Griffey Jr.

1568   What event did Gail Devers win an Olympic gold medal for in 1996?

A   100-meter run
B   110-meter hurdles
C   200-meter run
D   High jump

1569   What city were the Black Barons of the Negro League from?

A   Boston
B   Atlanta
C   Birmingham
D   Philadelphia

1570   Which college did football legend Walter Payton attend?

A   Florida State
B   Grambling
C   Jackson State
D   Mississippi State

1571   How many gold medals did Jesse Owens win in the 1936 Berlin Olympics?

A   Three
B   Four
C   One
D   Seven

1572   What is the nickname of teams at Virginia Union?

A   Panthers
B   Lions
C   Spiders
D   Tigers

1573   What number did football legend and Hall of Fame member Jim Brown wear in the pros?

A   44
B   33
C   34
D   32

1574   What college did basketball star Hakeem Olajuwon attend?

A   UCLA
B   Georgetown
C   Houston
D   Louisville

1575   What is basketball player Mahmoud Abdul-Rauf's birth name?

A   Keith Wilkes
B   Chris Jackson
C   Olivier Saint-Jean
D   Walt Hazzard

1576 Which of the following won the 2007 American League Cy Young Award?

A Edwin Jackson
B Dontrelle Willis
C CC Sabathia
D David Price

1577 What college did Heisman Trophy winner Lamar Jackson attend?

A Louisville
B Florida State
C Clemson
D Notre Dame

1578 Which of the following was an outstanding lacrosse player?

A Jim Brown
B Jackie Robinson
C Allen Iverson
D Venus Williams

1579 How many home runs did Reggie Jackson hit in his career?

A 660
B 586
C 563
D 755

1580   What is the name of the high school Kareem Abdul-Jabbar (Lew Alcindor at the time) attended?

A   Crenshaw
B   Oak Hill Academy
C   Power Memorial
D   Booker T. Washington

1581   Which Negro League team did Buck Leonard play for (1934–1950)?

A   New York
B   Chicago
C   Kansas City
D   Homestead

1582   In what year was the Negro National League founded?

A   1914
B   1893
C   1959
D   1920

African American Desk Reference, page 510

1583   What position did Basketball Hall of Fame member George Gervin play in the pros?

A   Center
B   Forward
C   Guard
D   Point guard

1584   What is basketball legend and Hall of Fame member Kareem Abdul-Jabbar's birth name?

A   Cassius Clay
B   Curtis Rowe
C   Lew Alcindor
D   Sidney Wicks

1585   What is Negro League legend and Hall of Fame member Cool Papa Bell's first name?

A   John
B   James
C   Leroy
D   William

1586   Who set the American League record for most home runs hit by a rookie with 52 in 2017?

A   Kenny Griffey Jr.
B   Aaron Judge
C   Barry Bonds
D   Hank Aaron

1587   What number did Baseball Hall of Fame member Eddie Murray wear?

A   44
B   34
C   33
D   45

1588   In what city were the Lincoln Giants of the Negro League located?

A   Kansas City
B   Chicago
C   New York
D   Miami

1589   Which of the following men supposedly had romantic involvement with twenty thousand women?

A   Muhammad Ali
B   Wilt Chamberlain
C   Willie Mays
D   A. C. Green

1590   Who was the second black quarterback to win the Heisman Trophy?

A   Donovan McNabb
B   Doug Williams
C   Charlie Ward
D   Michael Vick

1591   What college did Heisman Trophy winner George Rogers attend?

A   Southern California
B   South Carolina
C   Notre Dame
D   Syracuse

1592   Which is the only major title in tennis that Arthur Ashe did not win?

A   Wimbledon
B   Australian Open
C   French Open
D   US Open

1593   Who was the first black jockey to ride three winners in the Kentucky Derby?

A   Isaac Murphy
B   Jimmy Winkfield
C   Willie Simms
D   Oliver Lewis

1594   Who was the first black to win a gold medal in the Winter Olympics?

A   Rafer Johnson
B   Grant Fuhr
C   Vonetta Flowers
D   Jesse Owens

1595   In 2017, who became the first black woman, other than the Williams sisters, to win a Grand Slam event in tennis since 1958?

A   Madison Keys
B   Zina Garrison
C   Sloane Stephens
D   Chanda Rubin

1596   What number did football star Lee Roy Kelly wear in the pros?

A   40
B   44
C   42
D   34

1597   What position did baseball star Jimmie Crutchfield play in the Negro Leagues?

A   Third base
B   First base
C   Pitcher
D   Outfield

1598   What position did football star Jack Tatum play in college?

A   Tight end
B   Defensive lineman
C   Linebacker
D   Defensive back

1599   Which of the following led the American League in stolen bases from 1992 through 1996?

A   Kenny Lofton
B   Rickey Henderson
C   Willie Wilson
D   Harold Reynolds

1600   In what year did Tiger Woods become the youngest player to win the Masters?

A   2003
B   2001
C   1997
D   1995

Television, Arts, and Literature

1601   Where was the Fresh Prince of Bel-Air born and raised?

A   Bel Air
B   East Philadelphia
C   South Philadelphia
D   West Philadelphia

1602   Who was the first black Bond girl?

A   Gloria Hendra
B   Trina Parks
C   Naomi Harris
D   Halle Berry

1603   Which of the following creates problems for Neville Flynn (played by Samuel L. Jackson) on a plane?

A   Alligators
B   Snakes
C   Aliens
D   Spiders

1604   Which of the following was crowned Miss Fire Protection in a Tennessee beauty pageant?

A   Tina Turner
B   Halle Berry
C   Lena Horne
D   Oprah Winfrey

African American Lives, page 904

1605   Halle Berry won an Emmy Award for her portrayal of _____.

A   Josephine Baker
B   Coretta Scott King
C   Catwoman
D   Dorothy Dandridge

1606   Which white performer wrote the hit song "I Will Always Love You" that Whitney Houston sang in the film *The Bodyguard*?

A   Loretta Lynn
B   Faith Hill
C   Dolly Parton
D   Tammy Wynette

1607   What was the Fresh Prince of Bel-Air doing when a couple of guys started causing trouble in the neighborhood?

A   Playing video games
B   Playing basketball
C   Shooting pool
D   Dancing with a girlfriend

1608   Morgan Freeman was the narrator of the movie *March* _____.

A   *on Washington*
B   *of the Penguins*
C   *of the Soldiers*
D   *of Dimes*

1609   What is the middle initial of Fred Sanford, the character from *Sanford and Son*?

A   P.
B   G.
C   B.
D   C.

1610   Dewey Markham was a famous comedian who was known by his nickname. What is it?

A   Pig Eye
B   Pigmeat
C   Pig Feet
D   Mr. Piggy

1611   Who buys the Banks's house in the final episode of *The Fresh Prince of Bel-Air*?

A   George and Louise Jefferson
B   Arnold and Willis Jackson
C   James and Florida Evans
D   Heathcliffe and Claire Huxtable

1612   Who was the director of *12 Years a Slave*?

A   Spike Lee
B   John Singleton
C   Steve McQueen
D   Ava DuVernay

1613   Mr. T's signature saying is "I pity the _____."

A   fool
B   drunk
C   punk
D   crook

1614   Which of the following actresses played the character who married Reverend Gregory on *Amen*?

A   Anne Marie Johnson
B   Anna Maria Horsford
C   Denise Nicholas
D   Jo Marie Payton-France

1615   What is the name of the man Don Cheadle portrays in the movie *Hotel Rwanda*?

A   Desmond Tutu
B   Paul Rusesabagina
C   Idi Amin
D   Nelson Mandela

1616   Mable Simmons is a popular movie and television character. Who is she best known as?

A   Madea
B   Cutie Pie
C   Bertha Butt
D   Big Momma

1617   Nell Harper was a character on a television sitcom. What is the name of the family Harper worked for?

A   The Winlows
B   The Jeffersons
C   The Kaniskys
D   The Tates

1618   Which of the following actresses played the character who married Carl Winslow on *Family Matters*?

A   Anne Marie Johnson
B   Jo Marie Payton
C   Denise Nicholas
D   Lisa Bonet

1619   Who was the first black woman to make a record?

A   Bessie Smith
B   Pearl Bailey
C   Memphis Minnie
D   Mamie Smith

Black Firsts, page 64

1620   Which of the following movies has a character named Celie?

A   *The Color Purple*
B   *Rosewood*
C   *Shaft*
D   *The Learning Tree*

1621 Who played Mister in the movie *The Color Purple?*

A Sidney Poitier
B Lou Gossett Jr.
C Morgan Freeman
D Danny Glover

1622 What television show was Napoleon Whiting a regular on?

A *Sanford and Son*
B *Good Times*
C *The Big Valley*
D *Room 222*

1623 Who was the first black to win a Tony Award?

A Hattie McDaniel
B Juanita Hall
C Diahann Carroll
D James Earl Jones

Black Firsts, page 16

1624 Who portrayed the main character in the movie *Sister Act?*

A Tamara Dobson
B Whoopi Goldberg
C Vanessa Williams
D Phylicia Rashad

1625   Who was the first black person to receive an Oscar for his or her performance in a movie?

A   Hattie McDaniel
B   Whoopi Goldberg
C   Butterfly McQueen
D   Sidney Poitier

1626   The movie *Cool Runnings* is the story about the Jamaican _____.

A   soccer team
B   basketball team
C   sprinters
D   bobsled team

1627   Which of the following television characters did Gail Fisher play?

A   Gail Mannix on *Mannix*
B   Peggy Fair on *Mannix*
C   Harriet DeLong on *In the Heat of the Night*
D   Moesha on *Moesha*

1628   What is the name of Will Smith's daughter who was in the movie *I Am Legend*?

A   Wilamena
B   Jada
C   Jennifer
D   Willow

1629   What is the name of the play that Suzan-Lori Parks wrote that earned her a Pulitzer Prize for Drama?

A   *Topdog / Underdog*
B   *Underdog / Favorite*
C   *Underdog / Sweet Polly*
D   *Old Dog / Young Dog*

And Still I Rise, page 212

1630   Which movie soundtrack is the song "Earned It" by the Weekend on?

A   *The Fast and the Furious*
B   *Fifty Shades of Grey*
C   *Selma*
D   *42*

1631   Who is the author of *How Stella Got Her Groove Back*?

A   Terry McMillan
B   Maya Angelou
C   Gwendolyn Brooks
D   Toni Morrison

1632   Who is the star of the 1999 *Shaft* movie?

A   Richard Roundtree
B   Samuel L. Jackson
C   Bill Cosby
D   Wesley Snipes

1633   Who was the first black woman to win an Obie Award?

A   Alice Walker
B   Juanita Hall
C   Alice Childress
D   Lorraine Hansberry

African American Almanac, page 140

1634   Which actor played Lionel Jefferson on the television show *All in the Family*?

A   Damon Evans
B   Johnny Brown
C   Mike Evans
D   Ralph Carter

1635   Who won the Pulitzer Prize for *The Piano Lesson*?

A   Charles Fuller
B   August Wilson
C   Charles Gordone
D   James McPherson

1636   Arnold Jackson was a character on a television sitcom. What is the last name of the family he lived with?

A   Drummond
B   Coleman
C   Jackson
D   Peterson

1637   Which of the following men starred in *Showboat* and *The Emperor Jones*?

A   Ira Aldridge
B   Sidney Poitier
C   Paul Robeson
D   James Earl Jones

1638   Laurence Fishburne won the Tony Award for Best Featured Actor in a Play in 1992 for his performance in _____.

A   *Two Trains Running*
B   *Midnight Train*
C   *Two Planes Flying*
D   *One Train Running*

1639   What is the name of the TV character played by Keisha Knight Pulliam on the television show *The Cosby Show*?

A   Rudy Huxtable
B   Ronny Huxtable
C   Cleo Huxtable
D   Vanessa Huxtable

1640   How is *Sanford and Son* character Aunt Esther related to Fred?

A   The two are not related at all
B   She is his cousin
C   She is his aunt
D   She is his sister-in-law

1641 Who won a 1978 Best Featured Actress Tony for her performance in *Ain't Misbehavin'*?

A   Isabel Sanford
B   Marla Gibbs
C   Esther Rolle
D   Nell Carter

1642 Who played the title role in the movie *Akeelah and the Bee*?

A   Raven Goodwin
B   Keke Palmer
C   Paige Hurd
D   Willow Smith

1643 Which of the following characters did Reginald Val Johnson play?

A   Carl Winslow on *Family Matters*
B   Ernest Frye on *Amen*
C   Hampton Forbes on *In the Heat of the Night*
D   Henry Jefferson on *The Jeffersons*

1644 Who played Cedric Robinson on the television show *The Steve Harvey Show*?

A   Steve Harvey
B   Cedric the Entertainer
C   Todd Bridges
D   Charles Dutton

1645   What is the name of the character Danielle Spencer portrayed on the television show *What's Happening?*

A   C. J. Thomas
B   Dee Thomas
C   Lucy Thomas
D   Kay Thomas

1646   Which of the following plays the title role in the movie *Jackie Brown?*

A   Wesley Snipes
B   Tamara Dobson
C   Samuel L. Jackson
D   Pam Grier

1647   What was George Jefferson's mother's name?

A   Olivia
B   Holly
C   Molly
D   Harriet

1648   Which of the following is a movie Wesley Snipes starred in?

A   *Passenger 57*
B   *Passenger 55*
C   *Passenger 42*
D   *Passenger 99*

1649   What is the subject of Moneta Sleet's photograph that won him the Pulitzer Prize for Photography in 1969?

A   Myrlie Evers at Medgar's funeral
B   The Watts riots
C   Malcolm X's pallbearers
D   Coretta Scott King at Martin's funeral

African American Desk Reference, page 457

1650   Which of the following is not a Tyler Perry movie?

A   *Why Did I Get Married?*
B   *Precious*
C   *Good Deeds*
D   *Alex Cross*

1651   Lena James was a character on the television show *A Different World*. Which actress played James?

A   Jada Pinkett
B   Queen Latifah
C   Karyn Parsons
D   Lisa Bonet

1652   Will Smith is the star of the television show *The Fresh Prince of Bel-Air*. What is the last name of the family his character lived with?

A   Drummond
B   Banks
C   Papadapolis
D   Smith

1653   What television show has a character named Geoffrey who is a butler?

A   *The Fresh Prince of Bel-Air*
B   *Good Times*
C   *The Cosby Show*
D   *The Jeffersons*

1654   What character does LL Cool J portray on the television show *NCIS: Los Angeles*?

A   Hanna Barbera
B   Sam James
C   Sam Hanna
D   Cool James

1655   Lynn Whitfield won an Emmy Award for her portrayal of _____.

A   Dorothy Dandridge
B   Harriet Tubman
C   Tina Turner
D   Josephine Baker

1656   Ben Vereen won the 1973 Tony Award for Best Actor in a Musical for his performance in _____.

A   *Roots*
B   *Slippin'*
C   *Pippin*
D   *Webster*

1657   Which character is the only one that Eddie Murphy did not portray in the movie *The Nutty Professor II: The Klumps*?

A   Papa Klump
B   Sherman Klump
C   Ernie Klump Jr.
D   Mama Klump

1658   Who played Cleopatra Jones in the movie *Cleopatra Jones*?

A   Pam Grier
B   Tamara Dobson
C   Vanessa Williams
D   Whoopi Goldberg

1659   What is the name of Spike Lee's first feature movie?

A   *Do the Right Thing*
B   *Jungle Fever*
C   *School Daze*
D   *She's Gotta Have It*

1660   What is J. J. Evans's famous catchphrase?

A   "I'm coming to join you, Elizabeth."
B   "Did I do that?"
C   "Dynomite!"
D   "What you talking about?"

1661   Which character gave *Star Trek*'s Lieutenant Uhura television's first interracial kiss?

A   Captain Kirk
B   Luke Skywalker
C   Mr. Spock
D   Scotty

And Still I Rise, page 29

1662   What character does Dule Hill portray on the television show *West Wing*?

A   Charlie Young
B   Wilbur Young
C   Gus Guser
D   President Bartlet

1663   Whom does Viola Davis portray in the television show *How to Get Away with Murder*?

A   Alice Keating
B   Annalise Keating
C   Andrea Marino
D   Lisa Johnson

1664   Who is the author of *Oak and Ivy*?

A   Maya Angelou
B   James Porter
C   Paul Laurence Dunbar
D   Zora Neale Hurston

1665   Which actress portrays Cookie on the hit television show *Empire*?

A   Gabrielle Union
B   Regina King
C   Sanaa Latham
D   Taraji B. Henson

1666   What is the name of the movie in which Halle Berry stars as a drug-addicted mother who loses her son?

A   *Losing Isaiah*
B   *Losing Curtis*
C   *Losing Eddie*
D   *Losing Ivory*

1667   Who released a comedy album titled *Wanted*?

A   Martin Lawrence
B   Richard Pryor
C   Redd Foxx
D   Eddie Murphy

1668   Who starred in the movie *Guess Who's Coming to Dinner*?

A   William Perry
B   Sammy Davis Jr.
C   Lou Gossett Jr.
D   Sidney Poitier

1669   Who played Coffey in the movie *Coffey*?

A   Tamara Dobson
B   Pam Grier
C   Vanessa Williams
D   Whoopi Goldberg

1670   Cynthia Erivo won the Tony for Best Actress in a Musical in 2016 for her performance as _____ in *The Color Purple*.

A   Shug
B   Nettie
C   Sophia
D   Celie

1671   Which of the following movies received eleven Oscar nominations but did not win a single Oscar?

A   *Selma*
B   *The Color Purple*
C   *The Help*
D   *12 Years a Slave*

1672   Who said "I would rather make seven hundred dollars a week playing a maid than earn seven dollars a day being a maid"?

A   Olivia Spencer
B   Butterfly McQueen
C   Whoopi Goldberg
D   Hattie McDaniel

1673   Chuck Cooper and Lillias White won the Tony Awards for Best Featured Actor and Best Featured Actress, respectively, in 1997 for their performances in _____.

A   *The Resurrection*
B   *The Afterlife*
C   *The Death*
D   *The Life*

1674   With which of the following women did former football star Michael Strahan cohost a television show?

A   Ellen DeGeneres
B   Rosie O'Donnell
C   Kelly Ripa
D   Nancy Grace

1675   According to the title of the Walter Mosley book, what color dress is the devil in?

A   Black
B   Blue
C   Red
D   White

1676   The movie *Fruitvale Station* is about which of the following men who was killed by police?

A   Oscar Grant III
B   Eric Garner
C   Tamir Rice
D   Walter Scott

1677   What is TV character Reuben Gregory's occupation and the name of the television show he appears on?

A   Policeman on *Sanford and Son*
B   Reverend on *Amen*
C   Politician on *West Wing*
D   Policeman on *Homicide*

1678   What is the name of the musical for which Brian Stokes Mitchell won the Tony for Best Actor in 2000?

A   *Kiss Me, Fred*
B   *Kiss Me, Cathy*
C   *Kiss Me, Kate*
D   *Kiss Me, Suzanne*

1679   Which of the following actors won an Emmy for his performance in *Roots*?

A   Lou Gossett Jr.
B   LeVar Burton
C   John Amos
D   Ben Vereen

1680   In the movie *Casablanca*, what is Sam asked to play again?

A   Basketball
B   A song on the piano
C   A tune on the harmonica
D   A video game

1681　What character does Aisha Tyler portray on the television show *Ghost Whisperer*?

A　Melinda Gordon
B　Andrea Marino
C　Olivia Pope
D　Delia Banks

1682　Which of the following women married Lenny Kravitz?

A　Lisa Bonet
B　Whitney Houston
C　Sabrina Le Beauf
D　Tempestt Bledsoe

1683　How did Gordon Parks Jr. die?

A　Killed in a plane crash
B　Killed in a car wreck
C　Killed in a train derailment
D　Killed by a snakebite

1684　What is the name of Aaron McGruder's politically laced comic strip?

A　*Jumpstart*
B　*Blackstreet*
C　*Boondocks*
D　*The 'Hood*

1685   Who starred on Broadway in *The Tap Dance Kid* as an eleven-year-old?

A   Savion Glover
B   Florence Mills
C   Gregory Hines
D   Alfonso Ribeiro

1686   Which of the following actresses played the character who married Lionel Jefferson on *The Jeffersons*?

A   Roxie Roker
B   Denise Nicholas
C   Marla Gibbs
D   Berlinda Tolbert

1687   Which of the following is the host of the television show *Family Feud*?

A   Wayne Brady
B   Cedric the Entertainer
C   Anthony Anderson
D   Steve Harvey

1688   Robert Guillaume won the Emmy for Outstanding Supporting Actor in a Comedy Series for which television show?

A   *Room 227*
B   *Room 222*
C   *Benson*
D   *Soap*

1689 Julie Gillette was a character on the television show *Hotel*. Which actress played Gillette?

A   Diahann Carroll
B   Shari Belafonte
C   Halle Berry
D   Vanessa Williams

1690 Delores Hall won the 1977 Tony for Best Featured Actress for the musical *Your Arms Are Too Short to Box with* ____.

A   *Ali*
B   *Kareem Abdul-Jabbar*
C   *a Kangaroo*
D   *God*

1691 Which of the following won the Tony for Best Actress in a Play for her performance in *A Raisin in the Sun*?

A   Kathleen Cora Beane
B   Phylicia Rashad
C   Viola Davis
D   Mary Alice

1692 Who is the author of *Fences*?

A   James Porter
B   August Wilson
C   Lloyd Richards
D   Walter Mosley

1693   Which character was a friend of Forrest Gump?

A   Bubba
B   Sammy
C   Jimmy
D   Johnny

1694   Who was the first black to obtain a contract with a major Hollywood studio?

A   Lena Horne
B   Esther Rolle
C   Juanita Hall
D   Diahann Carroll

African American Desk Reference, page 429

1695   Who won the 2015 and 2016 Emmy Award for Best Supporting Actress in a Movie or Miniseries for her role in *Crime Story*?

A   Viola Davis
B   Kerry Washington
C   Taraji P. Henson
D   Regina King

1696   Will Smith was the star of the television show *The Fresh Prince of Bel-Air*. What is the name of the character he portrayed?

A   Will Banks
B   Will Smith
C   Will Prince
D   Carlton Banks

1697   Who was the first black prima ballerina at the Metropolitan Opera?

A   Janet Collins
B   Dorothy Dandridge
C   Katherine Dunham
D   Kathleen Cora Beane

Black Firsts, page 9

1698   Who is the narrator for the television show *Everybody Hates Chris*?

A   Chris Rock
B   Morgan Freeman
C   James Earl Jones
D   Terry Crews

1699   Which of the following is the host of the television show *Little Big Shots*?

A   Nick Cannon
B   Michael Strahan
C   Alfonso Ribeiro
D   Steve Harvey

1700   Which television show has an area in the city or town called the Bottoms?

A   *Good Times*
B   *Homicide*
C   *In the Heat of the Night*
D   *New York Undercover*

1701　What were the call letters for the first black-owned television station in the United States?

A　WDET
B　WORD
C　WOLF
D　WGPR

Black Saga, page 464

1702　Which television show had a character named Officer Smitty?

A　*Sanford and Son*
B　*Homicide*
C　*In the Heat of the Night*
D　*The Jeffersons*

1703　What Spike Lee movie focuses on interracial romance?

A　*School Daze*
B　*Four Little Girls*
C　*Jungle Fever*
D　*She's Gotta Have It*

1704　Halle Berry won an Oscar for her role in what movie?

A　*Kidnap*
B　*Monster's Ball*
C　*Bulworth*
D　*Catwoman*

1705   Who is the author of *Native Son*?

A   Alice Walker
B   Ralph Ellison
C   Richard Wright
D   William Wells Brown

1706   In which of the following television shows do students attend Hillman College?

A   *Amen*
B   *A Different World*
C   *Diff'rent Strokes*
D   *Facts of Life*

1707   The character Florence Johnston is employed by which TV family?

A   The Tates
B   The Bunkers
C   The Kaniskys
D   The Jeffersons

1708   Who is the author of *The Street*?

A   Maya Angelou
B   Ann Lane Petry
C   Terry McMillan
D   Toni Morrison

1709   Who is the author of *Passing*?

A   Nella Larsen
B   Alice Walker
C   Nikki Giovanni
D   Toni Cade Bambara

1710   Which actress plays Rochelle Rock on the television show *Everybody Hates Chris*?

A   Jackée Harry
B   Tichina Arnold
C   Imani Hakim
D   Tisha Campbell

1711   Who produced, directed, and starred in the movie *Hollywood Shuffle*?

A   Gordon Parks Sr.
B   Sidney Poitier
C   Eddie Murphy
D   Robert Townsend

African American Almanac, page 251

1712   Which television show has a character named Waldo Faldo?

A   *Family Matters*
B   *Amen*
C   *Family Ties*
D   *Fat Albert and the Cosby Kids*

1713 Who is the author of *Go Tell It on the Mountain*?

A Langston Hughes
B Martin Luther King Jr.
C Ralph Ellison
D James Baldwin

1714 What is the name of Spike Lee's movie that focuses on the different complexions of blacks?

A *School Daze*
B *Jungle Fever*
C *Do the Right Thing*
D *She's Gotta Have It*

1715 Who did Will Smith portray in the movie *The Pursuit of Happiness*?

A Muhammad Ali
B Chris Gardner
C Steven Hiller
D Alex Hitchens

1716 Which state is the birthplace of legendary actor James Earl Jones?

A Mississippi
B Florida
C Georgia
D Texas

1717   Which of the following does Aunt Esther frequently call Fred on the television show *Sanford and Son*?

A   Big dummy
B   Lover boy
C   Heathen
D   Old dummy

1718   T. K. Anderson is a character on a television sitcom. What is the last name of the family he lives with?

A   Drummond
B   Peterson
C   Papadapolis
D   Jefferson

1719   What is the name of the movies that spoof horror movies?

A   *Fright Nights*
B   *Pee Yo Pantz*
C   *Scary Movie*
D   *Halloween*

1720   Who is the author of *Unsung Heroes*?

A   Toni Morrison
B   Terry McMillan
C   Maya Angelou
D   Elizabeth Ross Haynes

1721   Whom did Steve Harvey play in the television sitcom *The Steve Harvey Show*?

A   Steve Little
B   Steve Hightower
C   Steve Big Shots
D   Steve Harvey

1722   Who was the first black to win the Pulitzer Prize for Photography?

A   Phillis Wheatley
B   Moneta Sleet
C   Harriet Jacobs
D   William Raspberry

African American Desk Reference, page 457

1723   Where was the Cotton Club located?

A   Compton
B   Watts
C   Detroit
D   Harlem

1724   Which of the following married actress Phylicia Allen in real life?

A   Heathcliffe Huxtable
B   Bill Cosby
C   Ahmad Rashad
D   Norm Nixon

1725 Who won the Pulitzer Prize for *Elbow Room*?

A Charles Gordone
B Charles Fuller
C James McPherson
D August Wilson

1726 Who won the Oscar for Best Supporting Actress for her role in *12 Years a Slave*?

A Octavia Spencer
B Lupita Nyong'o
C Halle Berry
D Viola Davis

1727 Who stars as the Notorious B.I.G. in the movie *Notorious*?

A Forest Whitaker
B Cedric the Entertainer
C Charles Dutton
D Derek Luke

1728 Which of the following played Jelly Roll Morton in *Jelly's Last Jam*?

A Gregory Hines
B Maurice Hines
C Fayard Nicholas
D Harold Nicholas

1729   Who is the author of *I Know Why the Caged Bird Sings*?

A   Zora Neale Hurston
B   Gwendolyn Brooks
C   Toni Morrison
D   Maya Angelou

1730   Who does the voice for the princess in the Disney movie *The Princess and the Frog*?

A   Halle Berry
B   Beyoncé
C   Cicely Tyson
D   Anika Noni Rose

1731   For what movie did Dorothy Dandridge earn an Academy Award nomination for Best Actress?

A   *Coffy*
B   *Porgy and Bess*
C   *Carmen Jones*
D   *Foxy Brown*

1732   Which of the following portrayed Buckwheat in the short film titled *Our Gang*?

A   Billie Thomas
B   Eddie Murphy
C   Tim Moore
D   Stepin Fetchit

1733   Who stars as Etta James in the movie *Cadillac Records?*

A   Jennifer Hudson
B   Fantasia
C   Beyoncé
D   Taraji P. Henson

1734   Which of the following won a Tony Award for *No Strings?*

A   Jennifer Holliday
B   Diahann Carroll
C   Mary Alice
D   Nell Carter

1735   Lester Holt became the full-time evening news anchor of which network in 2015?

A   ABC
B   Fox
C   NBC
D   CBS

1736   Whom did Jamie Foxx portray in the movie *Ray?*

A   Sugar Ray Robinson
B   Sugar Ray Leonard
C   Ray Rice
D   Ray Charles

1737   What Disney movie features the character of Tiana as a black princess?

A   *Black Beauty*
B   *The Princess and the Frog*
C   *Sleeping Beauty*
D   *The Black Princess*

1738   For which movie did Denzel Washington receive the Best Actor Oscar?

A   *Philadelphia*
B   *Training Day*
C   *Malcolm X*
D   *Hurricane*

1739   Who played Rachel Robinson in the 1950 movie *The Jackie Robinson Story?*

A   Rachael Robinson
B   Dorothy Dandridge
C   Louise Beavers
D   Ruby Dee

1740   Weezie is a character on the television show *The Jeffersons.* Which actress played Weezie?

A   Esther Rolle
B   Isabel Sanford
C   Lawanda Page
D   Marla Gibbs

1741   For which movie did Denzel Washington win an Oscar for Best
Supporting Actor?

A   *Training Day*
B   *John Q*
C   *Malcolm X*
D   *Glory*

1742   The movie *Drumline* is about the marching band at which
college?

A   Florida A&M
B   Grambling
C   Atlanta A&T
D   Morehouse

1743   According to a song by D. J. Jazzy Jeff and The Fresh Prince,
who does not understand?

A   Gangsters
B   Children
C   Chickenheads
D   Parents

1744   What is TV character Venus Flytrap's occupation and the name
of the television show he appears on?

A   Hobo on *The Littlest Hobo*
B   Policeman on *Homicide*
C   Deejay on *WKRP in Cincinnati*
D   Vampire on *Dark Shadows*

1745   Which actor played Arnold Jackson?

A   Jaleel White
B   Emmanuel Lewis
C   Gary Coleman
D   Todd Bridges

1746   What is the name of the fictional African nation in the movie *Black Panther*?

A   Kawanda
B   Wakanda
C   Bonkongo
D   Conbongo

1747   Who starred in the movie *Driving Miss Daisy*?

A   Morgan Freeman
B   Lou Gossett Jr.
C   Sammy Davis Jr.
D   Sidney Poitier

1748   Eddie Murphy is the voice for which character in *Shrek*?

A   Shrek
B   The king
C   The dragon
D   The donkey

1749   Who portrayed Ike Turner in the movie *What's Love Got to Do with It*?

A   Laurence Fishburne
B   Ike Turner
C   Dennis Haysbert
D   Lou Gossett Jr.

1750   Which actor stars as Tre in the movie *Boyz n the Hood*?

A   Ice Cube
B   Laurence Fishburne
C   Cube Gooding Jr.
D   Morris Chestnut

1751   Which man has a character named Dolemite in his comedy albums?

A   Eddie Murphy
B   Redd Foxx
C   Richard Pryor
D   Rudy Ray Moore

1752   Who played the role of Tina Turner in the movie *What's Love Got to Do with It*?

A   Vanessa Williams
B   Gabriel Union
C   Angela Bassett
D   Debbie Allen

1753   What is the name of the sitcom in which Tia Lowry plays the character Tia Landry?

A   *The Campbells*
B   *Girlfriends*
C   *Sister, Sister*
D   *That's So Raven*

1754   Who is the author of *Beloved*?

A   Gwendolyn Brooks
B   Maya Angelou
C   Terry McMillan
D   Toni Morrison

1755   The Nicholas Brothers were a great tap dance duo. What were their names?

A   Fayard and Harold
B   Lamont and Fred
C   Gregory and Maurice
D   Sam and Dave

1756   Who is the author of *Love and Marriage*?

A   James Earl Jones
B   Bill Cosby
C   Sammy Davis Jr.
D   Sidney Poitier

1757   Which TV show has a character named Winifred Brooks?

A   *In the Heat of the Night*
B   *A Different World*
C   *The Cosby Show*
D   *The Parent 'Hood*

1758   Who does David Mann portray in the television show *Meet the Browns*?

A   Larry Brown
B   Harry Belton
C   Tyler Brown
D   Leroy Brown

1759   Which of the following won the 1975 Tony for Best Featured Actor in a Musical for his performance in *The Wiz*?

A   Ted Ross
B   Nipsey Russell
C   Richard Pryor
D   Michael Jackson

1760   Who does Kerry Washington portray in the television show *Scandal*?

A   Olivia Jones
B   Mellie Grant
C   Janice Pope
D   Olivia Pope

1761   Who is the first black to have played the lead on Broadway in *Phantom of the Opera*?

A   Paul Robeson
B   Norm Lewis
C   Sidney Poitier
D   Bill Robinson

Playbill, May 12, 2014

1762   What is the name of the character Laverne Cox plays in the television show *Orange Is the New Black*?

A   Taystee Jefferson
B   Piper Chapman
C   Sophia Burset
D   Cindy Hayes

1763   Rolly Forbes is a character on the television show *Amen*. Which actor played Rolly Forbes?

A   Hal Williams
B   Carl Weathers
C   Jester Hairston
D   Sherman Hemsley

1764   Fred Sanford is a character on the television show *Sanford and Son*. Whom did Sanford have a crush on?

A   Lena Horne
B   Hattie McDaniel
C   Lawanda Page
D   Ruby Dee

1765   Which actress played the role of Tia Landry's mother in the sitcom *Sister, Sister*?

A   Jackée Harry
B   Marla Gibbs
C   Gabrielle Union
D   Viola Davis

1766   What is the name of the character Ben Vereen portrayed in the television miniseries *Roots*?

A   Chicken Charles
B   Kunta Kinte
C   Chicken Heart
D   Chicken George

1767   Which TV show has a character named Donna Harris?

A   *Good Times*
B   *Room 222*
C   *Sanford and Son*
D   *The Jeffersons*

1768   What is the character George Jefferson's wife's name?

A   Jenny
B   Helen
C   Louise
D   Florence

1769   Which actress played Jackie Robinson's mother in the 1950 movie *The Jackie Robinson Story*?

A   Ruby Dee
B   Lena Horne
C   Lillian Randolph
D   Louise Beavers

1770   Who is the author of *Gemini: An Extended Autobiographical Statement on My First Twenty-Five Years of Being a Black Poet*?

A   Nikki Giovanni
B   Nella Larsen
C   Rita Dove
D   Toni Cade Bambara

1771   Which actor plays Big Momma in the movie *Big Momma's House*?

A   Big Momma Thornton
B   James Avery
C   Martin Lawrence
D   Tyler Perry

1772   Which of the following created the role of the Dark Star?

A   Josephine Baker
B   Dorothy Dandridge
C   Billie Holiday
D   Judith Jamison

African American Desk Reference, page 425

1773   Which of the following won the 1975 Tony for Best Featured Actress in a Musical for her performance in *The Wiz*?

A   Lena Horne
B   Mabel King
C   Diana Ross
D   Dee Dee Bridgewater

1774   On the television show *Webster*, Ben Vereen played Webster's uncle. What is the uncle's name?

A   Phillip
B   Michael
C   Ben
D   Tom

1775   The movie *Lean on Me* is based on the life of which of the following men?

A   Jesse Owens
B   James Earl Jones
C   Joe Clark
D   Morgan Freeman

1776   Who is the author of *The Blacker the Berry*?

A   Lewis Allen
B   Wallace Thurmond
C   Richard Wright
D   Gwendolyn Brooks

1777   Which of the following has a Chinese grandmother?

A   Singer Mariah Carey
B   Singer and actress Janet Jackson
C   Singer and actress Vanessa Williams
D   Model Naomi Campbell

1778   In which movie does Denzel Washington play an angel?

A   *John Q*
B   *Hurricane*
C   *Remember the Titans*
D   *The Preacher's Wife*

1779   What is the name of the television soap opera on which Ellen Holly regularly appeared?

A   *The Young and the Restless*
B   *Peyton Place*
C   *One Life to Live*
D   *Days of Our Lives*

The Timetables of African American History, page 305

1780   Who was the first female to win two Pulitzer prizes for Drama?

A   Alice Childress
B   Beah Richards
C   Lynn Nottage
D   Alice Walker

Black Enterprise, April 12, 2017

1781   In what television show does Hollie Robinson Peete portray Detective Judy Hoffs?

A   *21 Jump Street*
B   *Love, Inc.*
C   *CSI: Miami*
D   *Hangin' with Mr. Cooper*

1782   Who played Private Peterson in the movie *A Soldier's Story*?

A   Adolph Caesar
B   Denzel Washington
C   Howard Rollins
D   Samuel L. Jackson

1783   What is the character George Jefferson's daughter-in-law's name?

A   Kisha
B   Florence
C   Jenny
D   Louise

1784   What character does Ice-T portray on the television show *Law and Order*?

A   John Munch
B   Tracy Marrow
C   Fin Tutuola
D   Ken Randle

1785   What is Mr. T's birth name?

A   Lawrence Tureaud
B   Theodore Johnson
C   Lawrence Thomas
D   Thomas Lawrence

1786   Who portrayed Martin Luther King Jr. in the movie *Selma*?

A   Samuel L. Jackson
B   David Oyelowo
C   Paul Winfield
D   Morgan Freeman

1787   Who is the author of *The Invisible Man*?

A   Ralph Ellison
B   Maya Angelou
C   Richard Wright
D   William Wells Brown

1788   Fred Berry was an actor on the television show *What's Happening?*
What is the name of the character Berry portrayed?

A   Repeat
B   Roger
C   Rerun
D   Dwayne

1789   What is the name of the airline Nashawn Wade (played by Kevin Hart) founds in the movie *Soul Plane*?

A   Red Tail Airlines
B   NWA Airlines
C   Soul Plane Airlines
D   Hip-Hop Airlines

1790   Which of the following won the 1987 Emmy for Best Supporting Actress in a Comedy?

A   Marla Gibbs
B   Jackée Harry
C   LaWanda Page
D   Ja'Net Dubois

1791   Which of the following is Jackie Torrence's profession?

A   Rapper
B   Gospel singer
C   Sprinter (track and field)
D   Storyteller and author

1792   Which of the following won a Tony Award for *Fences*?

A   Jennifer Holliday
B   Mary Alice
C   Diahann Carroll
D   Nell Carter

1793   Who did Oprah Winfrey play in the movie *The Color Purple*?

A   Celie
B   Odessa
C   Sophia
D   Miss Millie

1794   Who is the author of *The Salt Eaters*?

A   Toni Cade Bambara
B   Nikki Giovanni
C   Ralph Ellison
D   William Melvin Kelley

1795   Who played Mr. Tibbs in the movie version of *In the Heat of the Night*?

A   Samuel L. Jackson
B   Richard Roundtree
C   Sidney Poitier
D   Howard Rollins

1796   Which TV show has a character named Olivia Kendall?

A   *The Cosby Show*
B   *Good Times*
C   *Homicide*
D   *Amen*

1797 Who plays the title role of a basketball coach in the movie *Eddie?*

A   Samuel L. Jackson
B   Denzel Washington
C   Whoopi Goldberg
D   Morgan Freeman

1798 Who was the first black to win the Emmy for Lead Actor in a Comedy Series?

A   Redd Foxx
B   Robert Guillaume
C   Bill Cosby
D   Sherman Hemsley

1799 Which of the following is a main character in Zora Hurston's book *Moses, Man of the Mountain?*

A   A psychic
B   A blind mountain woman
C   A voodoo doctor
D   A rebellious slave

1800 What Spike Lee movie deals with the Birmingham church bombing?

A   *Do the Right Thing*
B   *Jungle Fever*
C   *School Daze*
D   *Four Little Girls*

1801   What was Redd Foxx's birth name?

A   John Elroy Sanford
B   Redford Foxison
C   James Foxx
D   Fred Sanford

1802   Who won an Emmy for a guest appearance as a widowed woman on the television show *Frank's Place*?

A   Beau Richards
B   Halle Berry
C   Daphne Reid
D   Esther Rolle

1803   Which of the following is Carmen McRae's profession?

A   Jazz singer
B   Playwright
C   Poet
D   Sculptor

1804   Deacon Frye is a character on the television show *Amen*. What is his first name?

A   Eugene
B   Edward
C   Ernest
D   Samuel

1805 The birth name of which of the following women was Loretta Mary Aiken?

A   Esther Rolle
B   Katherine Dunham
C   Moms Mabley
D   Roxie Roker

African American Lives, page 551

1806 Which one of the following characters did Morgan Freeman portray in the *Batman* movies?

A   The Riddler
B   The Penguin
C   The Joker
D   Lucius Fox

1807 What character does Hill Harper portray on the television show *CSI: NY*?

A   Mack Taylor
B   Sheldon Hawkes
C   Sam Hanna
D   Adam Ross

1808 On the television show *The Jeffersons*, how is Mel Stewart's character related to George Jefferson?

A   He is his brother-in-law
B   He is his brother
C   He is his son
D   He is his uncle

1809   Charles Fuller won a Pulitzer Prize for which play?

A   *A Soldier's Play*
B   *Fences*
C   *Glory*
D   *A Lesson Before Dying*

African American Desk Reference, page 341

1810   What city is the birthplace of actress Hattie McDaniel?

A   Wichita
B   Miami
C   Tampa
D   Kansas City

1811   Which of the following plays the title role in the movie *Black Panther*?

A   Michael B. Jordan
B   Chadwick Boseman
C   Denzel Washington
D   Daniel Kaluuya

1812   Bryant Gumbel was an anchor of what major network morning news show?

A   *Morning Bryan*
B   *CBS This Morning*
C   *The Today Show*
D   *Fox and Friends*

1813   What is Billy Dee Williams's middle name?

A   Delicious
B   David
C   December
D   Eddie

1814   Who directed the movie *Superfly*?

A   John Singleton
B   Gordon Parks Jr.
C   Gordon Parks Sr.
D   Spike Lee

1815   Who played the title role in the 1950 movie *The Jackie Robinson Story*?

A   Morgan Freeman
B   Jackie Robinson
C   Sidney Poitier
D   Ossie Davis

The 50 Most Influential Black Films, page 73

1816   In what movie does Jamie Foxx play a slave who tries to free his wife?

A   *Django Unchained*
B   *Ray Unchained*
C   *Bundini Unchained*
D   *Annie Unchained*

1817   Who won the 2017 Oscar for Best Supporting Actress?

A   Octavia Spencer
B   Kerry Washington
C   Taraji P. Henson
D   Viola Davis

1818   Which actor played Steve Erkel on the television show *Family Matters*?

A   Gary Coleman
B   Jaleel White
C   Emmanuel Lewis
D   Todd Bridges

1819   Sabrina Le Beauf was an actor on *The Cosby Show*. What is the name of the character she portrayed?

A   Denise
B   Rudi
C   Sondra
D   Vanessa

1820   What is Jackie Brown's occupation in the movie *Jackie Brown*?

A   Lawyer
B   Flight attendant
C   Detective
D   Pilot

1821   Which of the following best describes Miss Evers's boys?

A   They were unfairly jailed
B   They had syphilis
C   They were Negro League players
D   They were pilots

1822   Who won an Emmy Award for her performance in *Miss Evers' Boys*?

A   Lynn Whitfield
B   Cicely Tyson
C   Whoopi Goldberg
D   Alfre Woodard

1823   In the movie *The Lion King*, who does the voice for King?

A   Dennis Haysbert
B   James Earl Jones
C   Chris Rock
D   Morgan Freeman

1824   Which of the following starred in the 2000 action film *Romeo Must Die*?

A   Aaliyah
B   Rhianna
C   Janet Jackson
D   Monica

1825   Who won the 2010 Tony Award for Lead Actor for his portrayal of Tony Maxson in *Fences*?

A   Samuel L. Jackson
B   Terrence Howard
C   Morgan Freeman
D   Denzel Washington

1826   Which of the following starred in the movie *Soul Food*?

A   Whoopi Goldberg
B   Tamara Dobson
C   Robin Givens
D   Vanessa Williams

1827   Which of the following actresses played the character who married Virgil Tibbs on *In the Heat of the Night*?

A   Anne Marie Johnson
B   Anna Maria Horsford
C   Denise Nicholas
D   Jo Marie Payton-France

1828   Who is the author of *The Bluest Eye*?

A   Pauline Hopkins
B   Toni Morrison
C   Alice Walker
D   Maya Angelou

1829   Whoopi Goldberg is an Academy Award–winning actress and comedian. What is her birth name?

A   Goldie Whoopinberg
B   Caryn Elaine Johnson
C   Marguerite Anne Johnson
D   Nellie Conley

1830   Leilani Jones won the Tony for Best Featured Actress in a Musical in 1985 for her performance in_____.

A   *Rotate*
B   *Wiggle*
C   *Gyrate*
D   *Grind*

1831   Morgan Freeman plays a(n) _____ in the movie *The Sum of All Fears*.

A   CIA director
B   evil dictator
C   FBI director
D   president

1832   Who is the author of *Black Boy*?

A   Walter White
B   James Porter
C   Walter Mosley
D   Richard Wright

1833   Which of the following is the name of a movie starring Michael Clarke Duncan?

A   *The Blue Mile*
B   *The Green Mile*
C   *The Yellow Brick Mile*
D   *The Red Mile*

1834   Which TV show has a character named Meldrick Lewis?

A   *Homicide*
B   *NYPD*
C   *In the Heat of the Night*
D   *L.A. Undercover*

1835   Who won the 2010 Tony Award for Best Lead Actress for her portrayal of Rose Maxson in *Fences*?

A   Octavia Spencer
B   Taraji P. Henson
C   Viola Davis
D   Halle Berry

1836   Which of the following is a character on the television show *Amos and Andy*?

A   Sinbad
B   Kunta Kinte
C   Meadowlark Lemon
D   Kingfish

1837   Cicely Tyson won the Tony Award for Best Actress in a Play in 2013 for her performance in *The Trip to* _____.

A   *Bountiful*
B   *Chicago*
C   *New York*
D   *Wonderful*

1838   On the television show *The Jeffersons*, what is the maid's name?

A   Holly
B   Lucille
C   Florence
D   Molly

1839   What is the cause of death for choreographer and dancer Alvin Ailey?

A   A car wreck
B   Cancer
C   A fall while practicing
D   AIDS

1840   Which of the following is Evelyn Preer's profession?

A   Playwright
B   Blues singer
C   Actress
D   Sculptor

1841   Who played Moesha on the television show *Moesha*?

A   Brandy
B   Foxy Brown
C   Kim Fields
D   Moesha

1842   What is Sippie Wallace's birth name?

A   Caryn Elaine Johnson
B   Beulah Belle Thomas
C   Marguerite Anne Johnson
D   Nellie Conley

1843   Who played Officer Smitty on the television show *Sanford and Son*?

A   Mel Stewart
B   Carl Weathers
C   Lou Gossett Jr.
D   Hal Williams

1844   What is the name of the TV character played by Kellie Shanygne Williams on the television show *Family Matters*?

A   Laura Winslow
B   Laura Johnson
C   Judy Winslow
D   Linda Winslow

1845   Who played Prissy in the movie *Gone with the Wind*?

A   Ruby Dee
B   Hattie McDaniel
C   Lena Horne
D   Butterfly McQueen

1846   Who was the first black to receive an Oscar for Best Actor?

A   Bill Cosby
B   James Earl Jones
C   Lou Gossett Jr.
D   Sidney Poitier

1847   Who is the author of *Jonah's Gourd Vine*?

A   James Porter
B   Zora Neale Hurston
C   Richard Wright
D   Gwendolyn Brooks

1848   What is the name of the character portrayed by Bern Nadette Stanis on the television show *Good Times*?

A   Tina Evans
B   Thelma Evans
C   Tonya Evans
D   Tracy Evans

1849   Sidney Poitier was nominated for an Oscar for what 1958 movie?

A   *The House Behind the Cedars*
B   *In the Heat of the Night*
C   *The Exile*
D   *The Defiant Ones*

1850   What is the name of the family the television show *Empire* is centered around?

A   Lyon
B   Leon
C   Brown
D   Jackson

1851   Which of the following TV characters did Denise Nicholas portray?

A   Nadine Thomas
B   Donna Harris
C   Liz McIntyre
D   Thelma Frye

1852   Who is the author of *Twilight: Los Angeles, 1992*?

A   Maya Angelou
B   Anna Deavere Smith
C   Terry McMillan
D   Toni Morrison

1853　Who recorded a comedy album titled *Raw*?

A　Eddie Murphy
B　Martin Lawrence
C　Richard Pryor
D　Rudy Ray Moore

1854　Pecola is a character in which Toni Morrison book?

A　*Song of Solomon*
B　*The Bluest Eye*
C　*Sula*
D　*Beloved*

1855　Which character is from Zora Hurston's book *Jonah's Gourd Vine*?

A　John Buddy Pearson
B　Jamie Killicks
C　Arvay Henson
D　Jonah Mason

1856　Which actor portrayed Webster on the television show *Webster*?

A　Todd Bridges
B　Gary Coleman
C　Jaleel White
D　Emmanuel Lewis

1857   Who was the first black male to win a Tony Award?

A   Sidney Poitier
B   Harry Belafonte
C   James Earl Jones
D   Paul Robeson

1858   The movie *American Gangster* is the portrayal of which man's life?

A   Lucas McCain's
B   Frank Lucas's
C   Freddie Lucas's
D   Tom Lucas's

1859   In the James Bond movie *Die Another Day*, what is the name of Halle Berry's character?

A   Double O Eight
B   Lucky
C   Jinx
D   Sizzler

1860   Nikki M. Jones won the 2010 Tony Award for Best Featured Actress in a Musical for her performance in *The Book of* _____.

A   *Genesis*
B   *Mark*
C   *Mormon*
D   *John*

1861   Which artist recorded "Supermodel"?

A   Naomi Campbell
B   Tara Banks
C   Sade
D   RuPaul

1862   Which of the Tyler Perry television shows has a predominantly white cast?

A   *Meet the Browns*
B   *House of Payne*
C   *Too Close to Home*
D   *The Haves and the Have-Nots*

1863   Who was the first black person to receive an Oscar nomination for Best Director?

A   Gordon Parks Sr.
B   Gordon Parks Jr.
C   Spike Lee
D   John Singleton

1864   Which actress played Mrs. Prentice in the movie *Guess Who's Coming to Dinner?*

A   Denise Nicholas
B   Ruby Dee
C   Beah Richards
D   Lena Horne

1865   What first name was Spike Lee given at birth?

A   Shelton
B   Elton
C   Felton
D   Stephen

1866   *Stormy Weather* is a movie starring Lena Horne. What year was the movie released?

A   1964
B   1943
C   1945
D   1950

The 50 Most Influential Black Films, page 60

1867   Arnold Jackson is a character on the television show Diff'rent Strokes. What is his famous catchphrase?

A   "I'm coming to join you, Elizabeth."
B   "Dynomite!"
C   "What you talking about?"
D   "Did I do that?"

1868   Who played Mr. Tibbs in the television series *In the Heat of the Night*?

A   Howard Rollins
B   Hal Williams
C   Carl Weathers
D   Sidney Poitier

1869 What is Curtis Payne's occupation in the television show *House of Payne*?

A Fire chief
B Unemployed
C Mayor
D Police chief

1870 Which actor played Lionel Jefferson on *The Jeffersons* but never played the role on *All in the Family*?

A Ralph Carter
B Johnny Brown
C Mike Evans
D Damon Evans

1871 At which college or university was the first black Greek-lettered sorority, Alpha Kappa Alpha (AKA), founded?

A Howard University
B Spelman College
C Morehouse College
D Grambling State University

Black Saga, page 296

1872 Which of the following starred as Sheneneh on the television show *Martin*?

A Garrett Morris
B Martin Lawrence
C Tichina Arnold
D Tisha Campbell

1873   On what network or cable station was the show *Wild 'n Out* broadcast?

A   MTV
B   BET
C   ESPN
D   VH1

1874   Which of the following is not Lucious's son on the television show *Empire*?

A   Jamal
B   Andre
C   Hakeem
D   Marcus

1875   James Earl Jones won a Best Actor Tony Award for which of the following plays?

A   *Fences*
B   *Showboat*
C   *Hamilton*
D   *The Emperor Jones*

1876   What is the name of the family the character Benson works for on the television show *Benson*?

A   The Tates
B   The Jeffersons
C   The Kaniskys
D   The Gatlings

1877 Former football star Michael Strahan is a cohost of which of the following morning news shows?

A *Fox and Friends*
B *Good Morning America*
C *Today Show*
D *CBS This Morning*

1878 What is TV character Phillip Banks's occupation and the name of the television show he appears on?

A Reverend on *Amen*
B Banker on *The Fresh Prince of Bel-Air*
C Policeman on *Homicide*
D Attorney on *The Fresh Prince of Bel-Air*

1879 Nathaniel Taylor was an actor on *Sanford and Son*. What is the name of the character he portrayed?

A Bubba
B Officer Smitty
C Rollo
D Woody

1880 Who is the author of *The Road to Memphis*?

A Jim O'Connor
B Mildred D. Taylor
C Joyce Carol Thomas
D Walter Mosley

1881   What is TV character Frank Pembleton's occupation and the name of the television show he appears on?

A   Policeman on *In the Heat of the Night*
B   Policeman on *Hill Street Blues*
C   Policeman on *Homicide*
D   Policeman on *NYPD*

1882   Which actor played Hampton Forbes, a police chief on the television show *In the Heat of the Night*?

A   Hal Williams
B   Howard Rollins
C   Carl Weathers
D   LeVar Burton

1883   Which movie won the Oscar for Best Picture in 2017?

A   *Hidden Figures*
B   *I Am Not Your Negro*
C   *Moonlight*
D   *Fences*

1884   Which of the following was a regular on the television show *Out All Night*?

A   Whitney Houston
B   Janet Jackson
C   Roberta Flack
D   Patti LaBelle

1885   Which of the following portrayed Harriet Tubman in the 2019 movie *Harriet?*

A   Viola Davis
B   Cynthia Ervo
C   Zarinah Reed
D   Viola Davis

1886   Who is the author of *Tongues Untied?*

A   Marlon Riggs
B   Maya Angelou
C   Terry McMillan
D   Toni Morrison

1887   What is the character Shaft's first name in the movie *Shaft?*

A   Willie
B   John
C   LeRoy
D   Isaac

1888   On which cable network did Joy Reid began hosting the talk show *AM Joy* in 2016?

A   MSNBC
B   Fox News
C   BET
D   TV One

1889   Who played Michael Evans on the television show *Good Times*?

A   Mike Evans
B   Johnny Brown
C   Ralph Carter
D   Jimmie Walker

1890   Courtney B. Vance won an Emmy for his performance in *The People v. O.J. Simpson*. Whom did he portray?

A   Christopher Darden
B   Mark Fuhrman
C   O. J. Simpson
D   Johnnie Cochran

1891   Which of the following was a regular on the television show *Living Single*?

A   Queen Latifah
B   Patti LaBelle
C   Janet Jackson
D   Whitney Houston

1892   Who is the author of *Tar Baby*?

A   Alice Walker
B   Maya Angelou
C   Terry McMillan
D   Toni Morrison

1893 In the movie *Kazaam*, Shaquille O'Neal's character is a _____.

A genie
B basketball player
C pirate
D ghost

1894 Who does Shemar Moore portray on the television show *Criminal Minds*?

A Derek Morgan
B Hank Morgan
C JJ Jareau
D Derrick Moore

1895 Who starred in a stand-up comedy film titled *I'm a Grown Little Man*?

A Lavell Crawford
B Bruce Bruce
C Kevin Hart
D Katt Williams

1896 Who is the author of *The Color Purple*?

A Gwendolyn Brooks
B Alice Walker
C Maya Angelou
D Zora Neale Hurston

1897   On the television show *Family Matters*, how is Reginald Val Johnson's character related to Eddie Winslow?

A   He is his brother-in-law
B   He is his father
C   He is his son
D   He is his uncle

1898   Who is the author of *Wouldn't Take Nothing for My Journey Now*?

A   Maya Angelou
B   Richard Wright
C   Terry McMillan
D   Toni Morrison

1899   In which of the following movies does Denzel Washington play a boxer?

A   *John Q*
B   *Glory*
C   *Hurricane*
D   *Remember the Titans*

1900   Which of the following actresses portrayed the character who married Chief Gillespie on *In the Heat of the Night*?

A   Jo Marie Payton-France
B   Anne Marie Johnson
C   Marla Gibbs
D   Denise Nicholas

1901   Which of the following is Clementine Hunter's profession?

A   Film director
B   Belly dancer
C   Artist
D   Playwright

1902   Aunt Esther is a character on the television show *Sanford and Son*. Which actress played Aunt Esther?

A   Marla Gibbs
B   Isabel Sanford
C   Esther Rolle
D   LaWanda Page

1903   In the movie *Tommy*, what is the name of the character that Tina Turner portrays?

A   The Acid Queen
B   The Cokehead
C   Tommy
D   The Reefer Princess

1904   What is Fred Sanford's famous catchphrase?

A   "Dynomite."
B   "I'm coming to join you, Elizabeth."
C   "Did I do that?"
D   "What you talking about?"

1905   Which of the following is a character from the television miniseries *Roots*?

A   Sinbad
B   Kanye West
C   Meadowlark Lemon
D   Kunta Kinte

1906   Lisa Bonet was an actor on the television show *The Cosby Show*. What is the name of the character she portrayed?

A   Denise
B   Rudi
C   Sondra
D   Vanessa

1907   Which of the following did not win a Tony Award in 1982 for the musical *Dreamgirls*?

A   Loretta Devine
B   Jennifer Holliday
C   Cleavant Derricks
D   Ben Harney

1908   What year did Bill Cosby become the first black to win a prime time Emmy Award?

A   1982
B   1961
C   1966
D   1973

1909 Tempestt Bledsoe was an actress on *The Cosby Show.* What is the name of the character she portrayed?

A Vanessa
B Rudi
C Sondra
D Denise

1910 Which of the following played Catwoman in *Batman*?

A Lisa Bonet
B Diahann Carroll
C Eartha Kitt
D Lena Horne

1911 For how many years was *Soul Train* on TV?

A Twenty-seven
B Sixty-one
C Thirty-five
D Eighteen

1912 Which character did Ice Cube play in the movie *Boyz n the Hood*?

A Pillsbury
B Doughboy
C Dooky
D Mad Dog

1913   Who starred in the movie *The Great White Hype*?

A   Wesley Snipes
B   Sylvester Stallone
C   Tommy Morrison
D   Samuel L. Jackson

1914   What was the first movie with sound by a black company?

A   *She's Gotta Have It*
B   *The Defiant Ones*
C   *The Exile*
D   *The House Behind the Cedars*

African American Desk Reference, page 431

1915   Which actress played the butler's wife in Lee Daniels's *The Butler*?

A   Olivia Spencer
B   Oprah Winfrey
C   Viola Davis
D   Gabrielle Union

1916   Whitman Mayo is an actor on *Sanford and Son*. What is the name of the character he portrays?

A   Woody
B   Lamont
C   Officer Smitty
D   Grady

1917 Which of the following wrote the script for the movie *Friday*?

A LL Cool J
B Ice-T
C Ice Cube
D Tupac Shakur

1918 Who is the author of *Along This Way*?

A John Johnson
B James Weldon Johnson
C Langston Hughes
D Sammy Davis Jr.

1919 What was the cause of death for actress Hattie McDaniel, who starred in *Gone with the Wind*?

A House fire
B Drug overdose
C Heart attack
D Cancer

1920 Who played the lead role in *Lady Sings the Blues*?

A Diana Ross
B Billie Holiday
C Whitney Houston
D Marian Anderson

1921   For what movie did Morgan Freeman win the Oscar for Best Supporting Actor in 2005?

A   *Lean on Me*
B   *Unforgiven*
C   *March of the Penguins*
D   *Million Dollar Baby*

1922   What is the name of the church in the sitcom *Amen?*

A   Brooklyn AME
B   First Community
C   First Baptist
D   First Episcopal

1923   Who is the author of *If He Hollers Let Him Go?*

A   Nella Larsen
B   Chester Himes
C   Nikki Giovanni
D   Toni Cade Bambara

African American Desk Reference, page 356

1924   Who was the director of the 2014 movie *Selma?*

A   Steve McQueen
B   John Singleton
C   Spike Lee
D   Ava DuVernay

1925   What character does Victor Williams portray on the television show *The King of Queens*?

A   The King
B   Kelly Palmer
C   Deacon Palmer
D   Dallas Kirkland

1926   On the television show *The Jeffersons*, how is Damon Evan's character related to George Jefferson?

A   He is his son
B   The two are not related at all
C   He is his brother
D   He is his son-in-law

1927   Will Smith plays the title role in the movie *Hancock*. What is Hancock's first name?

A   Harry
B   John
C   James
D   William

1928   For which movie was the song "Glory" nominated for an Oscar?

A   *Selma*
B   *Red Tails*
C   *42*
D   *Glory*

1929 Webster is a character on a television sitcom. What is the last name of the family he lives with?

A Evans
B Drummond
C Papadapolis
D Peterson

1930 Who played Jack Jefferson in the movie *The Great White Hope*?

A Jack Johnson
B Lou Gossett Jr.
C James Earl Jones
D Morgan Freeman

1931 Who played the voice of Chef in the animated series *South Park*?

A Ruben Studdard
B Barry White
C Al Green
D Isaac Hayes

1932 What is the name of the film for which Sidney Poitier won an Oscar for Best Actor?

A *Guess Who's Coming to Dinner*
B *To Sir, with Love*
C *Lilies of the Field*
D *In the Heat of the Night*

1933   What is the name of the have-not family in *The Haves and the Have-Nots*?

A   Young
B   Payne
C   Harrington
D   Cryer

1934   Which of the following actors won the Emmy for Lead Actor in a Drama Series for his performance in *Gabriel's Fire*?

A   James Earl Jones
B   Harrison Page
C   Lou Gossett Jr.
D   Greg Morris

1935   In what movie does Bernie Mac star as a baseball player?

A   *The Jackie Robinson Story*
B   *Mr. 3000*
C   *42*
D   *Mr. 500*

1936   Steve Erkel is a character on the television show *Family Matters*. What is his famous catchphrase?

A   "I'm coming to join you, Elizabeth."
B   "Dynomite!"
C   "Did I do that?"
D   "What you talking about?"

1937   Which character is from Zora Hurston's book *Their Eyes Were Watching God*?

A   Buddy Pearson
B   Jamie Killicks
C   Arvay Henson
D   John Pearson

1938   What city is the location of the television show *The Wire*?

A   New York
B   Baltimore
C   Los Angeles
D   Chicago

1939   Which of the following movies stars Ron O'Neal?

A   *Trouble Man*
B   *Shaft*
C   *Truck Turner*
D   *Superfly*

1940   Who created the *Bootsie* comic strip?

A   Nat Love
B   George Herriman
C   Ollie Harrington
D   Bootsie Collins

African American Lives, page 376

1941   Which of the following married actress Debbie Allen?

A   Norm Nixon
B   Magic Johnson
C   Michael Jordan
D   Samuel L. Jackson

1942   Who played the television character Geraldine Jones?

A   Kim Fields
B   Flip Wilson
C   Isabel Sanford
D   Marla Gibbs

1943   Which character does Terrence Howard portray in the hit television show *Empire*?

A   Andre
B   Marcus
C   Lucious
D   Hakeem

1944   Who directed the movie *The Great Debaters*?

A   Spike Lee
B   Denzel Washington
C   Lee Daniels
D   Steve McQueen

1945   Who is the author of *Fatherhood*?

A   James Baldwin
B   Bill Cosby
C   Richard Wright
D   Walter White

1946   Who is the author of *Waiting to Exhale*?

A   Terry McMillan
B   Maya Angelou
C   Richard Wright
D   Toni Morrison

1947   In which movie does Denzel Washington portray a minister?

A   *Malcolm X*
B   *John Q*
C   *Hurricane*
D   *Philadelphia*

1948   Which of the following characters does Sherman Hemsley play?

A   Henry Jefferson on *The Jeffersons*
B   Carl Winslow on *Family Matters*
C   Hampton Forbes on *In the Heat of the Night*
D   Ernest Frye on *Amen*

1949   Who won the Tony for Best Featured Actress in a Musical in 1996 for *Bring in 'da Noise, Bring in 'da Funk*?

A   Ann Duquesnay
B   Whoopi Goldberg
C   Audra McDonald
D   Tina Turner

1950   Hinton Battle won the Tony for Best Featured Actor in a Musical in 1991 for his performance in _____.

A   *Miss Saigon*
B   *Mr. Big Stuff*
C   *Miss Tokyo*
D   *Miss Peking*

1951   What is legendary poet Maya Angelou's birth name?

A   Nellie Conley
B   Caryn Elaine Johnson
C   Angel Mayalou
D   Marguerite Annie Johnson

1952   Whom did Sinbad portray on the television show *A Different World*?

A   Walter Oakes
B   Kevin Franklin
C   Myron Larabee
D   David Bryan

1953 Who directed *Precious*?

A Spike Lee
B Steve McQueen
C Denzel Washington
D Lee Daniels

1954 What is the name of Will Smith's son who costars with Smith in the movie *The Pursuit of Happiness*?

A Wilbur
B Robert
C Jaden
D Wilbert

1955 Tootie is a character on the television show *Facts of Life*. Which actress played Tootie?

A Kim Fields
B Karyn Parsons
C Todd Bridges
D Lisa Bonet

1956 In the movie *Nurse Betty*, Chris Rock and Morgan Freeman star as_____.

A policemen
B patients
C hitmen
D doctors

1957   Bookman is the maintenance man on the television show *Good Times*. Which actor played Bookman?

A   Ralph Carter
B   John Amos
C   Mike Evans
D   Johnny Brown

1958   Who received an Academy Award nomination for Best Supporting Actress for her role in the movie *American Gangster*?

A   Dorothy Dandridge
B   Ruby Dee
C   Olivia Spencer
D   Viola Davis

1959   What is the name of the character that Will Smith portrays in the *Men in Black* movies?

A   Agent K
B   Agent J
C   Special K
D   Doctor J

1960   Which of the following is Pearl Bailey's profession?

A   Singer and actress
B   Playwright
C   Sculptor
D   Track star

1961   Which of the following characters did Eddie Murphy portray on *Saturday Night Live*?

A   Pat
B   Buckwheat
C   The Church Lady
D   The Ladies' Man

1962   What city is the birthplace of Academy Award–winning actor Lou Gossett Jr.?

A   New Orleans
B   New York
C   Miami
D   Newark

1963   What is the name of the character Wesley Snipes portrays in the movie *New Jack City*?

A   Nino Brown
B   Noxeema Jackson
C   Simon Phoenix
D   Roemello Skuggs

1964   Officer Sweet is a character on the television show *In the Heat of the Night*. What is Officer Sweet's first name?

A   John
B   Wilson
C   Sammy
D   Bubba

1965　The maintenance man on the television show *Good Times* is called Bookman. What is his first name?

A　Nathan
B　Barry
C　Larry
D　Harry

1966　Which of the following won the Best Featured Actor Tony in 1984 for his performance in *The Tap Dance Kid*?

A　Hinton Battle
B　Savion Glover
C　Alan Weeks
D　Alfonso Ribeiro

1967　Who was the first black concert singer?

A　Memphis Minnie
B　Mamie Smith
C　Bessie Smith
D　Elizabeth Greenfield

1968　Which television show is Al Roker best known for being the weatherman?

A　*CBS This Morning*
B　*Fox and Friends*
C　*Good Morning America*
D　*Today Show*

1969   Gwendolyn Brooks is a Pulitzer Prize–winning author. In what state was she born?

A   Missouri
B   Arkansas
C   Kansas
D   Oklahoma

1970   Who is the author of *Zeely*?

A   Terry McMillan
B   Maya Angelou
C   Toni Morrison
D   Virginia Hamilton

1971   Which comedian was seriously injured in a 2014 automobile accident?

A   Kevin Hart
B   Tracy Morgan
C   Katt Williams
D   Chris Rock

1972   Which actress portrayed Florida Evans on the television show *Good Times*?

A   Isabel Sanford
B   Esther Rolle
C   LaWanda Page
D   Marla Gibbs

1973 What is the name of the movie in which Denzel Washington plays an attorney who defends a client with AIDS?

A *Philadelphia*
B *San Francisco*
C *Atlanta*
D *Chicago*

1974 Audra McDonald won the Tony for Best Featured Actress in a Musical in 1994 for her performance in _____.

A *Ferris Wheel*
B *Roller Coaster*
C *Tunnel of Love*
D *Carousel*

1975 Who starred in the 2014 movie *Annie*?

A Keke Palmer
B Nicole Beharie
C Quvenzhané Wallis
D Willow Smith

1976 Which former football star acted in three *Naked Gun* movies?

A Bernie Casey
B Jim Brown
C O. J. Simpson
D Tony Dorsett

1977   What movie won the Best Picture Oscar for 2014?

A   *12 Years a Slave*
B   *The Help*
C   *42*
D   *Selma*

1978   A boy discovers the history of the Negro League in the movie _____.

A   *Finding Satchel Paige*
B   *Finding Josh Gibson*
C   *Finding Buck McHenry*
D   *Finding Cool Papa Bell*

1979   Who won the Oscar for Best Supporting Actress for her role in *The Help*?

A   Alfre Woodard
B   Viola Davis
C   Taraji P. Henson
D   Octavia Spencer

1980   According to John Cutter, a character in *Passenger 57*, you should always bet on _____.

A   black
B   white
C   gold
D   red

1981   What is the name of the vampire Eddie Murphy plays in the movie *A Vampire in Brooklyn*?

A   Maximillian
B   Bela
C   Fango
D   Blacula

1982   In the play *The Emperor Jones*, what is the emperor's first name?

A   Popeye
B   Caesar
C   Julius
D   Brutus

1983   Who won the 1970 Tony for Best Featured Actress in a Musical for her performance in *Purlie*?

A   Aretha Franklin
B   Freda Payne
C   Melba Moore
D   Gladys Knight

1984   What character does Alfre Woodard portray on the television show *Desperate Housewives*?

A   Betty Applewhite
B   Ruby Reynolds
C   Joyce McQueen
D   Renee Perry

1985   In what state was Lena Horne born?

A   California
B   Illinois
C   New York
D   New Jersey

1986   Who won the Pulitzer Prize for *No Place to Be Somebody*?

A   Richard Wright
B   Charles Fuller
C   Charles Gordone
D   James McPherson

1987   Which network aired the television show *Smart Guy*?

A   WB
B   Fox
C   HBO
D   NBC

1988   Which actor played Willis Jackson on the television show *Diff'rent Strokes*?

A   Jaleel White
B   Gary Coleman
C   Todd Bridges
D   Emmanuel Lewis

1989 Who is the author of *Annie Allen*?

A Maya Angelou
B Terry McMillan
C Gwendolyn Brooks
D Annie Allen

1990 Which of the following movies stars Lou Gossett Jr.?

A *Rosewood*
B *An Officer and a Gentleman*
C *Shaft*
D *The Color Purple*

1991 In the television show *Empire*, how many years does Cookie serve in jail for drug dealing?

A Twenty-one
B Eleven
C Seventeen
D Eight

1992 What is the name of the genius Tahj Mowry plays in the television show *Smart Guy*?

A Marcus Henderson
B Malcolm Einstein
C Michael Evans
D T. J. Henderson

1993   Which TV show has a character named Liz McIntyre?

A   *Room 227*
B   *Room 123*
C   *Room 222*
D   *WKRP in Cincinnati*

1994   Which character is from Zora Hurston's book *Seraph on the Suwanee*?

A   Arvay Henson
B   Jamie Killicks
C   John Buddy Pearson
D   Seraph Franklin

1995   Who was the first black female to win the Oscar for Best Actress?

A   Halle Berry
B   Cicely Tyson
C   Hattie McDaniel
D   Whoopi Goldberg

1996   Don Bexley is an actor on the television show *Sanford and Son*. What is the name of the character he portrays?

A   Officer Smitty
B   Bubba
C   Rollo
D   Woody

1997   Which of the following television characters did Roxie Roker portray?

A   Helen Kravitz of *Good Times*
B   Helen Willis of *The Jeffersons*
C   Thelma Frye of *Amen*
D   Peggy Fair of *Mannix*

1998   Which character did Eddie Murphy portray in the movie *Beverly Hills Cop*?

A   Axl Rose
B   Buckwheat Klump
C   Axel Foley
D   Randy Watson

1999   Which Jackson posed in *Playboy*?

A   Katherine
B   LaToya
C   Janet
D   Rebbie

2000   In the movie *Hustle and Flow*, DJay (played by Terrence Howard) is a(n) _____.

A   detective
B   pimp
C   undercover policeman
D   astronaut

A VERY SPECIAL THANKS TO DOCTOR PETER WALLENSTEIN (VIRGINIA TECH) WHO ASSISTED ME IN THE WRITING AND EDITING FOR SOME OF THE FOLLOWING PEOPLE AND EVENTS

FAMOUS PEOPLE AND EVENTS

DRED SCOTT DECISION (questions 28-30)

Sam Blow was born into slavery around 1800 in Southampton County, Virginia. Peter Blow, Sam's master, his family and slaves lived in Virginia, Alabama and eventually moved to St. Louis, Missouri where Sam was sold in 1833 to Dr. John Emerson. Emerson was a military doctor and took Blow with him to his places of deployment including Illinois, a free state, and the Wisconsin territory, which was also free. John, with his wife Irene, moved back to Missouri in 1838. John died in 1843 leaving his slaves, including Blow (who was now going by the name Dred Scott) to his wife. Scott and his wife, Harriet, sued for their freedom in 1846 on the grounds that since they had lived in a free state, they are free. In 1857, the United States Supreme Court ruled that a slave remains a slave even if they are transported to a free state and blacks were not citizens and had no right to file a federal lawsuit. The Supreme Court also ruled blacks had "no rights the white man is bound to respect".

HARRIET TUBMAN (questions 34-38)

Araminta Ross was born a slave in Dorchester County, Maryland in the early 1820's. She would become a fugitive slave, Underground Railroad conductor, and scout and spy for the Union army during the civil war. Araminta began using her mother's name, Harriet, and married John Tubman. Harriet escaped slavery in 1849 mostly through the Underground Railroad. Tubman went back to Maryland in 1851 to help her husband escape but he had remarried. She would return to the south numerous times to help other slaves escape. During the civil war, Tubman's spying helped the Union army free 756 slaves in South Carolina.

FREDERICK DOUGLASS (questions 39-43)

Frederick Augustus Washington Bailey was born a slave in February 1818 in Dorchester County, Maryland. He was an abolitionist, civil rights advocate and orator. Disguised as a sailor he escaped in 1838. He used the last name Douglass to help avoid being captured. Douglass becomes involved in the abolitionist movement in 1841 and publishes Narrative of the Life of Frederick Douglass, An American Slave in 1845. He founds the North Star, his weekly newspaper, in 1847. In a speech delivered July 5,1852, Douglass criticizes the hypocrisy of the July 4th celebrations. Douglass states "you celebrate and we mourn" emphasizing July 4th means nothing to people who are not free. Slavery would finally be abolished more than eighty eight years after July 4, 1776. Another hundred years would pass before many of the other inequities would be addressed.

JIM CROW LAWS

Jim Crow laws were United States laws, most frequently found in the south, that denied equal rights to blacks. These laws were used in the eighteen and nineteen hundreds to promote segregation. They prevented blacks from using the same public facilities (water fountains, restrooms, theatres, swimming pools, libraries) as whites. The integration of schools and housing was often denied by these laws. Blacks were often denied the most American of all rights: the right to vote by racist rules and laws. Poll taxes and literacy tests were designed to deny blacks their rights. Among the literacy tests were laws like Alabama's Boswell amendment. A poll worker could require a voter to explain any part of the constitution to the worker's satisfaction as a prerequisite to voting. Some localities instituted even more racist laws such as "grandfather clauses". These clauses stated a person could not vote if their grandfather did not vote. Since the grandfathers' of many blacks could not vote because they were slaves, it prevented their descendants from voting. To assure the the denial of their voting rights, some blacks were threatened, beaten, and even murdered.

SECESSION (question 177)

In December 1860, soon after the election of Abraham Lincoln as president, a convention in South Carolina voted to take the state out of the Union. The South Carolina convention, in explaining its radical action, focused entirely on race and slavery as the cause. Northerners were charged with seeking to prevent the expansion of slavery into new territories, resisting the return of fugitive slaves to white southerners who claimed them, and violating the Dred Scott decision by treating blacks as citizens and permitting them to vote - in support of Republican candidates like Lincoln. South Carolina asserted that each state had always had "separate control over it's own institutions", including "the right of property in slaves". With Lincoln considered "hostile to slavery", coming to power " the equal rights of the states will be lost" - the right of a state's citizens to own slaves.

CONFEDERACY (questions 178-184)

In December 1860 South Carolina became the first of eleven states to leave the Union. The confederate constitution was written in 1861. The constitution said no laws could be made that impedes on the rights of slave owners. This meant slavery could never be abolished in the confederate states. The confederates often did not respect the rights of black soldiers they captured. The black captives were often executed. At Fort Pillow, Tennessee, confederate troops killed black women and children and executed 238 black soldiers. Nathan Bedford Forrest was the Confederate commander at Fort Pillow. The confederates also murdered the captured black troops at Poison Spring in Arkansas.

CIVIL WAR (questions 185-189)

The American Civil War was fought between the Confederate States of America (eleven southern states that seceded from the Union)and the rest of the United States. The war began April 12, 1861 when Confederate troops bombarded Fort Sumter in South Carolina. It largely ended on April 9, 1865, when Confederate General Robert E.

Lee surrendered to Union General Ulysses S. Grant at Appomattox Court House in Virginia. While slavery was not the only reason for the Civil War, it was without question a major factor. Other reasons were tariffs, state's rights and preservation of the Union. One of the issues involving states rights was the right to own slaves. When slave states were contemplating seceding is when preservation of the Union became critical. Even though the Civil War did not begin until 1861, factors leading to the war began centuries earlier. In 1619, one hundred fifty seven years before the founding of the United States of America, the enslavement of African blacks was introduced to the colonies. The decade prior to war had numerous events that contributed to the confrontation. Among those factors were the publication of Uncle Tom's Cabin, the Dred Scott decision, John Brown's raid on Harper's Ferry and the election of Abraham Lincoln. On January 1, 1863, Lincoln issued the Emancipation Proclamation which stated that all slaves living in the rebelling states were free. The 13th amendment, which was ratified on December 18, 1865, made slavery and involuntary servitude illegal in the United States. Blacks played various roles for the Union during the war. Among them were Mary Ann Shadd Cary (army recruiter), Alexander Augusta (surgeon), Susie King (nurse and teacher), and Harriet Tubman (scout and spy). Of the 2.7 million Union troops over 178,000 were black. Nicholas Biddle was the first black wounded during the war when he was struck by a rock thrown by a proslavery demonstrator. The first black regiment to be involved in a battle was the 1st Kansas at Island Mound, Missouri (October 27 and 28, 1862). William Carney, a member of the Massachusetts 54th regiment, was the first black to receive the Congressional Medal of Honor. Carney earned the award for his valor at the battle of Fort Wagner (South Carolina). Carney was one of twenty-nine Union blacks to earn the award for their Civil War heroism. On March 13,1865, less than a month before the end of the war, the Confederates authorized the arming of slaves. This was a desperate measure because a Union victory was no longer in doubt. America paid a tremendous price for the four year conflict. The death toll for both sides exceeded 620,000. This total is more than

American deaths in World War 1 (116,516), World War II (405,399), Korea (36,516) and Vietnam (58,209) combined.

ROBERT SMALLS (questions 190-193)

Robert Smalls was born into slavery April 5,1839 in Beaufort, South Carolina. Smalls was working on a Confederate ship, Planter, in 1862. One night while the Confederates were off the ship, Smalls and a group of slaves boarded the vessel. Smalls sailed the ship into Union territory and surrendered, thus becoming a Civil War hero. After the war, he served five terms from South Carolina in the United States Congress.

AMENDMENTS (questions 194-199)

Abraham Lincoln issued the Emancipation Proclamation January 1,1863. It freed the slaves that were in the states that were still in rebellion. Slavery did not officially end in the United States until the 13th amendment. The 13th amendment, which was ratified on December 18, 1865, made slavery and involuntary servitude illegal in the United States. The 14th amendment (ratified July 28, 1868) made blacks citizens and the 15th amendment (ratified March 30, 1870) stated citizens of the United States could not be denied the right to vote because of "race, color or condition of servitude". The 19th amendment, fifty years later (ratified August 18,1920) gave women the right to vote. The 24th amendment, ratified January 23, 1964 outlawed the use of poll taxes (people paying a tax to vote).

LYNCHINGS (questions 200-203)

Lynching is the execution (frequently by mobs) of an individual or group without the victim receiving due process of law. These executions were frequently performed by whites as vigilante justice against blacks in the eighteen and nineteen hundreds. Blacks were lynched for a variety of reasons, real and contrived. The reason for lynching's could be the accusation of murder, rape, assaulting a white, disobeying a white or for committing any act that angers a white. Blacks could be lynched for being successful, for a business competing against whites, registering to vote or any act a white considered to be a black getting out of their place. Common methods of lynching were hangings, shootings, burning at stake and other forms of murder. Sometimes the lynching would be a combination of the preceding acts. The victim was often tortured prior to their death and mutilated after death. Sometimes bystanders would take body parts of the victim for souvenirs. Some lynching had few spectators other than the participants, but others were huge spectacles drawing more than five thousand spectators to watch the sadist event. The first year in the twentieth century with no known lynching was 1952. These horrible terrorist acts continued into the fifties and sixties during the civil rights movement. The lynching of Emmett Till was in 1955 and the murder of three civil rights workers in Mississippi occurred in 1964. Michael Donald was lynched by the Ku Klux Klan in Alabama in 1981. According to the NAACP statistics, 3446 of the 4743 known lynching victims between 1882 and 1968 in the United States were black. The word 'known' is used because some lynching victims were never found and numerous lynchings were not reported due to intimidation. The lynchers were almost never prosecuted. The United States Congress made a formal apology to lynching victims and their descendants in a 2005 resolution.

IDA B. WELLS (questions 204-210)

Ida B. Wells was born July 16,1862 in Holly Springs, Mississippi. She was an educator, journalist and fierce anti-lynching advocate. After her parents died of yellow fever in 1878, Ida supported herself and her younger siblings by teaching. She refused to sit in the Jim Crow section of a train in 1883 and was forcibly removed. She sued and was awarded 500 dollars in the case, but the decision was overturned by the Tennessee Supreme Court. In 1891 Wells was fired from a teaching job for writing about the sexual exploitation of black teachers by their white board members. Wells' editorial condemning the lynching of blacks in

Memphis resulted in an angry white mob burning her newspaper office in 1892. She moved to Chicago where the Ida B. Wells Club, of which she was president, started one of the first black kindergartens in 1893. She spent much of her life investigating and compiling statistics about lynching, and her research utterly disputed the racist justifications of lynching. Wells also protested the hangings of thirteen black soldiers who were convicted of murder after the 1917 riots near Houston. Her courage, perseverance and continued fight against lynching makes her one of the greatest figures in not only black history, but in world history. The United States Congress made a formal apology to lynching victims and their descendants in a 2005 resolution.

BOOKER T. WASHINGTON (questions 211-216)

Booker Taliaferro Washington was born April 5, 1856 in Franklin County, Virginia. He was a prominent leader of blacks in the late 1800's and early 1900's. He is known for a compromising tone in his attempts to fight for equality, while his contemporary W.E.B. DuBois had a more direct and aggressive approach. In 1881 Washington founded Tuskegee Institute in Alabama. He was the college's president from 1881 to 1915. Washington's autobiography is titled Up From Slavery.

W.E.B. DuBOIS (questions 217-221)

William Edward Burghardt DuBois was born on February 23,1868, in Great Barrington, Massachusetts. He was a scholar, educator, and author. DuBois studied at Fisk University and then earned a BA, an MA, and, in 1895, a doctoral degree at Harvard University in Massachusetts, the first African American to earn a PhD there. He briefly taught at Wilberforce University in Ohio and at Tuskegee Institute and for a far longer time at Atlanta University. For a time in the 1890s he shared common goals with Booker T. Washington, but by the next decade he had become committed to full civil and political rights for all African Americans. He was one of the founders of the National Association for the Advancement of Colored People in 1909, and he edited its crusading magazine (The Crisis) from 1910 to 1934. He participated in many international conferences, all focused on the people of the African diaspora, from London in 1900 to Paris in 1919 and England again in 1945. In 1961 he moved to Ghana, the first of the newly independent nations in Sub-Saharan Africa. There he continued his work until his death on August 27, 1963, shortly after he had become a citizen of his adopted country, and the day before the March on Washington for Freedom and Jobs. W. E. B. DuBois many books include The Souls of Black Folks (1903) and Black Reconstuction in America (1935).

EMMETT TILL (questions 231-235)

Emmett Louis Till was born in Chicago, Illinois, on July 25, 1941. In August 1955, the fourteen year old was visiting relatives in Money, Mississippi, when he was kidnapped and brutally murdered for supposedly flirting with a white female store clerk. Abducted at the home of his great-uncle Moses Wright, Till was beaten, mutilated, shot in the head, tied to a cotton gin and dumped in the Tallahatchie River. His body was later found and returned to Chicago with orders that the casket cannot be opened. His mother, Mamie Till Bradley defied those orders and Till had an open-casket funeral. Jet magazine put a picture of Till's body on it's cover to show the world how horrible the lynching was. An all-white jury acquitted Till's murderers Roy Bryant (the store clerk's husband) and his half brother J.W. Milam- of kidnapping and murdering the teenager. The pair sold their story to Look magazine and admitted killing Till. This episode produced fury and sadness for African Americans and sympathy among many white northerners, and helped propel the emerging Civil Rights Movement.

PLESSY VS FERGUSON (questions 238-239)

In 1892 Homer Plessy boarded a whites only train in Louisiana. Plessy, who had a black grandmother, was commanded to leave the train. He refused the orders and was arrested. Plessy filed suit and the case reached the United States Supreme Court in 1896. In the Plessy vs. Ferguson case the court ruled separate-but-equal was legal. Separate-but-equal was a policy which promoted segregation. The policy contended that as long as blacks were receiving the same accommodations as whites, racist policies such as segregation could still be permitted.

BROWN VS THE BOARD OF EDUCATION (questions 240-243)

The case began in Topeka, Kansas in 1951 when Linda Brown and her sister, Terry, were not allowed to attend the white public school. Their father joined in a NAACP suit with four other cases. Thurgood Marshall, who would later become the first black justice on the United States Supreme Court, was the lead attorney for the NAACP. In 1954 the United States Supreme Court ruled separate-but-equal was unconstitutional thus paving the way for the integration of schools. Some localities were still in defiance despite the court ruling. Governor Orval Faubus sent the Arkansas National Guard to Little Rock's Central High to prevent the blacks from integrating the school in 1957. President Dwight Eisenhower then sent army troops to escort the Little Rock Nine to their classes. In 1958 Governor Faubus closed the public schools in Little Rock, Arkansas. Prince Edward County, Virginia chose to close their public schools in 1959.

ROSA PARKS (questions 244-250)

Rosa McCauley was born February 4, 1913, in Tuskegee, Alabama. She had, as she put it, " a life history of being rebellious against being mistreated because of my color," but she is best known for a single gesture. On December 1, 1955 she refused to give up her seat to a white man on a segregated local bus in Montgomery, Alabama. When she was arrested, another local activist, E. D. Nixon, paid her bond. Convicted, she paid a fine of ten dollars for disorderly conduct and an additional four dollars for court costs. Meanwhile, her act of civil disobedience sparked the Montgomery bus boycott. This brought the leader of the boycott, Martin Luther King Jr., to national prominence. The boycott, which lasted a year, ended in a victory at the United States Supreme

Court. The court ruled that racial segregation on public transportation was unconstitutional. While her act led to future generations giving her the legendary status as "mother of the civil rights movement", her brave act caused her to lose her job as a department store seamstress, and threats against her physical safety continued. She and her husband, Raymond Parks, felt forced to leave Montgomery and moved to Detroit, Michigan in 1957. She worked for several years as a seamstress and in 1965 she was hired by congressman John Conyers as an administrative assistant. Parks received the NAACPs highest honor in 1977 and was the recipient of the nation's highest civilian award, the Presidential Medal of Freedom in 1977. Parks died October 24, 2005 at the age of 92. She was the first woman to lay at state at the Capital Rotunda after death.

MARTIN LUTHER KING, JR. (questions 251-268)

Michael King Jr. was born in Atlanta, Georgia, on January 15, 1929. His father, Michael King Sr. - as a great admirer of Martin Luther (16th century German monk and theologian)- changed his own name name to Martin Luther King Sr. and changed his son's name to Martin Luther King Jr. King, Jr. was ordained as a minister at the age of 18 and graduated from Morehouse College at age 19. He married Coretta Scott in 1953. In 1955 he became the leader of the Montgomery bus boycott after Rosa Parks was arrested for refusing to give up her seat on a city bus to a white man. This role catapulted King into national prominence as a civil rights leader. In 1957, King became the first president of the Southern Christian Leadership Conference. In 1963, at the March on Washington, King delivered his "I Have A Dream Speech". King won the 1964 Nobel Peace Prize for his non-violent fight against the injustices blacks faced in the United States. King continued to fight for poor people and all African Americans until he was shot and killed on April 4, 1968, on the balcony of the Lorraine Motel in Memphis, Tennessee. King left behind his widow and their four children, ages 5,7,10 and 12 when he was murdered. At his funeral in Atlanta, Ossie Davis performed King's eulogy, and Mahalia Jackson sang "Take My

Hand, Precious Lord". The King family would endure another tragedy six years later when, on June 30, 1974, King's mother, Alberta, was shot and killed at Ebenezer Baptist Church in Atlanta as she played the organ. In 1973 Illinois became the first state to honor Reverend Dr. Martin Luther King, Jr. with a holiday and a national holiday began in 1986. The National Football League removed Phoenix as the site for the 1993 Super Bowl because the state of Arizona did not recognize the King holiday.

MALCOLM X (questions 269-275)

Malcolm Little, one of eight siblings, was born May 19, 1925 in Omaha, Nebraska. His father, Earl Little, who was an outspoken Baptist minister and supporter of black nationalist Marcus Garvey, apparently fell victim twice to a white supremacist group. The family home was destroyed by a suspicious fire in 1929 and Mr. Little was found beaten and dead on a train track in 1931. Malcolm's mother suffered a nervous breakdown and was institutionalized, and the children were split up. As a young adult Malcolm turned to crime. During a long prison sentence, he joined the Nation of Islam, a black nationalist organization led by Elijah Muhammad. He rejected his slave name and adopted the name Malcolm X. During the decade after his release from prison in 1952, he emerged as a charismatic leader of the organization. He grew profoundly disillusioned with Elijah Muhammad and the Nation of Islam in 1963 and broke with both the following year. Also in 1964, he went on a pilgrimage to Mecca, Saudi Arabia, an experience that transformed his understanding of race, as he discovered that Muslims could be any race, including white. He changed his name yet again, to el-Hajj Malik el-Shabazz. Several months after his return to the United States, on February 21, 1965, gunmen from the Nation of Islam assassinated him in Harlem's Audubon Ballroom. The Autobiography of Malcolm X, published later that year, was based on interviews over the preceding two years with writer Alex Haley.

FANNIE HAMER (questions 276-278)

Fannie Lou Townsend was born on October 6, 1917 in Montgomery County, Mississippi. Townsend, who had nineteen siblings, was one of the many people who played a major role in obtaining voting rights for blacks. In 1944 she married Perry Hamer. Fannie Hamer became a member of the Student Nonviolent Coordinating Committee. After registering to vote in 1963 she was arrested and severely beaten in jail. In 1964, Hamer with others, founded The Mississippi Freedom Democratic Party. She continued her effort to improve the rights of blacks. She was the founder of Freedom Farms Corporation which helped provide food for poor blacks and whites.

MEDGAR EVERS (questions 279-284)

Medgar Wiley Evers was born July 2, 1925 in Decatur, Mississippi. He joined the NAACP in 1952 and became the Mississippi field secretary of the NAACP from 1954 until his death in 1963. Evers was assassinated in the driveway of his home. Evers children was 3, 8 and 9 years old at the time of his murder. It would take over thirty years before Evers' murderer would be convicted. In 1994, Byron De La Beckwith was sentenced to life in prison for the murder. Evers widow, Myrlie Evers-Williams became the first female chairperson of the national NAACP in 1995 and held the position until her resignation in 1998.

SELMA TO MONTGOMERY MARCHES FOR VOTING RIGHTS (questions 285-290)

On February 18,1965, blacks were protesting for voting rights in Marion, Alabama (a little more than twenty five miles from Selma). State troopers were beating 82 year old Cager Lee. When his daughter, Viola, got involved she too was beaten. Her son, Jimmie Lee Jackson, intervened in an attempt to protect his mother. He was shot by a state trooper and died eight days later. Frustrated by the situation a march from Selma to the state capital in Montgomery to voice their complaints to Governor George Wallace was planned. On March 7 approximately 600 civil rights marchers began the 54 mile journey. When the marchers reached the bottom of Selma's Edmund Pettus Bridge (named for the former confederate general and Klansman), they were stopped by state troopers. The troopers began beating the marchers with billy clubs and spraying them with tear gas. Many marchers including future congressman John Lewis would be severely beaten. This event would become known as Bloody Sunday. This was the first of three attempts for the civil rights activist to march from Selma to Montgomery. On March 9, the second attempt was made. Once again the state troopers were there to prevent the march. The marchers retreated. Protester James Reeb, a white minister from Boston, would be severely beaten later that day and die March 11th from his wounds. On March 20, President Lyndon Johnson mobilized the Alabama National Guard under federal authority to protect the marchers. The third march began March 21 and ended March 25 when approximately 25,000 activist reached Montgomery. That evening Viola Liuzzo, a white mother of five from Detroit, who had transported marchers was murdered by the Ku Klux Klan. (Hosea Williams and John Lewis led the first Selma march. Martin Luther King, Jr. led the second and third marches.)

BIRMINGHAM CHURCH BOMBINGS (questions 291-294)

The Sixteenth Street Baptist Church was the location of the Birmingham church bombing. Nineteen sticks of dynamite exploded on Sunday, September 15, 1963 at the church. The explosion killed four young girls. The murder victims were Addie Mae Collins, Carole Robinson and Cynthia Wesley, all fourteen year olds. The other victim was eleven-year-old Denise McNair. The same evening thirteen year old, Virgil Ware, was shot and killed by racist.

OTHER VOTING RIGHTS VICTIMS OF
VIOLENCE (questions 295-300)

Lamar Smith (1955), Reverend George Lee (1955), Herbert Lee (1961), and Vernon Dahmer (1966) were murdered by racist for registering to vote or registering others to vote. Three civil rights volunteers who were investigating the burning of a black church and working on the Freedom Summer Project to help black voter registration were also murdered. In 1964 James Chaney, who was black, and a pair of whites (Andrew Goodman and Michael Schwerner) were shot and their bodies were recovered in an earthen dam near Philadelphia, Mississippi in 1964.

WHITNEY ELAINE JOHNSON (question 336)

Whitney Elaine Johnson is one of the youngest victims of racism. Named for the singer Whitney Houston, little Whitney was born in Thomasville, Georgia in 1996. Whitney lived only nineteen hours. Whitney's white mother, Jaime Wireman, wanted her daughter buried next to her father, the baby's grandfather, so she would not be alone. Whitney, who's father was black, was buried in the previously all-white cemetery. Three days after her funeral the deacon's board voted to have her body removed. Due to the criticism the board and the town received, she was allowed to remain in the cemetery beside her grandfather.

BARACK OBAMA

Barack Obama was born in Hawaii on August 4, 1961. His father was a black Kenyan and his mother was a white American from Kansas. He graduated from Harvard law school and married Michelle Robinson, another Harvard law school graduate. In 2004, Obama won a senatorial election in Illinois and became the lone black in the United States Senate. In 2008 Obama defeated Hillary Clinton in the Democratic primary thus becoming their nominee for president. He defeated the Republican nominee, John McCain. On January 20, 2009 Barack Obama was sworn in as the first black president of the United States of America. President Obama was re-elected in 2012 when he defeated Mitt Romney.

LAWS (questions 47-102)

1641   Virginia law decreeing that white and black runaway servants would be branded

1662   Virginia law stating that white Christians who had sex with blacks would pay double the fine of other offenders

1663   Maryland law that a white woman and her offspring would become slaves if she married a black man

1680   Virginia law stating that slaves could be executed for carrying arms

1690   Pennsylvania court case, a white woman was ordered to receive 21 lashes for having a black baby

1691   Virginia law that levied a fine of £15 (fifteen pounds of sterling) on any white woman for having a black baby

1691   Virginia law, a mixed child with a white mother would be a ward of the state for thirty years

1705   Massachusetts law decreeing that any black would be beaten severely for striking a white

1712   South Carolina law made it legal to cut off a slave's ear if the slave was a three time runaway and was gone thirty days

1712   South Carolina law made it legal to execute a slave for being a four time thief

1715   New York law that prevented blacks from selling oysters

1716   South Carolina law Christian white men were the only people allowed to vote

1723   Virginia law stipulating that freed slaves could not vote or carry weapons

1724   Louisiana law stating that runaway slaves could be punished by being branded or having their ears cut off

1729   Maryland law that made the decapitation of a slave legal as punishment for some crimes

1730   Virginia decreeing that white males must carry arms to church

1735   South Carolina a freed slave has to leave the colony within six months

1735 South Carolina any freed slave who returned to the colony within seven years would become a slave again

1739 South Carolina a person could be fined 1000 dollars, in addition to being sentenced to a year in jail, for hiding a runaway slave

1739 South Carolina law stating that no slave could work over fifteen hours per day in the summer or fourteen hours in the winter

1753 Massachusetts law ordering that slaves be publicly whipped for breaking streetlamps

1770 Georgia enacted law that made assaulting a white a capital offense for a black

1770 Georgia law decreeing that a white man must be present at any gathering of six or more blacks

1774 New York law stating that a slave who served three years as a soldier would be freed

1780 Pennsylvania law that all offspring of slaves became free at age twenty-eight

1780 South Carolina law that gave a slave to each man who enlisted in the army

1792 Virginia law that sentenced any white who married a black to six months in jail

1739 South Carolina law to punish ($100 fine and six months in jail) anyone who gave alcohol to a slave

1780 Pennsylvania was the first state to allow interracial marriage by repealing the law against it

1784, Connecticut passed a law stating that no one could be held in slavery after they were 25 years old

1800 South Carolina law prohibiting free blacks from entering

1805 Virginia law stating that all freed slaves must leave the state

1806 Virginia law stipulating that all freed slaves had to leave the state within a year

1807 Ohio law decreeing that all blacks must pay a five-hundred-dollar good behavior bond

1808   was the year import of slaves outlawed in the United States (even though the law was not enforced)

1810   New York, slave children was required to read the Bible

1811   Delaware law decreeing that any black who entered must leave within ten days or be fined $10 per week

1820   Maine constitution allowed all men the right to an education and the right to vote

1832   Florida law any free black unable to pay his or her fine would be sold as a slave

1832   Virginia law stipulating that a slave could be executed for assaulting a white

1832   Virginia law stipulating that a slave could be executed for burning more than fifty dollars worth of wheat

1832   Virginia make it illegal for free blacks to purchase slaves

1835   New Orleans had its cemeteries zoned (one for whites, one for free blacks, and one for slaves)

1840   Indiana law stipulating that a minister could be levied a fine up to ten thousand dollars for performing an interracial wedding

1840   Indiana law stipulating that one could receive ten to twenty years in jail for having an interracial marriage

1841   Atlanta law stipulating that blacks and whites must be sworn in on different Bibles in court

1841   South Carolina law decreeing that black and white mill workers could not look out of the same window

1842   Mississippi law stipulating that blacks coming in from any other state would be whipped and deported

1851   Virginia law that made a free black a slave if he or she stayed in the state for a year

1915   US Supreme Court rule grandfather clauses (racist laws to prevent blacks from voting) unconstitutional. (The grandfather clause stipulated that if your grandfather did not vote, you could not vote. Therefore, blacks could not vote.)

1946   Alabama The Boswell Amendment said voters must be able to explain any part of the US Constitution to a poll worker in order to vote. This Alabama law was used to prevent blacks from voting.

1953   Supreme Court, segregation in Washington, DC, restaurants banned

1967   Supreme Court rules laws against interracial marriages unconstitutional

Fugitive Slave Law made harboring a runaway a crime

Neal v. Delaware court case ruled that excluding blacks from juries violated black defendants' rights

Vermont was the first colony to abolish slavery

age Jan Matzeliger, inventor of a shoe-lacing machine, when he died of tuberculosis	Thirty-seven
amendment outlawed the use of poll taxes, which were frequently used in the South to prevent blacks from voting	Twenty-Fourth
became famous for his scientific discoveries using soybeans	Percy Julian
city, Benjamin Banneker played a major role in the surveying and design	Washington, DC
common name of the national safety hood, invented by Garrett Morgan	Gas Mask
company was cofounded by Frederick Jones	Thermo King
developed many products from peanuts	George Washington Carver
first African American female neurosurgeon	Alexa Canady
first African American to receive a PhD in chemistry	Saint Elmo Brady
first black male surgeon general	David Satcher
first black nurse to enroll with the Red Cross	Fannie Elliott Davis

first black president of the American Medical Association	Roselyn Payne Epps
first black woman to obtain a medical degree in the United States	Rebecca Crumpler
first director of the American Red Cross Blood Bank	Charles Drew
first female bank president in the United States	Maggie Walker
first person to perform a successful open heart surgery	Daniel Hale Williams
first physician to aid President Garfield after he was shot	Charles Purvis
founded a hospital for blacks in Nashville in 1916	Millie Hale
founded Provident Hospital	Daniel Hale Williams
founded three hospitals with nurse training schools, and a free clinic in Columbia, South Carolina, before 1935	Matilda Evans
invented the induction telegraph system, which allowed trains to communicate with each other, thus preventing collisions	Granville Woods
invented the Super Soaker water gun	Lonnie Johnson
invented toggle harpoon that greatly improved whaling industry	Lewis Temple
invented vacuum pan evaporator for sugar industry	Norbert Rillieux
inventor created a refrigeration system for trucks	Frederick Jones
item sold by Madam C. J. Walker to obtain her wealth (she was a millionaire when she died at the age of fifty-two)	Hair-care products
known as the "Baby Doctor" because she delivered more than 7000 babies	Justina Ford

made the first clock in the American colonies	Benjamin Banneker
major medical concern Solomon Fuller (as a doctor) was fighting	Alzheimer's disease
major medical concern William Cardoza (as a doctor) was fighting	Sickle cell anemia
medical condition that is treated by synthetic physostigmine, which was created in a lab by renowned chemist Percy Julian	Glaucoma
name of the first black-owned hospital in the United States	Provident
patent for a beer keg tap	Richard Spikes
patent for a corn sheller	Lockrum Blue
patent for a dough kneading machine	Joseph Lee
patent for a feeding device for the handicapped	Bessie Blount
patent for a golf tee	George Grant
patent for a guided missile device	Otis Boykin
patent for a hearing aid	Harry Hopkins
patent for a lawn sprinkler in 1897	Joseph Smith
patent for a low-fuel helicopter engine	Joseph Logan
patent for a miner's lamp bracket	J. R. Watts
patent for a mortician's table	Leander Coles
patent for a permanent waving machine	Marjorie Joyner
patent for a radar search beacon	Ozzie Williams
patent for a shoe-lasting machine that dramatically increased the production of shoes	Jan Matzeliger
patent for a spark plug	Edmond Berger
patent for a stair-climbing wheelchair	Rufus Weaver
patent for a toaster	Ruane Sharon Jeter
patent for an airplane propeller	James Adams

patent for an automatic traffic symbol (the three-color traffic light)	Garrett Morgan
patent for an automatic train lubricator	Elijah McCoy
patent for an overhead conducting system for electric railways	Granville Woods
patent for carbon filament for electric lights	Lewis Latimer
patent for disposal panties	Tanya Allen
patent for ice cream	Augusta Jackson
patent for portable electric light	Cap Collins
patent for potato chips	Hyram Thomas
patent for the first elevator in 1887	Alexander Miles
patent for the jenny coupler, a device that attaches one train car to anther	Andrew Beard
patents for corn and cotton planters in 1836	Henry Blair
patents for tissue tests for cancer prevention drugs	Jane Cooke Wright
received a patent for a folding bed	Leonard Bailey
received a patent for a lock in 1889	W. A. Martin
received a US patent for inventing a lawn mower in 1899	J. A. Burr
resigned as head of a plasma drive because soldiers were permitted to receive blood only from donors of their own race	Charles Drew
Shirley Ann Jackson's profession	Scientist
slave who taught whites how to vaccinate against smallpox	Onesimus
state birth, Garrett Morgan the great inventor	Kentucky
state, birth of George Washington Carver, an agriculturist and inventor	Missouri
year Provident Hospital, the first black-owned hospital, was founded	1891
year sickle cell anemia, an inherited blood disease most common in blacks, discovered	1910

year Twenty-Fourth Amendment to the Constitution, which outlawed the use of poll taxes, was ratified	1964
year, Macon Allen become a licensed attorney	1844
year, Richard Spikes, engineer and inventor, develop the multiple-barrel machine gun	1940
year, the Red Cross stop segregating blood	1950
year, Tuskegee Syphilis Experiment (government experiments on black men with syphilis) ended	1972
years the Tuskegee Syphilis Experiment (government experiments on black men with syphilis) lasted	Forty

NAACP (questions 222-230)

birth city, Charles Houston, an attorney for the NAACP who played a major role in setting the strategy for legal battles to overturn racist laws	Washington, DC
executive director of the NAACP from 1955 to 1977	Roy Wilkins
executive director of the NAACP from 1977 to 1992	Benjamin Hooks
first female chairperson of the NAACP	Myrlie Evers-Williams
national field secretary of the NAACP, 1935–1947	Daisy Lampkin
state birth, Julian Bond, civil rights leader, politician, and chairperson of the NAACP	Tennessee
state, Edgar Nixon was the president of the NAACP	Alabama
youngest president of the NAACP in the history of the organization	Ben Jealous

year, Harry Moore, president of the Florida   1951
NAACP, and his wife murdered when racists
bombed their home on Christmas

year, National Association for the   1909
Advancement of Colored People (NAACP)
founded

CIVIL RIGHTS MARTYRS (questions 295-307)

activity Herbert Lee was engaged in when he was murdered by racists in 1961	registering voters
activity Lamar Smith was engaged in when he was murdered by racists in 1955	registering voters
activity Reverend George Lee was engaged in when he was murdered by racists in 1955	registering voters
activity Samuel Younge Jr. was engaged in when he was murdered by racists in 1966	dispute over a whites-only restroom
activity the three civil rights workers were engaged in when they were murdered in Mississippi in 1964	registering voters
activity Vernon Dahmer was engaged in when he was murdered by racists in 1966	registering voters
activity Viola Liuzzo, a white civil rights activist, was engaged in when she was murdered by white racists	transporting marchers
city or town where three civil rights (James Chaney, Andrew Goodman, and Michael Schwerner) workers murdered in 1964	Philadelphia, Mississippi
killed in Alabama by state troopers during the civil rights movement	Jimmy Lee Jackson
name the 1968 killing of three students (with twenty-seven wounded) by white policemen is known as	Orangeburg Massacre

number of Vietnam War protestors killed at Jackson State by law enforcement officials	Two
town 1966 murder of Samuel Younge Jr. occurred	Tuskegee, Alabama
university where three black students were killed and twenty-seven wounded by local policemen in 1968	South Carolina State
year white civil rights activist Viola Liuzzo, who was murdered by the KKK	1965
year, James Reeb, a white minister, was murdered by white racists in Selma, Alabama	1965

VICTIMS OF VIOLENCE (questions 308-313)

city and date, shooting of Latasha Harlins	Los Angeles, California, 1991
city a white racist murdered nine blacks at a church in 2015	Charleston, South Carolina
first year a white person was executed for killing a black in Florida	2017
how James Byrd Jr. murdered by racists in 1998	Dragged with a truck
murdered by a white mob in Bensonhurst, New York	Yusef Hawkins

RAPES (questions 314-320)

black woman who was abducted at gunpoint and raped by six white men in Alabama in 1944	Recy Taylor
civil rights icon helped with the investigation of the 1944 rape of black by six whites in Alabama?	Rosa Parks

number of blacks out of 45 men executed for   Forty-five
rape in Virginia before 1951

number of blacks were executed after the 1951   Seven
rape of a white woman in Martinsville, Virginia

number of Scottsboro Boys falsely accused of   Nine
raping two white women in Alabama (1931)

number of whites executed between 1619   Zero
and today (in the colonies and the United
States) for the rape of blacks

punishment for three white lacrosse players   They were briefly
from Duke University who were falsely   jailed
accused of rape

RIOTS (questions 321-329)

city, white mobs burn 1,115 black homes and   Tulsa, Oklahoma
businesses and murder over 200 people in
1921 riots (according to Red Cross statistics)

state, white mob destroyed a black   New York
orphanage in 1863

town, two hundred blacks were murdered by   Opelousas, Louisiana
white mobs in 1868

year, a major race riot in Detroit   1967

year, a major race riot occurred in Chicago   1919
after a black boy who ventured into the
"white section" of Lake Michigan and
drowned after whites threw rocks at him

year, major race riot in East Saint Louis   1917

year, major race riot in New York City   1863

AVIATION (questions 344-359)

black astronaut died when the *Challenger* space shuttle exploded, killing all seven aboard, in 1986	Ron McNair
college, US Army started a school for black pilots	Tuskegee
country, Bessie Coleman obtained her pilot's license because no flight school in the United States would give her lessons	France
employer of the women in the movie *Hidden Figures*	NASA
first African American woman in space	Mae Jemison
first black commander of a NASA space shuttle	Frederick Drew Gregory
first black female in the United States to have a commercial pilot's license	Willa Brown
first black NASA astronaut to walk in space	Bernard Harris
first person to have an international pilot's license	Bessie Coleman
name of the NASA space shuttle that Frederick Drew Gregory commanded	*Challenger*
nickname of the Tuskegee pilots	Red Tails
relation of astronaut Frederick Gregory to Dr. Charles Drew	He is his nephew
second black American astronaut in space	Ron McNair
state birth, Mae Jemison is the first African American female astronaut to enter space	Alabama
university, Mae Jemison earned her engineering degree	Stanford
year the first three blacks were accepted to NASA	1978

ORGANIZATIONS (questions 360-374)

city, Madame Bernard Couvent's school for orphans was located	New Orleans
city, the Student Nonviolent Coordinating Committee founded in 1960	Raleigh, North Carolina
cofounder of the Student Nonviolent Coordinating Committee	Marion Barry
executive director of the Urban League	Whitney Young
female was the executive director of PUSH (People United to Save Humanity) from 1986 to 1989	Willie Barrow
first black member of the Daughters of the American Revolution (DAR)	Karen Farmer
founder of PUSH (People United to Save Humanity)	Jesse Jackson
founder of the United Negro College Fund	Frederick Patterson
founder of the United Negro Improvement Association	Marcus Garvey
is a terrible thing to waste according to the motto of the United Negro College Fund	A mind
presidential award received by Whitney Young, executive director for the National Urban League, in 1968	Medal of Freedom
state birth, Ralph Abernathy, civil rights leader and head of the Southern Christian Leadership Conference	Alabama
year, Clara Hale founded The Hale House, was a home that cared for drug-addicted babies	1970
year, United Negro Improvement Association was founded	1914
year, United Negro College Fund was founded	1944

BLACK FIRSTS (questions 375-430)

city the first black-owned television station established	Detroit
college had the first black graduate	Middlebury
college had the first black nursing school	Spelman College
educator and civil rights leader who was born a slave and died in 1964	Anna Haywood Cooper
first black child born in the colonies	William Tucker
first black director of the Centers for Disease Control	David Satcher
first black director of the Peace Corps	Carolyn Robertson Payton
first black female admitted to practice before the US Supreme Court	Violette Anderson
first black female dentist license to practice in the United States	Ida Gray
first black female federal judge	Constance Baker Motley
first black female lawyer in the United States	Charlotte Ray
first black female president of a major white university	Marguerite Ross Barnett
first black female president of the American Bar Association	Paulette Brown
first black female president of the National Bar Association	Arnette Hubbard
first black female principal in the United States	Fannie Jackson Coppin
first black female school superintendent of a major city	Barbara Sizemore
first black female surgeon general	Jocelyn Elders
first black female to receive a PhD from MIT	Shirley Jackson
first black female US Army nurse	Susie King Taylor
first black Harvard graduate	Richard Greener

first black in the United States to publish written material advocating the use of violence for equality and self-defense	David Walker
first black lawyer approved to practice before the US Supreme Court (but never did)	John Rock
first black lawyer to practice before the US Supreme Court	Samuel R. Lowery
first black licensed attorney in the United States	Macon Allen
first black man to be appointed to the United States Supreme Court	Thurgood Marshall
first black physician in the United States	James Durham
first black president of Atlanta Baptist College	John Hope
first black president of Howard University	Mordecai Johnson
first black president of the American Nursing Association	Barbara Lorraine Nichols
first black president of the Girl Scouts	Gloria Randle Scott
first black president of the National Organization of Women	Aileen Hernandez
first black president of the Southern Baptist Convention	Fred Luter
first black president of Wilberforce which was the first black-owned college and the first college to have a black president in the United States	Daniel Payne
first black professor at a white college	Charles Reason
first black student at Ole Miss	James Meredith
first black student at the University of Alabama	Autherine Lucy
first black Texas Ranger	Lee Roy Young
first black to earn a law degree in the United States	George Ruffin

first black to earn a PhD from Harvard	W. E. B. DuBois
first black to graduate from a United States college	Alexander Twilight
first black to graduate from the University of Alabama	Vivian Malone
first black to have a national monument in his honor	George Washington Carver
first black to receive a doctorate degree in the United States	Edward Bouchet
first black to win the Nobel Peace Prize	Ralph Bunche
first black woman elected to the US Congress from Florida	Carrie Meek
first black woman to earn a BA degree in the United States	Mary Jane Patterson
first black woman to earn a college degree in the United States	Lucy Stanton Session
first black woman to graduate from Yale Law School	Jane Bolin
first blacks to graduate from a United States medical school	Thomas and John White
president sent federal troops to protect James Meredith when he integrated Ole Miss	President Kennedy
second black woman to obtain a medical degree in the United States	Rebecca Cole
state Jane Bolin, the first black woman judge, presided	New York
year first black student was admitted to the University of North Carolina	1951
year first black student was admitted to the University of South Carolina	1873
year first black student was admitted to the University of West Point	1870

year Thurgood Marshall, first black appointed to the US Supreme Court — 1967

MILITARY (questions 431-468)

first black admiral in the US Navy	Samuel Gravely
first black admitted to West Point	James W. Smith
first black American to orbit the earth	Guion Bluford
first black chairman of the Joint Chiefs of Staff	Colin Powell
first black commander of a US warship	Samuel Gravely
first black female air force pilot	Marcella Hayes
first black female four-star admiral	Michelle Howard
first black female US Air Force general	Marcelite Harris
first black female US Army two-star general	Marcia Anderson
first black female US Navy pilot	Jill Brown
first black fighter pilot	Eugene Bullard
first black fighter pilot to shoot down a German airplane during World War II	Charles Hall
first black four-star general in the United States Air Force	Daniel "Chappie" James
first black four-star general in the US Army	Roscoe Robinson Jr.
first black general in the United States Marines	Frank Petersen
first black naval aviator	Jesse Brown
first black to be admitted to the US Naval Academy	James Henry Conyers
first black to graduate from the United States Military Academy at West Point	Henry Flipper
first black to graduate from the US Naval Academy	Wesley Brown
first black to receive the Medal of Honor in the Vietnam War after he dove on a live grenade to save fellow soldiers	Milton Olive

first black US Air Force general	Benjamin Davis Jr.
first United States military ship to be commanded by a black man	USS *Falgout*
kicked out of West Point for breaking a coconut dipper over the head of another cadet	James W. Smith
lost at sea during World War II	Dorie Miller
middle name is Ossian	Henry Flipper
name of the ship Dorie Miller was assigned to at Pearl Harbor	USS *West Virginia*
number, Medals Of Honor were awarded to Buffalo Soldiers for their heroic acts in the Indian Wars and the Spanish American War	23
received France's highest bravery award for fighting two dozen Germans in World War I to save a wounded soldier	Henry Johnson
shot down four Japanese planes at Pearl Harbor	Dorie Miller
state birth, Henry O. Flipper was the first black to graduate from West Point	Georgia
state, Port Chicago, where a mutiny occurred in 1944 after an explosion killed three hundred people (two hundred of them blacks), is located	California
year, first black graduate from the United States Naval Academy	1949
year, Henry O. Flipper graduate from the United States Military Academy at West Point	1877
year, John Green retired, leaving Benjamin Davis Sr. as the only black officer in the US Army	1929

year, Port Chicago mutiny occurred when   1944
sailors refused to handle munitions after
unsafe conditions continued following an
explosion that killed hundreds of people
year, President Truman order that all   1948
military personnel be treated equally
year, the US Air Force end its ban on   1981
applicants with sickle cell trait
year, United States begin a training program 1941
for black pilots in Alabama

POLITICS (questions 475-589)

15th president of the United States and not a James Buchanan
slave owner
1967 Carl Stokes became the first black   Cleveland
mayor of a major US city
age of Maynard Jackson when he graduated   Eighteen
from Morehouse College
Barack Obama's main competitor for the   Hillary Clinton
Democratic Party's nominee for president in
2008
birth city of Andrew Young is a civil rights New Orleans
activist, politician, and preacher
birth city Thurgood Marshall was the first   Baltimore
black appointed to the US Supreme Court
birth country Barack Obama's father   Kenya
birth name was Frizzell Gray   Kweisi Mfume
birth state of Blanche Bruce, the second   Virginia
black member of the United States Senate,
birthplace state
birth state of Jesse Jackson   South Carolina
birth state of President Barack Obama   Hawaii

birth state Willie Brown, member of the California legislature for thirty-one years and mayor of Oakland	Texas
black politician sued Barack Obama because he did not think Obama was born in the United States	Alan Keyes
black women have been US senators	Two
city born, Ralph Bunche, Nobel Peace Prize winner, born	Detroit
city born, Ron Brown first black chairman of the National Democratic Party	Washington, DC
city Coleman Young the mayor	Detroit
city Cory Booker became the mayor in 2006	Newark, New Jersey
city Kasim Reed became the mayor in 2010	Atlanta
city Kurt Schmoke was the mayor	Baltimore
city Lionel Wilson was the mayor	Oakland
city where Harvey Gantt the mayor	Charlotte
city where Tom Bradley was the mayor	Los Angeles
city Wilson Goode was the mayor	Philadelphia
civil rights leader endorsed former Klansman David Duke for governor of Louisiana	James Meredith
college Hiram Revels became president of in 1872	Alcorn
defeated by Barack Obama in the 2008 presidential election	John McCain
defeated by Barack Obama in the 2012 presidential election	Mitt Romney
first American president of Liberia	Joseph Jenkins Roberts
first black attorney general (a President Obama appointee)	Eric Holder
first black chairman of the Republican National Committee in 2009	Michael Steele

first black Democrat elected to the US Congress	Arthur Mitchell
first black elected to the United States Senate	Edward Brooke
first black female attorney general was appointed by President Obama	Loretta Lynch
first black female mayor	Ellen Walker Craig-Jones
first black female United States senator	Carol Moseley Braun
first black mayor of Atlanta	Maynard Jackson
first black mayor of New York	David Dinkins
first black secretary of labor	Alexis Herman
first black to be appointed to the cabinet by a president	Robert Weaver
first black to be elected (but not seated) to the US Congress	John Menard
first black to be elected to a political office in the United States	John Mercer Langston
first black to give a speech at the US Capitol	Henry Garnet
first black US ambassador to a European country	Clifton Wharton Sr.
first black US ambassador to the United Nations	Andrew Young
first black US congressman after Reconstruction	Oscar DePriest
first black US senator	Hiram Revels
first black woman elected to the US Congress	Shirley Chisholm
first black woman in the United States cabinet	Patricia Roberts Harris
first black woman to run for vice president	Charlotta Bass
first female and first black secretary of energy	Hazel O'Leary

first secretary of state for George W. Bush	Colin Powell
had multiple sclerosis and leukemia	Barbara Jordan
HBCU that Jesse Jackson attended	North Carolina A&T
hidden black daughter of Strom Thurmond, who ran for president as a segregationist	Essie Mae Washington-Williams
killed in a plane crash in Ethiopia taking supplies to famine victims	Congressman Mickey Leland
last name was Walcott at birth	Louis Farrakhan
mayor of Atlanta from 1982 to 1989	Andrew Young
mayor of New Orleans when it was devastated by Hurricane Katrina	Ray Nagin
middle name is Eulion	Vernon Jordan
middle name is Mosiah	Marcus Garvey
middle name is Shepilov	Marion Barry
name of Barack Obama's father	Barack Obama
name of President Roosevelt's "Black Cabinet"	Federal Council of Negro Affairs
national security advisor for George W. Bush	Condoleezza Rice
nickname of Ernest Morial, the first black mayor of New Orleans	Dutch
only city in the United States where residents do not have representatives in the US Senate	Washington, DC
only decade before 2000 that had two black members of the United States Senate	1870s
president appointed Alexis Herman to the position of United States secretary of labor	Bill Clinton
president appointed Clarence Thomas to the Supreme Court	George Bush
president appointed Patricia Roberts Harris to the US cabinet	Jimmy Carter

president appointed Rod Paige, first black secretary of education	George W. Bush
president appointed the first black to his cabinet	Lyndon Johnson
president appointed Thurgood Marshall to the United States Supreme Court	Lyndon Johnson
President Barack Obama wife's maiden name	Michelle Robinson
president had a group of advisors called the Black Cabinet	Franklin Roosevelt
president when Elizabeth Keckly was a household assistant for his family	Abraham Lincoln
ran for the Democratic presidential nomination in 1984 and 1988	Jesse Jackson
ran for vice president in 1980 and 1984 with the Communist Party	Angela Davis
second black member of the US Senate	Blanche Bruce
second black US cabinet member	William Coleman
secretary of health and human services under George Bush	Louis Sullivan
security guard who discovered the break-in at Watergate Hotel	Frank Wills
state Douglas Wilder was the first elected black governor	Virginia
state elected Barack Obama to the United States Senate	Illinois
state elected Mia Love as the first black female Republican to the US Congress	Utah
state P. B. S. Pinchback served as acting governor from December 9, 1872, to January 13, 1873	Louisiana
state represented by Kamala Harris, the second black female US senator	California

state represented by Maxine Waters in Congress	California
state represented by Oscar DePriest, first black US congressperson after Reconstruction	Illinois
state represented by Senator Edward Brooke	Massachusetts
state represented by Shirley Chisholm in Congress	New York
state where the first black Democratic congressional member was elected	Illinois
total number of blacks that have been members of the United States Senate as of 2019	Ten
town first black was elected to a political office in the United States	Brownhelm, Ohio
town where Monroe Baker was elected the first black mayor in the US in 1867	Saint Martin, Louisiana
US ambassador to the United Nations under President Obama	Susan Rice
was defeated by Barack Obama in the 2004 United States Senate election	Alan Keyes
was once secretary of Housing and Urban Development	Patricia Roberts Harris
wife had twins after he was killed in a plane crash	Congressman Mickey Leland
winner of the 2009 Nobel Peace Prize	Barack Obama
won a Nobel Peace Prize for work on the Arab-Israeli conflict	Ralph Bunche
year Henry Garnet give his speech at the United States House of Representatives	1865
year Robert Weaver became the secretary of Housing and Urban Development	1966

year the first black elected to a political office in the United States	1855
year Barack Obama took office as the first black president of the United States	2009
year first black female Republican elected to the United States Congress	2014
year Kamala Harris, the second black female US senator took office	2017
year Mickey Leland, Texas congressman and advocate for the poor, was killed in a plane crash	1989
year Mississippi got its second black US senator	1874
year Ron Brown was killed in a plane crash	1996
year that Ralph Bunche won the Nobel Peace Prize	1950
year the first black female elected mayor in the United States took office	1972
year the first black mayor of Birmingham, Alabama, Richard Arrington was elected	1979
year the United States Senate got its first black member	1870

LITERATURE (questions 596-669)

"Father of Black History"	Carter Woodson
age, Ed Bradley, prominent black journalist on CBS's *60 Minutes*, when he died in 2006 of leukemia	Sixty-five
author *Before the Mayflower: A History of the Negro in America*	Lerone Bennett
author of *Autobiography of an Ex-Colored Man*	James Weldon Johnson

author of *Behind the Scenes: Or, Thirty Years a Slave and Four Years in the White House*	Elizabeth Keckley
author of *Black No More*	George Schuyler
author of *Black Women in White*	Darlene Hine
author of *Blues for Mr. Charlie*	James Baldwin
author of *If They Come in the Morning*	Angela Davis
author of *Immunological Studies in Sickle Cell Anemia*	William Cardozo
author of the book *April 4, 1968: Martin Luther King Jr.'s Death and How It Changed America*	Michael Eric Dyson
author of the first novel published by a black woman in the United States	Harriet Adams Wilson
author of the first short story published in the United States by a black woman	Frances Watkins Harper
author of *The Negro Family in the United States*	E. Franklin Frazier
author of *The Negro's Church*	Benjamin Mays
author of the poem "If We Must Die"	Claude McKay
author of *The President's Daughter*	William Wells Brown
author of *The Underground Railroad*	William Still
author of *Why Blacks Kill Blacks*	Alvin Poussaint
author, "The Slave Auction" is a gripping poem detailing the horrors of slavery	Frances Harper
authored the first slave narrative written by a female	Mary Prince
autobiography is titled *Incidents in the Life of a Slave Girl*	Harriet Jacobs's
autobiography is titled *My American Journal*	Colin Powell
autobiography is titled *The Good Fight*	Shirley Chisholm
Black History Month	February

book that listed names and addresses of locations Black travelers could dine or stay at during segregated times	The Green Book
city birth, Frances Harper was a women's rights advocate, antislavery advocate, and author	Baltimore
city, worst in the United States for a black to live in, according to the 1948 *Negro Digest*	Columbia, South Carolina
city, birth of news reporter and *60 Minutes* correspondent Ed Bradley	Philadelphia
first African American to play the lead role in Shakespeare's *Othello*	Paul Robeson
first black anchor of a major network morning news show	Bryant Gumbel
first black magazine	*Mirror of Liberty*
first black male author to have a poem published in the United States	Jupiter Hammon
first black network news commentator	Mal Goode
first black newspaper in United States founded by Samuel Cornish and John Russwurm	*Freedom's Journal*
first black on the cover of *Vogue* magazine	Beverly Johnson
first black owner of a major newspaper (the *Oakland Tribune*)	Robert Maynard
first black *Time* magazine Man of the Year	Martin Luther King Jr.
first black to have a book of poetry published in the United States	Phillis Wheatley
first black to publish an almanac	Benjamin Banneker
first black woman to have won a Pulitzer Prize for Drama	Suzan-Lori Parks
first known black to write a poem in English	Lucy Terry

first newspaper in North America with a female editor (Mary Ann Shadd Cary)	*Provincial Freedom*
first novel published by a black woman in the United States	*Our Nig*
founder Chicago Defender (a black newspaper)	Robert Abbott
founder Negro Associated Press, which supplied news to black papers	Claude Barnett
founder New York Freemen newspaper	T. Thomas Fortune
founder of *Encore* magazine	Ida Elizabeth Lewis
founder of Radio One and TV One	Cathy Hughes
fruit in the Billie Holiday song "Strange Fruit"	lynched men
Good Morning America co-host and breast cancer survivor	Robin Roberts
Harriet Jacob's autobiography *Incidents in the Life of a Slave Girl* is a detailed account of the suffering slaves had to endure. After Jacobs was willed to her master's niece, how old was her new master?	Three
joined Charlayne Hunter as one of the first two black students at the University of Georgia	Hamilton Holmes
magazine, published a caricature of President Barack Obama on its cover wearing Muslim attire and his wife, Michelle, with an afro and assault rifle	*The New Yorker*
name of David Walker's publication advocating the use of violence for equality and self-defense	*Appeal*
name of ship that brought Phillis Wheatley the great poet and the first black to have a book of poetry published in the United States to North America	*Phillis*

name of the 1915 film that portrayed Klansmen as heroes	*The Birth of a Nation*
name of the TV miniseries that traced the history of a black family from Africa into twentieth-century America	Roots
national news network Max Robinson, the first black anchorman, worked for	ABC
person portrayed in the book *Uncle Tom's Cabin*	Josiah Henson
poet died at the age of thirty-three after battling tuberculosis	Paul Laurence Dunbar
president *The President's Daughter* about	Thomas Jefferson's
pseudonym used by Harriet Jacobs in her autobiography, *Incidents in the Life of a Slave Girl*, which details the suffering slaves endured	Linda Brent
published the first magazine intended for a black audience	David Ruggles
regular news correspondent on the long-running CBS television show *60 Minutes*	Ed Bradley
reporter on the *MacNeil/Lehrer News Hour* (a news show on the Public Broadcasting Service)	Charlayne Hunter Gault
state birth of Carter Woodson, the "Father of Black History,"	Virginia
state birth, Harriet Jacobs	North Carolina
state birth, James Weldon Johnson poet, lawyer, novelist, and civil rights leader	Florida
state birth, Lerone Bennett author, editor, and historian	Mississippi
Time's Person of the Year for 2008	Barack Obama
University, *In My Place* is about the first black woman to attend	Georgia

white woman author of *Uncle Tom's Cabin*	Harriet Beecher Stowe
year, first issue of *Ebony* magazine published	1945
year, miniseries *Roots* first broadcast on television	1977

EDUCATION (questions 670-700)

city Fisk University is located	Nashville
city Howard University is located	Washington, DC
city Johnson C. Smith University is located	Charlotte
city Morehouse College is	Atlanta
city Morgan State University is located	Baltimore
city North Carolina A and T is located	Greensboro
city Spelman College is located	Atlanta
college was once known as Atlanta Baptist	Morehouse
first black president of Fisk University	Charles Spurgeon Johnson
first black woman president of Spelman College	Johnetta Cole
state Albany State is located	Georgia
state Alcorn State University is located	Mississippi
state birth, John Hope, first black president of Atlanta Baptist College (now Morehouse)	Georgia
state birth, Mary Bethune was a civil rights leader and educator	South Carolina
state Bluefield State College is located	West Virginia
state Bowie State University is located	Maryland
state Coppin State College is located	Maryland
state Elizabeth City State University is located	North Carolina
state Fayetteville State University is located	North Carolina
state Fort Valley State College is located	Georgia
state Grambling is located	Louisiana

state Hampton University is located	Virginia
state Knoxville College is located	Tennessee
state Jackson State University is located	Mississippi
state Prairie View A&M University is located	Texas
state Saint Paul's College is located	Virginia
state Shaw University is located	North Carolina
university Kappa Alpha Psi, a predominately black fraternity, founded	Indiana
year first black sorority, Alpha Kappa Alpha, was founded	1908
year Kappa Alpha Psi, a predominately black fraternity, founded	1911

VARIOUS (701-704)

civil rights icon died in 2005	Rosa Parks
civil rights icon died in 2006	Coretta Scott King
named Michael at birth	Martin Luther King Jr.
never married	George Washington Carver

OTHER COUNTRIES OR CULTURES (questions 705-709)

age, Nelson Mandela died	Ninety-five
country had a major earthquake in 2010	Haiti
South African massacre where sixty-nine blacks killed by police	Sharpeville
speaks Japanese, Russian, and Swahili	Mae Jemison
states Gullah, a language and culture of West Africa and the Caribbean, most often associated	South Carolina and Georgia

COURTS AND LAW (questions 710-716)

convicted (by an all-black jury) in Georgia for killing two law enforcement officers	Rap Brown
filibustered for over twenty-four hours against a civil rights bill	Strom Thurmond
Lani Guinier's profession	Professor and lawyer
last name of the couple in the Supreme Court case that resulted in the legalization of interracial marriage in the United States	Loving
number of women Barack Obama appointed to the U. S. Supreme Court	Two
state birth of Anita Hill, who accused Clarence Thomas of sexual harassment	Oklahoma
year lawyer Johnnie Cochran died	2005

SPORTS (questions 717-734)

had polio and scarlet fever as a child	Track star Wilma Rudolph
birth state of Bill Pickett, legendary black cowboy and rodeo star	Texas
cause of death for Bill Pickett, famous cowboy and rodeo star	A horse kick to the head
college Benjamin Mays was the president from 1940 to 1967	Morehouse
college Jackie Robinson attended	UCLA
congressman was a star quarterback at the University of Oklahoma	J. C. Watts
famous black cowboy	Deadwood Dick
first black female to win the all-around gold medal in gymnastics	Gabby Douglas
first black golfer to qualify to play in the Masters Tournament in Augusta, Georgia	Lee Elder
first black in Major League Baseball in 1947	Jackie Robinson

first black jockey to ride a winning horse in the Kentucky Derby	Oliver Lewis
founder of the Negro Baseball League	Rube Foster
Hall of Fame member became a supreme court justice in Minnesota	Alan Page
law boxer Jack Johnson broke when he was arrested for taking his white girlfriend (and future wife) across state lines for "immoral purposes"	The Mann Act
once a football coach at Morgan College	Charles Drew
scored 101 points in a high school basketball game that ended at halftime because the opponent quit	Lisa Leslie
university Don Imus made racist and sexist comments about basketball players	Rutgers
was the coach of Rutgers when Don Imus, radio host, made racist and sexist remarks about the team's basketball players	Vivian Springer

ENTERTAINMENT (questions 737-769)

birth city of comedian and social activist Dick Gregory	St. Louis
composed "Lift Every Voice and Sing" with James Weldon Johnson	John Rosamond Johnson
died of an epileptic seizure	Track star Florence Griffith Joyner
died of cancer at the age of thirty-four	Lorraine Hansberry
famous portrait painter in the late 1700s and early 1800s	Joshua Johnson
first African American woman entered the Miss America Pageant as a contestant in 1970	Cheryl Brown

first black female sculpture to exhibit her work in Rome	Edmonia Lewis
first black film	*The Railroad Porter*
first black person to appear regularly on a television soap opera	Ellen Holly
first black princess in a Disney movie	Tiana
first black to produce and direct a major Hollywood film	Gordon Parks Sr.
first black to sing before the Queen of England	Elizabeth Greenfield
first black woman nominated for an Oscar for Best Actress in a Leading Role	Dorothy Dandridge
first black woman to have her work performed on Broadway	Lorraine Hansberry
first black-owned radio station in the United States	WERD
first winner of the Miss Black America Pageant	Saundra Williams
Glamour magazine's 1991 Woman of the Year	Anita Hill
Josephine Baker's profession	Dancer and singer
Marian Anderson's profession	Opera singer
movie, John Singleton received the Best Director Oscar nomination	*Boyz n the Hood*
nickname of legendary dancer Bill Robinson	Bojangles
nineteenth-century Shakespearean actor	Ira Aldridge
played Mammy in *Gone with the Wind*	Hattie McDaniel
portrayed the character Jane Pittman in a movie	Cicely Tyson
second black Miss America	Suzette Charles
ship Stephen Spielberg made a movie about	*Amistad*

song asks the antiwar question "How you gonna make me kill somebody I don't even know"	Prince's "Party Up"
state birth of Oprah Winfrey	Mississippi
state the first black contestant in the Miss America Pageant represented	Iowa
The Great White Hope is based on the life of this man	Jack Johnson
year Dance Theatre of Harlem School was founded	1969
year Otis Redding famous rhythm and blues singer was killed in a plane crash	1967
year the first Miss Black America Pageant held	1968

RELIGION (questions 770-785)

"Wonder-Boy Preacher"	Al Sharpton
age of Al Sharpton when he began preaching	Four
city the Nation of Islam was founded	Detroit
founded the African Methodist Episcopal Church	Richard Allen
founded the Nation of Islam	Wallace Fard
location of the Greater Emmanuel Temple of Faith, founded by T. D. Jakes in 1979	Montgomery, West Virginia
member of the Nation of Islam was born with the last name Clay	Muhammad Ali
member of the Nation of Islam was born with the last name Poole	Elijah Muhammad
pastor of the Potter's House in Dallas, Texas	T. D. Jakes
state birth of Richard Allen, founder of the AME (African Methodist Episcopal) Church	Pennsylvania

state birth, Father Divine was a religious leader and advocate for equality	Maryland
title of the *New Yorker* magazine cover that depicted President Obama and Mrs. Obama as radical Muslims	"The Politics of Fear"
white wife of Father Divine	Sweet Angel
year Mormon Church ruled that a single drop of black blood made a person unfit to become a priest	1855
year South African archbishop Desmond Tutu won the Nobel Peace Prize	1984
year the Nation of Islam was founded	1930

BUSINESS (questions 786-792)

company John W. Thompson become chairman of in 2014	Microsoft
first black female CEO of a Fortune 500 company	Ursula Burns
first black woman to become a billionaire	Oprah Winfrey
first self-made female millionaire in the United States	Madam C. J. Walker
founder of North Carolina Mutual Insurance Company	John Merrick
owned a variety of businesses in Memphis and was nicknamed "the Boss of Beale Street"	Robert Church Sr.
year, National Negro Doll was a company that made black dolls, was founded	1911

PARENTAL ADVISORY (questions 793-800)

1712 South Carolina law make it legal to castrate a slave for this crime	Being a four-time runaway
1729 law stipulating that cutting a slave into four pieces and displaying the pieces in public was legal for some crimes	Maryland
1740 law that made it illegal to castrate, cut out the tongue of, put out an eye of, or scald a slave	South Carolina
impregnated twice as a result of rapes (one by a black man and one by a white sheriff)	Moms Mabley
place Abner Louima sodomized with a stick by a policeman	At a police precinct
raped as a seven-year-old	Maya Angelou
woman's parents were a twelve-year-old black girl and a white rapist	Ethel Waters
year Abner Louima sodomized by a policeman with a stick	1997

Sources

Books

Appiah, Kwame Anthony, and Henry Louis Gates, eds. *Africana.* New York: Civitas, 1999.

Bergman, Peter M. *Chronological History of the Negro in America.* New York: Harper and Row, 1969.

Berry, S. Torriano, and Venise T. Berry. *50 Most Influential Black Films.* New York: Kensington, 2001.

Boyd, Herb. *We Shall Overcome.* Naperville, Illinois: Sourcebooks, 2004.

Brooks, Christopher, ed. *African American Almanac.* Canton, Michigan: Visible Ink, 2012.

Bullard, Sara. *Free at Last.* New York: Oxford, 1998.

Carson, Clayborne, Mark Bauerlein, Todd Steven Burroughs, Ella Forbes, Jim Haskins, Paul Lee, Howard Lindsey, Jerald Podair and Jo Ellen Warner. *Civil Rights Chronicle.* Lincolnwood, Illinois: Legacy, 2003.

Christian, Charles M. *Black Saga.* Washington, DC: Civitas / Counterpoint, 1999.

Gates, Henry Louis Jr., and Kevin M. Burke. *And Still I Rise.* New York: Harper Collins, 2015.

Gates, Henry Louis Jr., and Evelyn Brooks Higginbotham. *African American Lives.* New York: Oxford, 2004.

————. *African American National Biography*. 8 vols. New York: Oxford, 2008.

Green, Richard L. *A Salute to Black Scientists and Inventors*. Chicago: Empak, 1985.

Harley, Sharon. *Timetables of African American History*. New York: Touchstone, 1995.

Heidler, David S. *Encyclopedia of the American Civil War*. New York: W. W. Norton and Company, 2002.

Hornsby, Alton Jr. *Chronology of African American History*. 2nd ed. Detroit: Gale Research, 1967.

Koslow, Phillip. *African American Desk Reference. New York: Stonesong Press,* 1999.

Lanning, Michael Lee. *African American Soldier.Secaucus, New Jersey: Carol,* 1999.

Low, W. Augustus, and Virgil A. Clift, eds. *Encyclopedia of Black America*. New York: McGraw-Hill, 1981.

Lyman, Darry. *Great African-American Women. New York: Gramercy Books,* 1994.

Miles, Johnnie H., Juanita L. Davis, Sharon Ferguson-Robertson, and Rita Giles. *Almanac of African American Heritage*. Paramus, New Jersey: Prentice Hall, 2001.

Newman, Richard. *African American Quotations*. New York: Checkmark, 1998.

Penrice, Ronda Racha. *African American History for Dummies*. Hoboken, New Jersey: Wiley, 2007.

Potter, Joan. *African American Firsts*. New York: Kensington, 2002.

Salzman, Jack. *Macmillan Information Now Encyclopedia: The African American Experience*. New York: MacMillan Library Reference, 1993.

Sauers, Richard A. *Civil War Chronicle*. Lincolnwood, Illinois: Legacy, 2004.

Shadwick, Keith. *Encyclopedia of Jazz and Blues*. Ann Arbor, Michigan: Borders, 2003.

Smith, Jessie Carney. *Black Firsts*. Detroit: Visible Ink, 2003.

Stewart, Jeffrey C. *1001 Things Everyone Should Know about Black History*. New York: Doubleday, 1996.

Syken, Bill. *Any Given Number*. Sports Illustrated, New York; Sports Illustrated, 2014.

Taylor, Quintard. *America I Am Black Facts*. New York: Smiley Books, 2009.

Woods, Michael D. *Afromation*. Henderson, Nevada: MYKCO Communications, 2000.

Magazines and Pamphlets
Hetrick, Adam, and Karu F. Daniel. "Norm Lewis Ends History-Making Engagement in Broadway's *Phantom of the Opera*." *Playbill*, February 7, 2015.

Wolff, Alexander. "Ground Breakers." *Sports Illustrated*, November 7, 2005.

Newspapers
Anderson, Dave. "Nine Votes from Unanimous." *New York Times*, January 13, 1982.

Associated Press. "Thomas of Chiefs Gets 7 Sacks." *New York Times*, December 12, 1990.

Green, Frank. "A Year of History: Martinsville Seven Executions Remain 'a Raw Spot' for Many." *Richmond Times Dispatch*, February 6, 2011.

Johnson, Katie. "Paulette Brown to Take Reins of American Bar Association." *Boston Globe*, September 7, 2014.

White, Lonnie. "Morningside's Lisa Leslie Scores 101 in One Half." *Los Angeles Times*, February 8, 1990.

Posters
Jones, Wilbert D. "Miracles Happen. Black Innovators, Then and Now." Nos. 4, 51, and 61.

Websites
Adams, Genetta M. "17 Top Blacks in the Military." November 11, 2014. The Root. https://www.the root.com/call-of-duty-17-top-blacks-military-officers.

"Blues Singer Bessie Smith Killed in Mississippi Car Wreck." "On This Day, October 4." History Channel. https://www.history.com/this-day-in-history/blues-singer-bessie-smith-killed-in-mississippi-wreck-is-buried.

"Ed Bradley biography." CBS. https.www.cbsnews.com/news/ed-bradley-08-07-1998.

Freelon, Kiratiana. "The Rape of Recy Taylor Looks Back at a Horrific but Largely Forgotten Case from The Jim Crow South." September 26, 2017. The Root. https://.www.theroot.com/the-rape-of-recy-taylor-looks-back-at-a-horrific.

"Hattie McDaniel quotes." https://quotefancy.com/hattie-mcdaniel-i-d-rather-make.

Quinn, Gwendolyn. "From Brooklyn to Broadway: Lynn Nottage Makes History as Two-Time Pulitzer Prize Winner." April 12, 2017. Black Enterprise. http://www.blackenterprise.com/playwright-lynn-nottage-pulitzer-prize-winner-sweat/.

"Mae Jemison Biography." NASA biography data. https://www.jsc.nasa.gov/bios/htmlbios/jemison-mc.htlm.

"Mickey Leland – Biography." University of Houston. https://www.uh.edu/class/hobby/interns/leland-fellows/bio-mickey-leland.php.

"Single Game Rushing Leaders." Pro-Football-Reference.com. https://www.pro-football-reference.com/leaders-rush-yds-single-game-htm.

St. Félix, Dorren. "Latasha Harlins, American Girl." April 27, 2017. MTV News. www.mtv.com/news/latasha-harlins-american-girl/.

Whack, Errin. "Who Was Edmund Pettus?" March 7, 2015. Smithsonian.com. https://www.smithsonianmag.com/history/who-was-edmund-pettus-180954501/.

"Year 1973 Illinois." King Center (chronology). www.thekingcenter.org/making-king-holiday.

1 D	45 D	89 D	133 C	177 B	221 A	265 A
2 D	46 A	90 C	134 D	178 C	222 C	266 C
3 B	47 D	91 A	135 A	179 C	223 D	267 D
4 C	48 D	92 D	136 C	180 D	224 A	268 A
5 A	49 A	93 D	137 C	181 D	225 B	269 B
6 D	50 D	94 C	138 B	182 B	226 A	270 D
7 C	51 B	95 C	139 C	183 A	227 A	271 A
8 B	52 A	96 C	140 D	184 C	228 D	272 B
9 D	53 D	97 A	141 D	185 D	229 A	273 D
10 B	54 A	98 B	142 D	186 C	230 D	274 B
11 A	55 D	99 D	143 A	187 A	231 C	275 D
12 C	56 B	100 A	144 A	188 D	232 A	276 C
13 B	57 B	101 C	145 A	189 A	233 D	277 C
14 B	58 C	102 D	146 B	190 B	234 C	278 B
15 C	59 B	103 D	147 C	191 C	235 B	279 A
16 D	60 D	104 A	148 A	192 C	236 C	280 B
17 A	61 B	105 A	149 C	193 D	237 C	281 D
18 B	62 C	106 D	150 D	194 D	238 A	282 D
19 A	63 C	107 A	151 B	195 B	239 C	283 B
20 D	64 A	108 C	152 C	196 C	240 A	284 D
21 A	65 A	109 B	153 D	197 C	241 B	285 C
22 A	66 D	110 A	154 B	198 A	242 C	286 D
23 D	67 D	111 D	155 D	199 B	243 C	287 D
24 C	68 A	112 B	156 D	200 A	244 B	288 A
25 B	69 D	113 A	157 D	201 C	245 D	289 A
26 D	70 B	114 D	158 A	202 D	246 B	290 C
27 C	71 B	115 A	159 D	203 C	247 C	291 D
28 A	72 A	116 C	160 B	204 C	248 D	292 A
29 C	73 D	117 D	161 D	205 B	249 A	293 B
30 C	74 A	118 A	162 C	206 D	250 C	294 C
31 B	75 C	119 B	163 D	207 C	251 B	295 D
32 A	76 B	120 A	164 D	208 B	252 A	296 D
33 C	77 D	121 C	165 A	209 C	253 D	297 B
34 C	78 A	122 B	166 D	210 B	254 C	298 D
35 D	79 B	123 D	167 B	211 A	255 A	299 A
36 D	80 C	124 A	168 D	212 D	256 B	300 C
37 A	81 C	125 A	169 D	213 A	257 A	301 B
38 C	82 B	126 C	170 A	214 C	258 D	302 A
39 A	83 C	127 A	171 A	215 A	259 D	303 D
40 B	84 A	128 D	172 C	216 A	260 C	304 B
41 D	85 C	129 B	173 D	217 B	261 B	305 A
42 D	86 A	130 C	174 C	218 D	262 C	306 A
43 B	87 D	131 B	175 D	219 D	263 B	307 C
44 B	88 B	132 C	176 A	220 C	264 C	308 A

309 D	353 D	397 D	441 B	485 C	529 C	573 D
310 C	354 A	398 A	442 A	486 C	530 A	574 C
311 D	355 A	399 D	443 D	487 A	531 D	575 A
312 B	356 B	400 A	444 D	488 C	532 D	576 A
313 C	357 D	401 C	445 C	489 A	533 A	577 C
314 A	358 D	402 C	446 B	490 D	534 D	578 A
315 D	359 C	403 A	447 B	491 A	535 A	579 D
316 D	360 C	404 B	448 D	492 B	536 A	580 A
317 B	361 C	405 B	449 B	493 B	537 C	581 B
318 D	362 A	406 B	450 C	494 C	538 A	582 D
319 A	363 D	407 D	451 B	495 B	539 A	583 C
320 D	364 D	408 D	452 A	496 C	540 A	584 D
321 A	365 C	409 C	453 C	497 B	541 B	585 A
322 D	366 C	410 C	454 C	498 A	542 C	586 B
323 A	367 A	411 A	455 A	499 B	543 B	587 C
324 B	368 B	412 A	456 D	500 C	544 A	588 A
325 A	369 A	413 D	457 B	501 A	545 B	589 D
326 B	370 A	414 C	458 D	502 B	546 D	590 B
327 B	371 D	415 A	459 B	503 A	547 B	591 D
328 C	372 A	416 B	460 C	504 D	548 D	592 A
329 A	373 D	417 D	461 B	505 A	549 D	593 A
330 B	374 D	418 B	462 B	506 D	550 A	594 D
331 A	375 B	419 A	463 B	507 B	551 A	595 D
332 A	376 C	420 C	464 B	508 D	552 B	596 C
333 C	377 D	421 B	465 C	509 A	553 A	597 C
334 B	378 A	422 B	466 A	510 B	554 D	598 D
335 C	379 D	423 A	467 C	511 A	555 C	599 C
336 B	380 D	424 A	468 D	512 D	556 C	600 D
337 B	381 B	425 B	469 C	513 B	557 C	601 D
338 C	382 B	426 A	470 B	514 B	558 A	602 C
339 C	383 A	427 C	471 A	515 A	559 A	603 B
340 A	384 D	428 D	472 B	516 C	560 B	604 B
341 A	385 D	429 B	473 C	517 A	561 D	605 B
342 C	386 A	430 C	474 A	518 C	562 A	606 A
343 A	387 B	431 A	475 B	519 C	563 A	607 C
344 B	388 B	432 D	476 D	520 D	564 D	608 C
345 A	389 A	433 D	477 C	521 B	565 D	609 B
346 D	390 C	434 C	478 D	522 A	566 B	610 D
347 D	391 C	435 C	479 B	523 B	567 D	611 B
348 B	392 C	436 A	480 D	524 B	568 C	612 C
349 B	393 D	437 B	481 D	525 A	569 A	613 B
350 B	394 B	438 A	482 C	526 D	570 C	614 B
351 C	395 B	439 C	483 C	527 A	571 D	615 C
352 B	396 D	440 B	484 B	528 B	572 B	616 D

617 D	661 A	705 D	749 C	793 B	837 D	881 D
618 B	662 D	706 D	750 C	794 D	838 B	882 C
619 A	663 B	707 D	751 A	795 B	839 D	883 C
620 B	664 B	708 C	752 B	796 B	840 B	884 C
621 B	665 B	709 B	753 C	797 C	841 A	885 B
622 D	666 A	710 B	754 D	798 D	842 C	886 C
623 C	667 A	711 A	755 B	799 A	843 D	887 B
624 B	668 C	712 D	756 A	800 D	844 D	888 C
625 C	669 B	713 D	757 B	801 D	845 A	889 D
626 D	670 A	714 B	758 B	802 A	846 A	890 D
627 C	671 A	715 C	759 A	803 C	847 D	891 B
628 A	672 B	716 C	760 B	804 D	848 C	892 D
629 B	673 D	717 C	761 D	805 A	849 B	893 C
630 A	674 D	718 D	762 C	806 D	850 C	894 B
631 D	675 B	719 C	763 B	807 D	851 D	895 C
632 A	676 C	720 A	764 B	808 C	852 B	896 B
633 D	677 D	721 D	765 A	809 C	853 B	897 C
634 C	678 A	722 D	766 D	810 A	854 D	898 B
635 D	679 D	723 B	767 A	811 C	855 B	899 D
636 A	680 C	724 B	768 A	812 B	856 A	900 D
637 B	681 B	725 D	769 C	813 C	857 A	901 C
638 D	682 A	726 D	770 C	814 C	858 B	902 D
639 A	683 D	727 A	771 C	815 B	859 A	903 C
640 C	684 C	728 B	772 D	816 A	860 D	904 D
641 A	685 C	729 B	773 B	817 D	861 A	905 B
642 A	686 D	730 D	774 B	818 C	862 B	906 A
643 B	687 A	731 C	775 D	819 B	863 A	907 A
644 A	688 C	732 D	776 D	820 A	864 C	908 D
645 C	689 A	733 B	777 C	821 A	865 A	909 D
646 B	690 A	734 A	778 D	822 D	866 B	910 C
647 D	691 C	735 D	779 B	823 A	867 B	911 A
648 C	692 D	736 D	780 B	824 C	868 A	912 A
649 A	693 B	737 D	781 D	825 B	869 A	913 D
650 C	694 A	738 C	782 D	826 A	870 B	914 A
651 D	695 D	739 A	783 C	827 D	871 B	915 D
652 B	696 C	740 D	784 B	828 C	872 D	916 A
653 D	697 D	741 C	785 C	829 B	873 A	917 B
654 C	698 D	742 D	786 D	830 B	874 D	918 A
655 C	699 D	743 B	787 A	831 D	875 B	919 B
656 B	700 C	744 A	788 A	832 A	876 B	920 D
657 A	701 A	745 A	789 D	833 A	877 D	921 C
658 B	702 D	746 D	790 D	834 B	878 D	922 A
659 C	703 D	747 C	791 D	835 A	879 C	923 D
660 D	704 A	748 B	792 B	836 D	880 B	924 B

925 D	969 C	1013 B	1057 C	1101 A	1145 C	1189 D
926 D	970 A	1014 D	1058 A	1102 C	1146 D	1190 D
927 A	971 D	1015 A	1059 D	1103 C	1147 B	1191 C
928 B	972 C	1016 A	1060 B	1104 D	1148 D	1192 C
929 D	973 B	1017 C	1061 C	1105 C	1149 C	1193 A
930 C	974 C	1018 A	1062 C	1106 C	1150 A	1194 B
931 C	975 D	1019 C	1063 A	1107 A	1151 C	1195 A
932 B	976 D	1020 C	1064 C	1108 A	1152 A	1196 D
933 C	977 B	1021 A	1065 A	1109 D	1153 A	1197 B
934 D	978 C	1022 C	1066 D	1110 B	1154 B	1198 C
935 A	979 D	1023 D	1067 A	1111 B	1155 D	1199 A
936 B	980 D	1024 D	1068 C	1112 A	1156 A	1200 A
937 D	981 B	1025 B	1069 A	1113 C	1157 C	1201 B
938 B	982 A	1026 D	1070 A	1114 C	1158 D	1202 C
939 D	983 C	1027 D	1071 B	1115 B	1159 C	1203 B
940 B	984 C	1028 C	1072 A	1116 D	1160 B	1204 D
941 D	985 D	1029 D	1073 A	1117 A	1161 B	1205 B
942 B	986 D	1030 C	1074 D	1118 B	1162 C	1206 D
943 C	987 C	1031 B	1075 B	1119 A	1163 A	1207 B
944 B	988 C	1032 C	1076 C	1120 A	1164 D	1208 B
945 D	989 A	1033 D	1077 B	1121 B	1165 D	1209 A
946 C	990 B	1034 B	1078 D	1122 A	1166 A	1210 B
947 B	991 C	1035 C	1079 B	1123 C	1167 D	1211 A
948 A	992 B	1036 D	1080 C	1124 C	1168 D	1212 C
949 A	993 D	1037 A	1081 C	1125 B	1169 C	1213 A
950 C	994 C	1038 B	1082 D	1126 D	1170 B	1214 B
951 B	995 D	1039 C	1083 A	1127 D	1171 D	1215 A
952 C	996 D	1040 D	1084 A	1128 A	1172 C	1216 B
953 C	997 C	1041 C	1085 C	1129 C	1173 C	1217 C
954 A	998 D	1042 D	1086 D	1130 D	1174 A	1218 C
955 C	999 B	1043 C	1087 A	1131 D	1175 B	1219 A
956 C	1000 B	1044 D	1088 D	1132 A	1176 C	1220 A
957 B	1001 D	1045 D	1089 B	1133 D	1177 A	1221 D
958 B	1002 C	1046 B	1090 B	1134 B	1178 A	1222 A
959 A	1003 C	1047 A	1091 A	1135 C	1179 C	1223 C
960 C	1004 B	1048 D	1092 C	1136 A	1180 A	1224 B
961 B	1005 C	1049 A	1093 C	1137 C	1181 A	1225 B
962 C	1006 D	1050 A	1094 D	1138 C	1182 C	1226 C
963 B	1007 C	1051 B	1095 D	1139 B	1183 C	1227 C
964 D	1008 C	1052 B	1096 C	1140 B	1184 D	1228 A
965 C	1009 B	1053 D	1097 B	1141 C	1185 B	1229 C
966 B	1010 C	1054 B	1098 D	1142 D	1186 A	1230 A
967 A	1011 A	1055 D	1099 D	1143 C	1187 B	1231 C
968 D	1012 B	1056 D	1100 C	1144 B	1188 A	1232 A

1233 C	1277 A	1321 A	1365 C	1409 D	1453 A	1497 A
1234 D	1278 C	1322 C	1366 C	1410 A	1454 B	1498 B
1235 D	1279 B	1323 C	1367 B	1411 C	1455 C	1499 B
1236 A	1280 A	1324 B	1368 A	1412 A	1456 D	1500 C
1237 C	1281 D	1325 A	1369 B	1413 D	1457 C	1501 A
1238 A	1282 C	1326 A	1370 C	1414 C	1458 C	1502 A
1239 B	1283 B	1327 D	1371 C	1415 B	1459 D	1503 D
1240 D	1284 B	1328 B	1372 C	1416 D	1460 B	1504 C
1241 A	1285 A	1329 C	1373 B	1417 B	1461 A	1505 C
1242 C	1286 D	1330 B	1374 D	1418 A	1462 C	1506 A
1243 A	1287 C	1331 D	1375 C	1419 C	1463 B	1507 A
1244 C	1288 A	1332 A	1376 C	1420 A	1464 A	1508 D
1245 A	1289 B	1333 A	1377 A	1421 A	1465 B	1509 B
1246 C	1290 C	1334 B	1378 C	1422 C	1466 D	1510 C
1247 D	1291 A	1335 D	1379 C	1423 C	1467 A	1511 C
1248 A	1292 D	1336 D	1380 A	1424 A	1468 D	1512 C
1249 D	1293 C	1337 D	1381 D	1425 B	1469 C	1513 B
1250 D	1294 B	1338 A	1382 C	1426 B	1470 C	1514 A
1251 C	1295 C	1339 A	1383 A	1427 B	1471 A	1515 D
1252 A	1296 C	1340 D	1384 B	1428 A	1472 C	1516 C
1253 B	1297 D	1341 C	1385 B	1429 C	1473 C	1517 B
1254 B	1298 A	1342 C	1386 C	1430 B	1474 B	1518 D
1255 C	1299 D	1343 B	1387 D	1431 D	1475 D	1519 C
1256 B	1300 A	1344 D	1388 C	1432 D	1476 A	1520 C
1257 D	1301 B	1345 B	1389 B	1433 B	1477 D	1521 B
1258 D	1302 A	1346 D	1390 C	1434 A	1478 D	1522 B
1259 B	1303 C	1347 B	1391 B	1435 B	1479 A	1523 D
1260 B	1304 C	1348 A	1392 D	1436 C	1480 B	1524 C
1261 A	1305 B	1349 A	1393 B	1437 A	1481 A	1525 A
1262 C	1306 A	1350 D	1394 C	1438 D	1482 C	1526 B
1263 D	1307 D	1351 B	1395 B	1439 A	1483 C	1527 C
1264 B	1308 B	1352 B	1396 A	1440 B	1484 A	1528 B
1265 A	1309 B	1353 C	1397 C	1441 B	1485 D	1529 C
1266 C	1310 A	1354 C	1398 A	1442 A	1486 B	1530 D
1267 B	1311 A	1355 C	1399 D	1443 C	1487 B	1531 D
1268 B	1312 D	1356 D	1400 C	1444 D	1488 C	1532 C
1269 C	1313 C	1357 A	1401 C	1445 B	1489 A	1533 C
1270 D	1314 D	1358 D	1402 D	1446 B	1490 B	1534 D
1271 B	1315 C	1359 B	1403 B	1447 A	1491 D	1535 D
1272 B	1316 D	1360 D	1404 C	1448 B	1492 C	1536 A
1273 C	1317 C	1361 D	1405 A	1449 D	1493 D	1537 B
1274 B	1318 A	1362 A	1406 B	1450 A	1494 A	1538 C
1275 A	1319 D	1363 B	1407 A	1451 A	1495 B	1539 A
1276 D	1320 D	1364 A	1408 D	1452 C	1496 A	1540 B

1541 C	1585 B	1629 A	1673 D	1717 C	1761 B	1805 C
1542 B	1586 B	1630 B	1674 C	1718 B	1762 C	1806 D
1543 A	1587 C	1631 A	1675 B	1719 C	1763 C	1807 B
1544 C	1588 C	1632 B	1676 A	1720 D	1764 A	1808 B
1545 A	1589 B	1633 C	1677 B	1721 B	1765 A	1809 A
1546 D	1590 C	1634 C	1678 C	1722 B	1766 D	1810 A
1547 C	1591 B	1635 B	1679 A	1723 D	1767 C	1811 B
1548 A	1592 C	1636 A	1680 B	1724 C	1768 C	1812 C
1549 C	1593 A	1637 C	1681 B	1725 C	1769 D	1813 C
1550 A	1594 C	1638 A	1682 A	1726 B	1770 A	1814 B
1551 B	1595 C	1639 A	1683 A	1727 D	1771 C	1815 B
1552 B	1596 B	1640 D	1684 C	1728 A	1772 A	1816 A
1553 C	1597 D	1641 D	1685 A	1729 D	1773 D	1817 D
1554 C	1598 D	1642 B	1686 D	1730 D	1774 A	1818 B
1555 B	1599 A	1643 A	1687 D	1731 C	1775 C	1819 C
1556 D	1600 C	1644 B	1688 D	1732 A	1776 B	1820 B
1557 D	1601 D	1645 B	1689 B	1733 C	1777 D	1821 B
1558 A	1602 B	1646 D	1690 D	1734 B	1778 D	1822 D
1559 C	1603 B	1647 A	1691 B	1735 C	1779 C	1823 B
1560 D	1604 D	1648 A	1692 B	1736 D	1780 C	1824 A
1561 A	1605 D	1649 D	1693 A	1737 B	1781 A	1825 D
1562 A	1606 C	1650 B	1694 A	1738 B	1782 B	1826 D
1563 C	1607 B	1651 A	1695 D	1739 D	1783 C	1827 A
1564 D	1608 B	1652 B	1696 B	1740 B	1784 C	1828 B
1565 B	1609 B	1653 A	1697 A	1741 D	1785 A	1829 B
1566 C	1610 B	1654 C	1698 A	1742 C	1786 B	1830 D
1567 B	1611 A	1655 D	1699 D	1743 D	1787 A	1831 A
1568 A	1612 C	1656 C	1700 C	1744 C	1788 C	1832 D
1569 C	1613 A	1657 C	1701 D	1745 C	1789 B	1833 B
1570 C	1614 B	1658 B	1702 A	1746 B	1790 B	1834 A
1571 B	1615 B	1659 D	1703 C	1747 A	1791 D	1835 C
1572 A	1616 A	1660 C	1704 B	1748 D	1792 B	1836 D
1573 D	1617 C	1661 A	1705 C	1749 A	1793 C	1837 A
1574 C	1618 B	1662 A	1706 B	1750 C	1794 A	1838 C
1575 B	1619 D	1663 B	1707 D	1751 D	1795 C	1839 D
1576 C	1620 A	1664 C	1708 B	1752 C	1796 A	1840 C
1577 A	1621 D	1665 D	1709 A	1753 C	1797 C	1841 A
1578 A	1622 C	1666 A	1710 B	1754 D	1798 B	1842 B
1579 C	1623 B	1667 B	1711 D	1755 A	1799 C	1843 D
1580 C	1624 B	1668 D	1712 A	1756 B	1800 D	1844 A
1581 D	1625 A	1669 B	1713 D	1757 B	1801 A	1845 D
1582 D	1626 D	1670 D	1714 A	1758 D	1802 A	1846 D
1583 C	1627 B	1671 B	1715 B	1759 A	1803 A	1847 B
1584 C	1628 D	1672 D	1716 A	1760 D	1804 C	1848 B

1849 D	1893 A	1937 B	1981 A
1850 A	1894 A	1938 B	1982 D
1851 C	1895 C	1939 D	1983 C
1852 B	1896 B	1940 C	1984 A
1853 A	1897 B	1941 A	1985 C
1854 B	1898 A	1942 B	1986 C
1855 A	1899 C	1943 C	1987 A
1856 D	1900 D	1944 B	1988 C
1857 B	1901 C	1945 B	1989 C
1858 B	1902 D	1946 A	1990 B
1859 C	1903 A	1947 A	1991 C
1860 C	1904 B	1948 D	1992 D
1861 D	1905 D	1949 A	1993 C
1862 C	1906 A	1950 A	1994 A
1863 D	1907 A	1951 D	1995 A
1864 C	1908 C	1952 A	1996 B
1865 A	1909 A	1953 D	1997 B
1866 B	1910 C	1954 C	1998 C
1867 C	1911 C	1955 A	1999 B
1868 A	1912 B	1956 C	2000 B
1869 A	1913 D	1957 D	
1870 D	1914 C	1958 B	
1871 A	1915 B	1959 B	
1872 B	1916 D	1960 A	
1873 A	1917 C	1961 B	
1874 D	1918 B	1962 B	
1875 A	1919 D	1963 A	
1876 D	1920 A	1964 B	
1877 B	1921 D	1965 A	
1878 D	1922 B	1966 A	
1879 C	1923 B	1967 D	
1880 B	1924 D	1968 D	
1881 C	1925 C	1969 C	
1882 C	1926 A	1970 D	
1883 C	1927 B	1971 B	
1884 D	1928 A	1972 B	
1885 B	1929 C	1973 A	
1886 A	1930 C	1974 D	
1887 B	1931 D	1975 C	
1888 A	1932 C	1976 C	
1889 C	1933 A	1977 A	
1890 D	1934 A	1978 C	
1891 A	1935 B	1979 D	
1892 D	1936 C	1980 A	